THE LIBRARY MANAGER'S DESKBOOK

102 EXPERT SOLUTIONS TO 101 COMMON DILEMMAS

Paula Phillips Carson
Kerry David Carson
Joyce Schouest Phillips

American Library Association
Chicago and London 1995

The paper used in this publication meets the minimum requirements of American National Standard for Information Sciences—Permanence of Paper for Printed Library Materials, ANSI Z39.48-1992. ∞

Cover designed by Richmond A. Jones
Text designed by Charles Bozett
Composed by Publishing Services, Inc.
   in ITC Galliard on Xyvision/Linotype.
Printed on 50-pound Glatfelter,
   a PH-neutral stock, and bound in 10-point CIS
   by Edward Brothers, Inc.

Library of Congress Cataloging-in-Publication Data

Carson, Paula Phillips, 1967-
     The library manager's deskbook : 102 expert solutions to 101 common
dilemmas / Paula Phillips Carson, Kerry David Carson, Joyce Schouest Phillips.
        p.   cm.
     Includes index.
     ISBN 0-8389-0655-9 (alk. paper)
     1. Library administration—United States.   2. Public libraries—United
States—Administration.   I. Carson, Kerry D. (Kerry David), 1946- .
II. Phillips, Joyce Schouest.   III. Title.
Z678.C345   1995
025.1'0973—dc20   95-17893

Printed in the United States of America.

99 98 97 96 95   5 4 3 2 1

To my mother—whose love for librarianship
is surpassed only by her love for life

P.P.C.

To my family

K.D.C.

To the joys and loves of my life . . . my parents,
Cullen and Florence Schouest, my daughters,
Shelly Phillips and Paula Carson, and
my son-in-law, Kerry Carson

J.S.P.

CONTENTS

Preface   *xiii*

Acknowledgments   *xv*

How to Use This Deskbook   *xvii*

PART I
Communication Issues   1

CHAPTER 1: (Mis) Communication   1

QUESTION 1: Why Does Communication So Often Break Down?   1

QUESTION 2: How Can Staff Members Ensure That Others Really Listen to What They Have to Say?   2

QUESTION 3: Why Is the Library Manager Often the Last to Know about "Bad News"?   3

QUESTION 4: How Do New Staff Members Acquire the Information They Need to Perform Their Jobs Effectively?   4

QUESTION 5: How Can the "Grapevine" Be Cultivated to Keep the Manager Better Informed?   6

QUESTION 6: What Can "Body Language" Tell Others?   7

CHAPTER 2: Patron and Staff Diversity   10

QUESTION 7: How Can Library Managers Respond to the Diversity of Their Patrons?   10

QUESTION 8: What Marketing Practices Are Required to Attract Minority Groups to the Library?   11

v

QUESTION 9: What Communication Techniques Are Required to Serve Minority Groups?   13

QUESTION 10: What Are the Library's Obligations in Recruiting Minority Applicants?   14

QUESTION 11: How Can Library Managers Successfully Retain a Diversified Staff?   16

CHAPTER 3: Personality Differences, Conflicts, and Creativity   19

QUESTION 12: How Do Staff Members Differ in Their Views of Fairness and Justice?   19

QUESTION 13: How Do Individual Differences in Thinking Styles Affect the Workplace?   20

QUESTION 14: What Is Intuition and How Does It Influence the Quality of Decisions?   21

QUESTION 15: How Should Conflicts among Staff Members Be Resolved?   22

QUESTION 16: How Can Library Managers Foster Creativity?   23

QUESTION 17: What Happens When Groups Are So Cohesive That Even Constructive Conflict Is Avoided?   24

CHAPTER 4: Power Use and Abuse   26

QUESTION 18: What Does "Power" Have to Do with Library Management?   26

QUESTION 19: Which Power Base Should the Library Manager Use?   27

QUESTION 20: How Can the Library Manager Determine Which Power Base Is Being Used?   28

QUESTION 21: How Can Using the Reward Power Base Backfire?   29

QUESTION 22: What Factors Diminish or Enhance the "Personal" Power Bases of Expertise and Reward?   30

Professional Issues   34

CHAPTER 5: Letting Professionals Be Just That   34

QUESTION 23: Exactly Who Is a "Librarian"?   34

QUESTION 24: Can Professionals Be Dually Committed to Both Their Employing Library and the Library Field?   35

QUESTION 25: How Do Issues of Professionalism Influence Managerial Activity in the Library?   36

QUESTION 26: How Should a Library Be Designed to Best Accommodate Professionals?   38

QUESTION 27: What Types of Problems Might Be Encountered When Library Professionals Are Excluded from Problem Diagnosis?   40

QUESTION 28: How Can Branch Managers Be Given the Autonomy They Need to Operate Effectively?   42

CHAPTER 6: *Supervising the Support Staff*   45

QUESTION 29: Who Are "Paraprofessionals" and Why Are They Important in the Library Setting?   45

QUESTION 30: How Should Library Employees Who Don't Possess an MLIS Degree Be Referred To?   46

QUESTION 31: How Can Library "Professionals" Be Distinguished from "Paraprofessionals"?   47

QUESTION 32: How Can Paraprofessionals Be Motivated in a Library Setting?   48

QUESTION 33: How Might the Jobs of Paraprofessionals Be Enriched?   51

QUESTION 34: How Should Library Volunteers Be Managed?   53

CHAPTER 7: *Career Management*   56

QUESTION 35: Does Mentoring Help with Career Advancement?   56

QUESTION 36: Why Do Supervisors Give Some Employees Exceptional Treatment?   57

QUESTION 37: What Are the Career Stages through Which Librarians Typically Progress?   58

QUESTION 38: What Are Some Alternative Career Paths Available to Librarians?   59

QUESTION 39: What Are the Common Coping Strategies Adopted by Plateaued Librarians?   60

QUESTION 40: How Can Library Administrators Help Staff Members Deal with Burnout and Career Plateauing?   62

Employment Issues   65

CHAPTER 8: Making the Roles Clear   65

QUESTION 41: What Information Should Be in a Job Description?   65

QUESTION 42: How Can Job Descriptions Benefit Both Employees and Library Managers?   68

QUESTION 43: Why Is There Often Resistance on the Part of Library Employees to Completing and Using Job Descriptions?   69

QUESTION 44: How Can the Development of Job Descriptions Assist the Library in Complying with the Americans with Disabilities Act (ADA) of 1990?   70

QUESTION 45: How Can the Development of Job Descriptions Assist the Library in Complying with Other Important Employment Legislation?   72

CHAPTER 9: Hiring the Right Person for the Job   74

QUESTION 46: What Activities Should Take Place before Screening Job Applicants?   74

QUESTION 47: What Questions Should Not Be Asked of Candidates Applying for Positions in the Library?   76

QUESTION 48: Is It Legal to Require Candidates for a Professional Librarianship Position to Have Obtained an MLIS Degree?   78

QUESTION 49: What Can and Should a Library Manager Say When Serving as a Reference for a Previous Employee?   79

QUESTION 50: What Is "Discrimination" and How Can It Be Avoided during the Selection Process?   81

CHAPTER 10: Complying with "Implied Contracts"   84

QUESTION 51: Given That Employee Manuals May Be Interpreted as "Implied Contracts," What Information Should They Contain?   84

QUESTION 52: How Should the Contents of Employee Manuals Be Communicated to Employees? 86

QUESTION 53: What Should the Library Manager Do If the Rules in an Employee Manual Are Broken? 88

QUESTION 54: What Are the Most Common Steps in Progressive Discipline? 89

QUESTION 55: Can a Library Manager Be Charged with Wrongful Termination for Discharging a Staff Member "at Will"? 89

QUESTION 56: What Are the Legal Limitations on Attempts to Ensure Contractual Compliance through Electronic Surveillance or Monitoring? 90

CHAPTER 11: *Work Scheduling That Works* 93

QUESTION 57: How Can the Library Manager Schedule So That Employees Have the Flexibility Needed to Fulfill Nonwork Obligations? 93

QUESTION 58: What Dysfunctional Outcomes Are Associated with Ineffective Scheduling? 95

QUESTION 59: What Are the Positive and Negative Aspects of Employee Turnover? 96

QUESTION 60: Should the Library Manager Attempt to Control "Moonlighting" by Staff Members? 97

QUESTION 61: Should a Library Give Special Attention to the Child-Care Needs of Staff Members? 99

Personnel Issues   *101*

CHAPTER 12: *Potential Pitfalls in Performance Evaluations* 101

QUESTION 62: Why Are Performance Appraisals So Often Met with Resistance? 101

QUESTION 63: Why Should Performance Appraisals Be Conducted at All? 102

QUESTION 64: Who Should Evaluate Staff Member Performance? 102

QUESTION 65: What Aspects of Staff Member Performance Should Be Evaluated?   103

QUESTION 66: How Can Personal Bias on the Part of the Evaluator Be Minimized during the Appraisal Process?   105

CHAPTER 13: Finding Value in Performance Evaluations   109

QUESTION 67: Should Pay Be Based on Performance Evaluations?   109

QUESTION 68: What Laws Should the Library Manager Be Aware of When Determining Compensation?   110

QUESTION 69: How Can Performance Evaluations Direct Training Initiatives?   111

QUESTION 70: What Educational Programming Should Supplement On-the-Job Training?   112

QUESTION 71: How Can the Library Manager Determine If Training Initiatives Are Successful?   113

QUESTION 72: What Effect Might Library School Closings Have on the Profession?   115

CHAPTER 14: Unionization   118

QUESTION 73: What Factors Encourage or Discourage Library Employees from Seeking Unionization?   118

QUESTION 74: To What Extent Do Librarians Believe That Union Membership Is Incompatible with Professionalism?   119

QUESTION 75: What Labor Relations Laws Should the Library Manager Facing Unionization Understand?   120

QUESTION 76: What Rights Do Library Staff Members Have during a Union Organizing Campaign?   121

QUESTION 77: What Issues Have to Be Negotiated with Unions during Collective Bargaining?   123

QUESTION 78: In Case of Negotiation Breakdowns, What Techniques Can Be Used to Avert a Strike?   124

QUESTION 79: What Factors Encourage Employees to File Grievances against the Library and Its Management?   126

Liability Issues   *127*

CHAPTER 15: Unethical Behavior   **127**

QUESTION 80: What Constitutes Sexual Harassment in the Library Setting?   127

QUESTION 81: How Can a Manager Eliminate Sexual Harassment in the Library Environment?   128

QUESTION 82: What Moral Philosophies Are Used for Making Ethical Decisions and How Does Morality Develop?   130

QUESTION 83: How Can Library Managers Be Encouraged to Make Ethical Decisions?   131

QUESTION 84: How Does the Library's Professional Association Address the Problem of Unethical Behavior?   133

CHAPTER 16: Managing Risk and Change   **136**

QUESTION 85: What Should a Library Manager Do in Preparation for a Natural Disaster?   136

QUESTION 86: How Should a Library Manager Respond to Staff Members Who Have Experienced a Disaster?   137

QUESTION 87: How Should Library Managers Deal with Risks Beyond Those of Natural Disasters?   138

QUESTION 88: What Are Some Fundamental Legal Issues That Library Managers Should Understand?   141

QUESTION 89: What Is the Nature of Organizational Change That Is Not Brought On by a Crisis?   142

CHAPTER 17: The Unhealthy Workplace   **146**

QUESTION 90: What Safety and Health Issues Are Most Problematic in the Library Setting?   146

QUESTION 91: How Can a "Sick" Building Be Made Healthy?   147

QUESTION 92: What Can Be Done to Avoid the Physical Hazards Posed by Working with Computers?   148

QUESTION 93: What Can Be Done to Minimize the Emotional Problems Associated with Computer Use?   149

QUESTION 94: How Can Libraries Avoid Worker's Compensation
Claims?   150

QUESTION 95: What Legal Obligations Does the Library Have to Protect
the Safety and Health of Staff Members?   152

CHAPTER 18: Workplace Crime and Violence   154

QUESTION 96: Is Workplace Violence an Issue That Should Concern
Library Managers?   154

QUESTION 97: How Should Staff Respond to Workplace
Violence?   155

QUESTION 98: How Can Librarians Respond to Homeless Patrons Who
Seem Potentially Volatile?   156

QUESTION 99: What Causes Staff Members to Engage in Violent
Acts?   157

QUESTION 100: What Steps Can Managers Take to Minimize Workplace
Violence?   159

QUESTION 101: Is There a Chance That Concerns about Personal Safety
May Induce Dysfunctional Responses among Library
Staff?   161

PART II
The 102nd Solution   *163*

CHAPTER 19: Total Quality Management   163

Appendix: Management Maxims: Guidelines for Browsers   187

Index   203

PREFACE

It was the hope and intent of the authors to provide a concise, practical, and readable compendium of common problems and solutions to assist librarians in their day-to-day management efforts. To this end, the *Library Manager's Deskbook: 102 Expert Solutions to 101 Common Dilemmas* is useful for all who supervise, coordinate, or otherwise manage human and inanimate resources in the library. And while this book is aimed at librarians currently occupying administrative positions, it was also written for those who aspire to climb the organizational ladder. In fact, the book can be used as a supplement to management texts adopted in MLIS programs. Keeping the intended audiences for this deskbook in perspective, it is comprehensible to those who have little or no background in management. Yet the information provided is also sophisticated, offering up-to-date insights and research findings to the experienced manager.

Library managers today are employed in challenging positions. While keeping pace with technological advances in their profession, they must simultaneously be aware of the latest administrative theories, practices, and mandates. As in other professional fields, graduate education in the information science and librarianship field provides for little formal management instruction. But without an astute awareness of the tools and techniques of management, librarians may find that their objectives and visions for their libraries are thwarted.

To clarify the complexities involved in day-to-day supervision of libraries, this book poses—and then provides answers to—the most commonly asked questions about managerial roles, expectations, and requirements. To ensure the practicality and accuracy of the solutions advanced, an extensive investigation was made of the literature in both the information science and business disciplines. Such inclusive research also ensured that the breadth and depth of coverage appropriately represented the field of library administration.

ACKNOWLEDGMENTS

The writing of any book represents considerable sacrifices, tireless efforts, and dedication by many. But we would like explicitly to acknowledge the support, encouragement, and enthusiasm of our colleagues and friends at Texas A&M University–Corpus Christi and at Delta State University in Cleveland, Mississippi. Within these academic communities, we solidified many of the ideas presented in this book. In particular, we wish to recognize Dr. Myra Macon, Jo Wilson, and the staff at the W. B. Roberts Library—especially Pat, Frances, Diane, and Loretta. Finally, we wish to express our appreciation to Arthur Plotnik, Marlene Chamberlain, Mary Huchting, and the ALA Editions staff for helping us turn the idea for this book into a reality.

HOW TO USE THIS DESKBOOK

Given the hectic and relentless pace demanded of library professionals, very few managers have the luxury of reading a book from cover to cover in one sitting (or even a couple!!).

Recognizing this. . . , we have designed this deskbook in such a way that, when managerial difficulties arise, the reader can immediately locate the problem and quickly find effective and legally defensible solutions.

Step 1: Locating a Problem

All 101 questions are listed in the Contents.
The 101 questions are organized into 18 topical chapters. The 18 chapters are organized into five sections:

1. Communication Issues—a section that should be consulted when interactions with staff members and patrons are more conflict-ridden and less productive than desired.

2. Professional Issues—a section that should be consulted when questions arise about the rights and responsibilities of either professional or support staff members.

3. Employment Issues—a section that should be consulted when the library manager is in the process of screening and hiring new job applicants.

4. Personnel Issues—a section that should be consulted when current staff members feel they are not being fairly treated or when they feel their contributions are not being adequately recognized.

5. Liability Issues—a section that should be consulted when the library is threatened by inappropriate staff behaviors, natural disasters, health risks, or even unsocialized patrons.

Step 2: Implementing the Proposed Solution

Once the reader has located the relevant problem . . .

Answers are presented in comprehensive, understandable terms.
Lingo and jargon are avoided, as are abstract solutions. Instead, the answers focus on solutions that are useful, effective, and legal.

Each solution offered has been tried and tested, and established as sound practice in the managerial literature.

Step 3: Preventing Problems Altogether

Importantly, the deskbook does not assume that the best time to think about a problem is after it occurs. Instead, the book offers a "102nd" solution—a solution aimed at preventing problems before they arise.

In the second part of the book—The 102nd Solution—the authors offer a simple, but integrated overview of the philosophy of Total Quality Management.

This management approach is introduced as a mechanism for anticipating and mitigating potential dilemmas before they escalate into problems that will require intervention by the library manager.

Thus, Chapter 19 differs from the earlier chapters that focus on detecting and resolving problems after they occur. Instead of adopting a retrospective vantage, the 102nd Solution is a continuous and prospective strategy.

In short, then, this book is aimed at assisting managers before, during, and after management crises surface.

Step 4: Detecting Problems of Which the Manager Is Unaware

In many organizations (including libraries), managers reach uninformed conclusions, implement suboptimal solutions, and adopt potentially illegal positions because they are unaware of preferable alternatives.

To highlight areas where these pitfalls are particularly likely, the "Management Maxims: Guidelines for Browsers" section is included at the end of the deskbook.

The "management maxims" are statements condensed from the solutions—statements intended to highlight common misperceptions, refute accepted myths, and dispel managerial fallacies.

By browsing through this section, the reader may find suggested solutions when it was believed there were none. Readers may also discover that solutions are available to problems that were not even recognized as such. In short, the Management Maxims may alert readers to questions that have not been, but perhaps should be, raised in the library setting.

PART I
Communication Issues

CHAPTER 1
(Mis) Communication

QUESTION 1
Why Does Communication So Often Break Down?

When students of library management study the process of communication, they can be falsely lulled into believing the "textbook" model works in practice as it is presented in theory. Unfortunately, this is usually not the case. Library managers spend about 80 percent of their working time communicating with others—including staff members, patrons, vendors, and other stakeholders of the library. But much of this communication is likely to be distorted by noise.

"Noise" can be interpreted literally to mean interference caused by phone line static, background chatter, or low-flying planes overhead. But there are also "figurative" forms of noise. One such form is semantic or linguistic noise, which results when the sender and receiver define the words in a message differently. The probability of such a breakdown is heightened by the fact that in the English language, the most common 500 words have nearly 5,000 different dictionary definitions. For example, the word "set" has 58 noun meanings, 126 verb meanings, and 10 adjective meanings:

Set the table.

Are you *set* to go?

The play was *set* against the backdrop of World War II.

Turn on the television *set*.

Set the vase down.

The storm *set* her on edge.

Contextual factors may also introduce noise, as when the sender and receiver possess different frames of reference resulting from differences in age, personality, education, and vocational training. For example, manager-specific lingo or jargon—which is uninterpretable by others outside the profession—is commonly used by administrators. Words such as *magnitude* (size), *accrue* (collect), *equitable* (fair), *increment* (increase), and *ameliorate* (improve) are integral components of managers' vocabularies. Potentially ambiguous phrases often used by managers include "kick it upstairs," "bite the bullet," and "put it on the back burner." While such terms may be perfectly understandable to the library manager, they may leave the staff clueless about what is to be done.

But the problem is not just with managerial communication. The use of jargon is both pervasive and problematic in the library and information science profession. Professionals habitually use terminology— ranging from *MARC records* to *ILLs*—that can be confusing to the general public.

Library Management Tip ————————————————————————————

The English language has been criticized for being sexist and using "male" words when referring to males and females alike. Examples of male-biased language include "mankind," "businessman," "brotherhood," "councilman," "chairman," "salesman," "mailman," "policeman," and "fireman." There are similarly some female-biased words, such as "stewardess," "chamber maid," "gal Friday," and "waitress," that ought to be avoided. Instead, gender-neutral language should be substituted. Such nonbiased language is preferred by many, mandated by some publishers for written works, perceived as more politically correct, and often less offensive to the receiver. Fortunately, in the librarianship field, gender-specific language is not particularly problematic. Labels such as "librarian," "information technician," or "library associate" do not imply gender. Whenever possible, staff members should be encouraged to use neutral language to avoid alienating patrons.[1]

QUESTION 2
How Can Staff Members Ensure That Others Really Listen to What They Have to Say?

Noise can be introduced by the individual initiating *or* by the individual receiving a communication. For example, messages the receiver is not prepared to accept are filtered, distorted, or screened out; that is, the receiver engages in *selective perception*. Receivers also use selective listening, a form of selective perception, when they block out new information that is inconsistent with previously held expectations.

Understanding oral transmissions requires "active listening," which goes beyond just hearing. Active listeners are empathetic and try to determine what the speaker is saying from the speaker's point of view. Listening effectively requires the receiver to act interested, remove distractions that may impede concentration, and avoid making the speaker defensive. The average person only listens at about 25 percent efficiency. This is because while humans can speak about 125 words per minute, the brain can process at a rate of 600 words per minute. Thus, minds will naturally wander—unless we purposely engage in actively hearing the speaker.

But active listening is diminished when the receiver is overwhelmed by the information to be processed. *Information overload* is caused by receiving information in too great a quantity, at too fast a rate, or of too much complexity. Alternatively, *information underload* results from receiving too little information upon which to make a decision or take action. Like overload, information underload creates stress and role ambiguity.

QUESTION 3
Why Is the Library Manager Often the Last to Know about "Bad News"?

As communications are passed upward from staff members to library managers, their content is often altered due to the *serial transmission effect*. The serial transmission effect refers to the changes a message undergoes as it is communicated from one individual to another. In the case of upward communication, serial transmission typically results in messages becoming more positive. Employees distort information in a manner they believe will be pleasing to the supervisor, conform with what they think the superior wants to hear, or is consistent with what they want the supervisor to know.

Distortion is particularly likely when the message will make staff members look bad or when an employee is afraid the supervisor will "shoot the messenger" bearing bad news. Such gatekeeping is perpetuated by managers who prefer positive to accurate, factual information. An example of upward distortion follows:

Library Technician to Systems Librarian: "The students seem to be having problems understanding how to operate the new CD-ROMs. In particular, they don't seem comfortable with using the mouse as an input device."

Systems Librarian to Assistant Director: "The students seem to be getting used to the new CD-ROMs. But to really help them take advantage of this new service, I think we should offer training."

Assistant Director to Dean of Libraries: "The students really seem to be adapting well to the new computers we purchased for them to do literature searches. In fact, they are so popular, we are thinking about offering seminars on advanced searching techniques."

Interestingly, downward communication—messages transmitted from library managers to staff members—may also be affected by the serial transmission effect. In fact, only about 20 percent of a message originated by library directors is transmitted correctly to lower-level employees. As messages travel downward, they typically expand and become more negative. This elaboration is caused by receivers either second guessing what the higher-ups really meant or interjecting details to make the message more dramatic before sending it down to the next level.

To attenuate the serial transmission effect, library managers might engage in "MBWA" (management-by-walking-around). Physically visiting staff members and inquiring about problems lets them know administration is concerned about the quality of their work life.[2]

QUESTION 4
How Do New Staff Members Acquire the Information They Need to Perform Their Jobs Effectively?

Newcomers entering a library setting are particularly in need of information—for even though they may have had occupational training or experience, they will lack specific knowledge about organizational culture and protocol. What is disallowed? What is rewarded? What are the collective values that permeate the institution? Such questions are sometimes difficult to answer from official pronouncements or handbooks. While newcomers may directly inquire about these issues, they may often be hesitant to do so—fearing ridicule or rejection. Instead, they may resort to the following six communication tactics identified by researchers studying the socialization process. Notably, these possible information-seeking techniques vary in terms of obtrusiveness, directiveness, and riskiness:

Tactics	Examples
Indirect Questions	"I guess I shouldn't plan to leave in the evening until the night security guard reports in."
Third-Party Inquiry	"I'm going to ask the director for a new microfilm reader. Should I wait until she asks if I need anything or just go ahead and request one now?"

Testing Limits	Observe reactions to rule-breaking, such as making an increasingly large number of long-distance phone calls until asked about them.
Disguising Conversations	Observe reactions to statements such as, "It seems to me that the system for allocating time off at this library is pretty arbitrary."
Observing Coworkers	Watch employees whose requests for new equipment are granted and emulate their specific behaviors.
Surveillance	Eavesdrop on peer conversations, pay attention at work-related social events, and monitor the environment for cues.

Obviously, some of these information-seeking tactics can have dysfunctional consequences for the library. To avoid this, managers may wish to establish an open-door policy—encouraging new and tenured employees alike to come in and clarify ambiguities.[3]

When library managers need to communicate with staff members, the channel through which messages are transmitted should be carefully considered. Methods of communication have evolved from the early cave wall drawings of prehistoric peoples, to root languages such as Latin, to written notes placed in bottles and cast into the sea, to hand signs for the hearing impaired, to modern day facsimile machines and electronic mail. With each advance, the capability for transmitting understanding has been enhanced. But given all the possible choices, the library manager needs to ensure the channel of transmission is appropriate to the message being sent.

The "richest" information is transmitted through face-to-face communication. In situations involving personal interaction, there is immediate feedback, and many cues such as body language and facial expressions are exchanged—cues that may be more revealing than words themselves. Information transmitted through the telephone and other electronic media (such as voice mail) tends to be less rich than information conveyed face to face. Although tone of voice and other verbal cues are available, visual cues are missing.

Moving from the oral to the written domain, media become "lean." While rich media should be used to transmit nonroutine messages, lean media are acceptable for routine communications. Other benefits of lean written communication are that: (a) it allows for processing at the receiver's own rate, (b) it facilitates documentation of interactions,

(c) it can be disseminated widely, (d) the writer can organize material at his or her leisure, (e) it tends to be well thought-out and accurate, (f) documents can be stored and retrieved at later dates, (g) it is most effective for communicating detailed or lengthy transmissions, and (h) it spans distance and time barriers.

QUESTION 5
How Can the "Grapevine" Be Cultivated to Keep the Manager Better Informed?

The "grapevine"—a term that dates back to the Civil War when soldiers draped telegraph wires across trees to resemble a wild vine—is the network of informal organizational communication that does not follow the formal, recognized paths. Information is disseminated by the grapevine quickly and accurately. In fact, up to 90 percent of informal communications are reliable, and errors are mostly due to omission rather than commission.

> With the rapidity of a burning powder train, [grapevine] infor-
> mation flows like magic out of the woodwork, past the water
> fountain, past the manager's door and the janitor's mop closet.
> As elusive as a summer zephyr, it filters through steel walls,
> bulkheads, and construction glass partitions, from office boy
> to executive.[4]

One advantage of the grapevine is that it tends to direct information to the recipients who most need it. The grapevine also fulfills employees' social needs (by perpetuating feelings of belonging), security needs (due to the grapevine's precision and dependability), and self-esteem needs (as recipients feel important when they know what is going on). As the grapevine is a natural outgrowth of organizational life, library managers should not try to kill it, but rather feed, fertilize, and cultivate it for use.

To take advantage of the grapevine, managers must first identify its roots. Some staff members are much more likely to be tuned into the grapevine than are others. Once identified, library managers might open channels of communication with these individuals, tapping into the network. If false rumors are revealed to the manager, she or he has a supervisory obligation to dispel them. This can be accomplished through either sending a contradictory message through the grapevine or calling a formal staff meeting. Unfortunately, nearly two-thirds of workers claim they receive more information about their workplace from the grapevine than from any other source. But on the hopeful side, three-quarters would prefer to get library-specific information directly from supervisors.

QUESTION 6
What Can "Body Language" Tell Others?

Research indicates that as much as 90 percent of a message is communicated through body language and other nonverbal signals. Experts believe this is because most nonverbal messages are unintended, and hence carry more meaning than actual words. Thus, when body language contradicts a spoken message—as when a library manager tells a staff member "I'm glad you stopped in to see me" while simultaneously picking up an ALA newsletter to read—the words will lose their impact. Alternatively, if that manager had leaned forward and smiled at the entrance of the staff member, his or her greeting would have been reinforced.

Body language refers to a broad array of nonverbal cues including posture, facial expressions, eye contact, touch, and spatial distance. Those attentive to a sender's bodily positions can detect signals about the communicator's true feelings. For example, removing hands from one's pockets and uncrossing one's arms indicate a desire to be open and helpful, while maintaining an erect stance implies confidence. The monitoring of posture is particularly important to the public service librarian who must communicate openness and confidence to a distressed, confused, or overwhelmed patron.

A second form of body language is the use of gestures. The hands are considered to be very fluent and expressive. For example, a clenched fist clearly implies irritation, touching oneself on the face or neck connotes tenseness, and pointing a finger or holding jacket lapels communicates dominance. But caution should be exercised when using hand gestures because of differing cultural interpretations. An "A-OK" sign with the thumb and index finger implies acceptance in the United States, money in Japan, and something worthless in France—but in Brazil and Italy it is an obscene gesture. Similarly, the "thumbs up" sign (originally used in Roman days to spare the lives of gladiators) is a sign of affirmation in the United States, but an obscene gesture in Greece.

"Keep a stiff upper lip" and "hold your chin up high" are mandates to communicate through nonverbal facial cues. Facial expressions such as smiling, frowning, yawning, and winking are the most universally understood nonverbal cues, as they transcend geographic and cultural barriers. The emotions of fear, excitement, frustration, confidence, and anger are easily interpreted by individuals in most societies through facial configurations.

Eyes have traditionally been referred to as "windows of the soul" because of their alleged capacity to reveal insights about communicators. However, old adages such as "a liar will never look you in the eye" have been scientifically shown to be false. In fact, skilled liars always look their victims in the eye, as maintaining eye contact is a sign of power. Because eye contact is viewed as a nontactile way to "touch" somebody, effective communicators often avoid eye shifting. However, extended eye contact can imply aggressiveness.

Touching is perhaps the most primitive form of nonverbal communication, as even a fetus in the womb can be stimulated by a touch. In an organizational setting, two functions are served by touching: expressing supportiveness and communicating power or dominance. To offer nonverbal support, a pat on the back and a friendly handshake are common. But since it is typically the person of higher status who has the power to touch, this nonverbal behavior can be interpreted as a form of dominance. For example, it is the police office who touches the perpetrator, the politician who touches the baby held by a voter, the coach who touches the football players, and the doctor who touches the patient. As touching is also a part of sexual expression, its use must be monitored carefully.[5]

Spatial distance—the distance people stand from each other when they interact—is a final interpretable cue of body language. Norms about *proxemics*—the placement of individuals relative to others—prescribe varying interpersonal distances for different forms of communication. Intimate distance (up to eighteen inches or an arm's length) is the space typically reserved for sensitive communications in a close relationship. Access into the personal zone (eighteen inches to four feet) is usually restricted to relatives and good friends. Social distance (four feet to eight feet or the width of a desk) is the territory in which ordinary business and social activities usually take place. Finally, public distance (greater than eight feet) exists during activities such as speeches and committee meetings.

Library Management Tip

In addition to interpersonal distance, environmental cues are provided to others through the arrangement of office furniture. For example, when a visitor is allowed to sit next to a desk, the power of the officeholder is minimized. But when a visitor is positioned across from the desk and against a wall, the officeholder retains a strong sense of power. Further, artifacts, decorations, aesthetic objects (such as sculptures or paintings), and interior design can transmit signals. Professional certificates, degrees, plaques, and awards serve to increase others' perceptions about the officeholder's credibility.[6]

REFERENCES

1. Anderson, A. J. (February 1, 1992). The "politically incorrect" librarian. *Library Journal,* 59–60.

2. Hulbert, D. (1990). Assertive management in libraries. *Journal of Academic Librarianship,* 16(1), 158–62.

3. Turner, B. G. (1992). Nonprofessional staff in libraries: A mismanaged resource. *Journal of Library Administration,* 16(4), 57–66.

4. Sheperd, J. K. (June 13, 1979). The spread of rumors. *Indianapolis Star Magazine,* 4.

5. Goodyear, M. L., and W. K. Black (February 1991). Combating sexual harassment: A public service perspective. *American Libraries,* 134–6.

6. Kniffel, L. (April 1992). Interior dialogue: Library design speaks volumes to users. *American Libraries,* 281–8.

CHAPTER 2
Patron and Staff Diversity

QUESTION 7

How Can Library Managers Respond to the Diversity of Their Patrons?

There is no such thing as a "typical" library patron. From faculty and nontraditional students in academic libraries, to children and senior citizens in public libraries, to lawyers and physicians in special libraries—the needs, values, and interests of patrons must be carefully considered. The recent focus on multiculturalism—a broad term that not only refers to recognized racial and ethnic groups but also includes differences in sexual orientation, gender, and social class—has further changed the way libraries respond to their patrons.[1]

Library managers are no longer trying to provide service to the "melting pot" of the American culture. Rather, most view the communities they serve as representing a "salad bowl." Here, each of the various patron groups requires distinct and differentiated services. This change in orientation has allowed librarians to be at the forefront in accepting and enfranchising individuals from diverse cultures.[2]

To respond to diversity issues, the library needs to provide collections that reflect its patrons' needs. In some cases, this involves going beyond mainstream publications and indexes to locate appropriate materials. However, some librarians have encountered resistance in this area because of collection policies against acquiring material that is not indexed in standard tools. To overcome the access problem in the area of sexual orientation, the Gay and Lesbian Task Force of the American Library Association has been advocating that periodicals of interest to them be included in standard indexes.

While this 25-year-old task force is meeting with some success, many gay and lesbian library users continue to experience discrimination. For example, they indicate that materials about heterosexuality are overly represented in libraries. Further, they feel that the mere addition of books on AIDS does not meet the needs of patrons. They point out that though a disproportion of gay men may indeed be vulnerable to this disease, the same is not true for lesbians. In addition, there are other informational requirements given the unique legal, interpersonal, financial, and cultural needs of these groups. Advocates point out that there is a great deal of material available—with over three hundred gay and lesbian magazines and papers published in the United States. In addition, there are over nine thousand books available on the topic of homosexuality.[3]

Another group requiring special services from libraries is the "graying" population. There are currently about thirty-one million elderly, comprising nearly 13 percent of the population. With the aging of the baby-boom generation (those born between the years of 1946 and 1964), the proportion of senior citizens will continue to rise throughout the twenty-first century. Every day, six thousand U.S. citizens celebrate their sixty-fifth birthday—and by the year 2000, there will be more than thirty-five million Americans over the age of sixty-five.

Librarians are aware that the needs of all older Americans are not the same. Those active in their earlier retirement years will have very different interests from those who are in their mid-eighties and nineties. Beyond the varying needs of the elderly is the information required by adult children who are caring for their parents. Thus, collections on aging must cover a wide range of topics including retirement planning, adult-care programs, and choosing nursing facilities. Since the elderly utilize health care services five to seven times more than younger populations, books on basic health issues are also required. Finally, the library may consider including up-to-date Medicare regulations available in readable print size in the collection.[4]

A library located in a small Oregon town has provided a special service for senior citizens for the past twenty-five years.[5] One librarian spends fifteen hours per week delivering books to homes, nursing facilities, senior meal sites, and retirement centers. In addition to books for and about seniors, the library collection includes multimedia kits (containing such items as slides, cassettes, photographs, crossword puzzles, games, and role-playing skits) designed to stimulate the sensory and intellectual capacities of the aged. This multimedia material also encourages group discussion and participation.

QUESTION 8
What Marketing Practices Are Required to Attract Minority Groups to the Library?

By the turn of the century, the majority of U.S. citizens in 95 percent of all urban areas will be from four "minority" groups: African-

Americans, Asian-Americans, Hispanics, and Native Americans. Throughout the United States, these groups will represent about 33 percent of the total population by the year 2000. One of the fastest growing populations in the United States is the Spanish-speaking minority. But even when librarians recognize this trend, appropriate collections are difficult to develop because publishers underemphasize the foreign-language market. In their defense, publishers point out that the U.S. Spanish-speaking population is extremely diverse—economically, politically, and educationally. So, in an effort to be responsive to this diversity, some libraries use their monies to purchase newspapers from patrons' home countries.[6]

But even when newspapers are available, it may be difficult to get the patron through the library's doors. Therefore, different types of marketing techniques have been used to bring members of the Hispanic group into the library. For example, the Miami-Dade County Public Library System makes regular public service announcements on the radio, on Hispanic TV programs, and in the daily paper, *El Nuevo Herald*. In library systems with branches near the Mexican border, managers should be aware of the confusion created by the Spanish word *libreria*—which means "bookstore" (*biblioteca* means "library"). In contrast, a library branch serving third-generation Hispanics might be less concerned with such language problems.

Marketing techniques will vary depending upon the background and acculturation of the patrons—as differences among people arise, in part, from their cultural heritage. Geert Hofstede, a Dutch researcher, offers a systematic framework for understanding people with divergent cultural backgrounds. He suggests that there are four concepts which differentiate national cultures: (1) strong uncertainty avoidance versus weak uncertainty avoidance, (2) centralized power versus diffused power, (3) masculine versus feminine gender orientation, and (4) individualism versus collectivism. These dimensions can be used as a theoretical framework for addressing marketing issues.

For example, Hofstede's research suggests that Mexican nationals have strong uncertainty avoidance needs, which result in ambiguous situations being interpreted as dangerous. Because of this orientation, clear rules, instructions, and policies are readily accepted and even desired. Hence, published procedures for using the library may enhance its attractiveness to this population. On the power dimension, Mexicans expect professionals to be more authoritarian than do U.S.-born citizens. However, Mexico is very similar to the United States in how social gender roles are viewed. Finally, the individual is subordinate to the group in Mexico. Everyone belongs to a collective (usually based on familial relationships) that fosters each member's well-being in exchange for loyalty and contribution to the group's legacy.

Because people with a Mexican cultural background tend to be strongly family oriented, some libraries focus on getting children and parents into the library through school-sponsored activities. With this technique, it is often important to provide the youngsters with bilingual books so that the Spanish-speaking parents can read along with their children who have mastered English.

QUESTION 9
What Communication Techniques Are Required to Serve Minority Groups?

Serving patrons in their preferred language can often lead to better utilization of the library. Five communication areas are important to multilingual service providers: symbols, written communication, speaker messages, face-to-face interaction, and telephone conversations.[7] First, widely understood symbols rather than words can be used in the library. For example, pictures can identify restrooms and telephone locations. Second, more complex information can be printed in multiple languages. Multilingualism can be applied not only to signs, but also to advanced technology such as computer systems that allow the patron to choose the language she or he prefers. Third, spoken messages—such as announcements about the closing time of the library—can be prerecorded in more than one language. The fourth important area is having multilingual staff available to help patrons.

When multilingual staff are not available, the library may want to have a series of brochures that provide answers to the most commonly asked questions. Also, phrase cards can be made available so that the staff member and patron can communicate by pointing to the relevant phrase. Finally, the library may have more than one telephone number so that a line can be assigned to a specific language group. But, of course, there are resource limitations on what the library can accomplish in the multilingual area. For example, within the Asian-American group alone, there are over one hundred Chinese dialects.

Multiculturalism goes beyond resolving linguistic problems to focus on other patron needs. To deal with the whole individual, some libraries have hired staff members who serve as "cultural brokers." These employees know the language of the patron, understand their nonverbal communications, and are familiar with the patron's culture.[8] Patrons often feel that the library is more adequately meeting their needs when there is a staff member present who understands them. As more and more library managers recognize this need, additional job requirements are being imposed on job applicants. For example, some south Texas university libraries are requiring that job seekers be able to speak Spanish. In other cases, so as not to exclude any qualified applicants, libraries are encouraging staff members to take classes on the language and customs of unfamiliar cultures.

QUESTION 10
What Are the Library's Obligations in Recruiting Minority Applicants?

By the year 2005, an additional twenty-six million people are expected to join the labor force. These workers are not coming from the traditional white male group—rather they are coming from groups that have historically been underrepresented in the workplace. Specifically, there is a projected 26 percent increase in women, 32 percent increase in African-Americans, 75 percent increase in Hispanics, and 74 percent increase in Asians and other minority laborers. Unfortunately, hiring practices in libraries have not reflected these trends. According to U.S. Census figures, of those currently employed in libraries only 8 percent are African-Americans and 2 percent are Hispanic.[9]

These figures represent a serious problem, as the pluralistic needs of patrons cannot be met by a homogeneous white staff—a diverse staff is essential. To provide better service, library administrators in culturally diverse areas are trying to increase the number of bilingual and bicultural staff members to better serve their diverse populations. Although a diverse staff may initially pose some problems for the library manager, in the long run, service quality may be improved through broader input into decision making and incorporation of divergent value systems into library policies.

Beyond service-quality reasons for hiring diverse staff, there are also legal reasons for doing so. Affirmative action guidelines require that those traditionally underrepresented in the labor market be given an opportunity to hold positions through which they can contribute. Affirmative action programs are designed to remedy past discrimination through the hiring and promotion of protected group members. Libraries receiving substantial federal monies ($50,000 or more) are required to abide by affirmative action guidelines. Those that fail to do so can come under a great deal of scrutiny. For example, Library of Congress administrators have been brought before a House subcommittee where two consultants testified that there was not an aggressive affirmative action program in place.

Library Management Tip

Although not all libraries are required to have affirmative action programs, those found guilty of discrimination might be forced to implement them through a court-ordered consent decree. Other libraries may, however, voluntarily implement affirmative action programs to correct past underutilization of protected group members or to facilitate an organization's commitment to proportional representation. In the case of voluntary programs, libraries should protect themselves against reverse discrimination claims by outlining specific timetables and goals.

Though affirmative action programs are designed to make up for past discrimination, current enrollment in library schools suggests that recruitment of minorities will continue to be a problem. Racial and ethnic minorities have been underrepresented in library schools through the past two decades.[10] For example, 9.63 percent of the 1979 graduates from library and information science schools were from ethnic minority groups. These figures declined to 6.01 percent in 1984 and then rose slightly to 6.3 percent in 1988. Today, about 8.5 percent of library school graduates are from minority groups.

There are a number of ways for the profession to increase the number of minorities receiving graduate training. First, there could be more partnerships formed between library educators and library administrators to promote the active hiring of minority graduates. Next, additional tuition waivers and monetary support could be targeted at underrepresented populations. Also, recruitment efforts could be aimed at the high school level so that first-year college students begin selecting librarianship as a career option. Further, nontraditional students from community colleges could be more aggressively recruited. And finally, the campus climate for minorities could be made more supportive.[11]

While there is need to bring more minorities into the profession, the American Library Association has been actively focusing on diversity issues for a few decades. Alex Boyd, president of the ALA Black Caucus, notes that diversity is not a passing fad. This caucus has long urged that members of minority groups be recruited for professional service roles within the association. Naomi Caldwell-Wood, president of the American Indian Library Association, adds that members of these groups should be given the opportunity to run for elected office and serve on committees beyond those dealing specifically with multicultural and diversity issues.[12]

Because the professional association is committed to providing equality of opportunity for all of its members, leadership has been cognizant of special issues for various groups. Because of this sensitivity, the American Library Association withdrew the 1995 Midwinter Meeting from Cincinnati and the 1998 Midwinter Meeting from Denver because the city councils there failed to protect gays and lesbians from discriminatory practices.

QUESTION 11
How Can Library Managers Successfully Retain a Diversified Staff?

As the demographic makeup of the labor force shifts from its traditional white male domination to a more heterogeneous composition, libraries are raising their levels of awareness about managing diversity. Managing diversity includes recognizing new types of staff members, learning to understand the needs and desires of nontraditional workers, and creating an environment in which minorities can succeed. Successful management of a diversified labor force can have many positive implications for a library. For example, it can improve service delivery by reducing turnover of females and racioethnic minorities, it can reduce discrimination litigation, and it can enhance recruitment efforts.

Library Management Tip ─────────────────────

A diverse staff is often viewed quite positively as improving decision making and increasing creativity. However, there can be some unexpected outcomes in multicultural settings. California researchers found that white males in a racially diverse work setting reported less organizational commitment than those in racially homogenous settings. In addition, men reported lower loyalty to the organization as the number of women in the unit increased. In contrast, women reported higher organizational commitment when a higher percentage of men were in the work setting.

Recruiting and retaining a multicultural staff may introduce some managerial complexities. White males may have some negative affective reactions. Women may need day-care services. Asian-American employees may be concerned about losing face from negative feedback at the performance appraisal interview. Health benefits for domestic partners may become a focal issue for gay and lesbian groups.[13] And conflicts and misunderstandings may surface between members of different groups. Because of the complexities of managing cultural diversity in the library setting, a three-pronged approach may be necessary: awareness building, discrimination control, and prejudice reduction.

First, to facilitate awareness building, library administrators must be committed to openly dealing with diversity issues. Interviews, focus groups, and survey questionnaires can be used to gather relevant information for administrative initiatives. Further, employee orientation and ongoing training programs can focus on multiculturalism.

After building awareness, management can engage in discrimination control. Discrimination—or the mistreatment of groups based upon irrelevant factors—can be controlled through appropriate role-modeling by managers and library professionals. These library leaders need to display cooperation, sensitivity, and empathy when dealing with members from minority groups. Staff members' evaluations of library managers can provide important feedback about the appropriateness of their role-modeling. Discrimination control can also be tackled through proper career management of minority groups. Providing equal opportunities for rising in the hierarchy can help all attain their potential.

The third step in handling cultural diversity is prejudice reduction. Prejudices—or inaccurate perceptions based on group membership—can be reduced through environmental and normative influences. Therefore, library administrators need to encourage a culture that is accepting of all members regardless of the group to which they belong.

Library Management Tip ———————————————————————

Diversity consultants offer ten ways for managers to deal with incidents of prejudicial treatment: (1) serve as an appropriate role model for staff, (2) let staff know what behaviors won't be tolerated, (3) refute assumptions about stereotypes, (4) help staff understand cultural differences, (5) use insensitive incidents as teaching opportunities, (6) build in opportunities for cross-cultural interaction, (7) provide training to deepen understanding, (8) assign diverse members to project teams, (9) note common objectives of the work group, and (10) be aware that none of us is free from the effects of stereotypes.[14]

REFERENCES

1. Smith, K. P. (1993). The multicultural ethic and connections to literature for children and young adults. *Library Trends,* 41(3), 340–53.

2. Stoffle, C. (October 1, 1990). A new library for the new undergraduate. *Library Journal,* 47–51.

3. Gough, C., and E. Greenblatt (January 1992). Services to gay and lesbian patrons: Examining the myths. *Library Journal,* 59–63.

4. Lovie-Kitchin, J., N. J. Oliver, A. Bruce, and M. S. Leighton (1994). The effect of print size on reading rate for adults and children. *Clinical and experimental optometry,* 77(1), 2.

5. Saunders, K. (February 1992). Expanding outreach services to seniors. *American Libraries,* 176–80.

6. Hoffert, B. (July 1992). ¡Se lea Espanol aqui! *Library Journal,* 34–7.

7. Lovelock, C. (April 1994). Going multilingual: A new marketing priority. *Marketing Forum,* 2.

8. Flagg, G. (January 1993). Racial controversy embroils West Las Vegas branch. *American Libraries,* 7.

9. Chadley, O. A. (May 1992). Addressing cultural diversity in academic and research libraries. *College & Research Libraries,* 206–14.

10. Knowles, E. M., and L. Jolivet (Fall 1991). Recruiting the underrepresented: Collaborative efforts between library educators and library practitioners. *Library Administration & Management,* 189–93.

11. McCook, K., and P. Geist (November 1, 1993). Diversity deferred: Where are the minority librarians? *Library Journal,* 35–38.

12. Liu, C. F. L. (Summer 1994). Cultural diversity: A conversation with the presidents of ALA's ethnic caucuses, Part 2. *Library Administration & Management,* 126–30.

13. St. Lifer, E., and M. Rogers (January 1993). Lesbian librarians win discrimination suit. *Library Journal,* 16.

14. Gardenswartz, L., and A. Rowe (1994). Dealing with prejudice and stereotypes on the job. *Managing Diversity,* 3(6), 1–4.

CHAPTER 3
Personality Differences, Conflicts, and Creativity

How Do Staff Members Differ in Their Views of Fairness and Justice?

Staff members want to be treated fairly compared to others—so they determine equitable treatment by comparing their inputs and outcomes to others' inputs and outcomes.[1] Inputs can include such factors as amount of work, quality of work, education and training, tenure in the library, tenure in the profession, workplace attitudes, and even personal attractiveness. Outcomes include such elements as pay, promotions, status, autonomy, recognition, approval, and favorable working conditions.

Staff members vary in their notions about what constitutes equitable treatment in the library setting. Many are "equity sensitives"—that is, they perceive equity when their outcome/input ratios are about the same as others' outcome/input ratios. However, a few staff members are "benevolents." They are very giving and actually prefer to have lower ratios than others. In contrast, some workers are "entitleds." Entitleds feel as if they are quite deserving, and they fully expect their ratios to exceed others.

As a general rule, most workers are rather tolerant of having higher ratios than other employees. Only when individuals feel they are being tremendously overcompensated compared to others do they tend to feel guilty. In response to this guilt, employees usually increase the *quality* of their output. However, most staff members are painfully sensitive to their outcome/input ratios being less than others'. When they feel slightly undercompensated, staff members tend to decrease their *quantity* of work.

Fairness of pay within the library is judged on two criteria—distributive justice and procedural justice. Distributive justice focuses on the fairness of the *amount* of rewards received, while procedural

19

justice deals with the *process* by which rewards are allocated. With procedural justice, the concern is with fairness of the administration of rules for promotions and pay increases. When there is a perception of distributive justice and procedural justice, staff members are likely to be both satisfied and committed to the library. Importantly, these members are less likely to look for another job as compared to those who feel that there is a lack of justice in the workplace.

Library Management Tip

The propensity to engage in "just" acts is influenced by three personality variables. First, those with an "internal locus of control" are more likely to do the right thing as compared to those with an "external locus of control." Individuals with an internal locus feel they exert control over their work environment. Therefore, these staff members tend to engage in helping behavior and resist pressures to harm or cheat. Second, an individual's "ego strength" influences his or her sense of justice. Individuals with high ego strength have the ability to resist impulsive behavior. They are led by the strength of their convictions and, thus, consistently engage in honest behavior. Finally, "field-independent" individuals function autonomously and don't depend upon others to guide their actions. Therefore, they are less likely to go along with the crowd than those who are field dependent.

QUESTION 13
How Do Individual Differences in Thinking Styles Affect the Workplace?

Conflict at work is often the result of personal differences among staff members who vary in age, social status, education, race, tenure, salary, and value systems.[2] Individuals also differ in their ways of thinking and of processing information about their environment; for example, some staff members are more analytical while others are more inventive. These dissimilarities in learning styles can cause friction between staff members, as they will have disparate perceptions of their world. Learning styles also influence the positions that staff members seek to fill in the library. For example, those with a logical style of thinking are attracted to jobs that are organized and detailed. Those with an imaginative style of thinking will seek out jobs compatible with creativity.[3]

One of the more sophisticated instruments for measuring differences in thinking styles is the Myers-Briggs Type Indicator. This personality measure, developed by a mother-daughter team (Katharine C. Briggs and Isabel Briggs Myers), is based on the theoretical formulations of Carl Jung. When individuals take this test, their learning style is evaluated on four dimensions: Extrovert/Introvert, Sensing/Intuitive,

Thinking/Feeling, and Judging/Perceiving. Of the 267 professional librarians listed in one large research database, the four-letter diagnostic code revealed that a majority scored as ISFJ: Introverted (61%), Sensing (54%), Feeling (67%), Judging (64%). Generally, this profile group consists of organized fact-gathers who are calm, quiet, deliberate, trustworthy, and patient. Also, they tend to be nice, diplomatic, supportive, steady, and conservative.[4] Those with an ISFJ profile are not only attracted to careers as librarians but also as clergy members, nurses, and teachers.

As people tend to pick careers that match their personalities, it is logical that there would be some similarities in thinking styles within a profession. And while there are indeed similarities among librarians, between 33 percent and 46 percent do not fit the ISFJ category. Thus, career and personality matches are not cast in stone.

QUESTION 14
What Is Intuition and How Does It Influence the Quality of Decisions?

While a majority of professional librarians are ISFJ, many library managers are INFJ. That is, managers tend to rely more on intuition (N) than do librarians who rely more on sensing (S). Intuitive decision making occurs when alternatives are selected without formal analysis. Although library administrators only reluctantly admit to reliance upon intuition, evidence suggests many good decisions are made based on managers' "gut feelings." Five explanations have been advanced to explain the source of an individual's intuition.[5]

Some suggest that intuition is a paranormal power, or sixth sense, made up of clairvoyance and telepathy. This school of thought believes that intuitive decision makers have extrasensory power that their non-intuitive counterparts lack or have not successfully cultivated. A second group feels that intuition is a personality trait—a stable personality attribute developed during formative years. Proponents of this explanation suggest that intuition cannot be cultivated during adulthood as reliance on hunches, inspiration, and insight results from early development of the left brain. Others suggest that intuition is a preconscious process, based on impressions collected in past experiences that cannot be verbalized. This explanation is often used to account for "eureka" experiences. A fourth explanation is that intuition is the result of gathering information from sources not typically consulted. Finally, some suggest that intuition occurs when a decision maker recognizes a situation as being similar to one experienced in the past. Here, intuition is seen as a learned response that facilitates quick problem recognition and instantaneous decisions.

Despite long-held skepticism, intuition is finding its way out of the closet and into library management circles. Indeed, management research has found a positive relationship between intuitive decision making and organizational performance. Furthermore, administrators who have risen to top management levels also tend to be more "intuitive" and have a good track record of making high quality decisions based on their hunches. To capitalize on the advantages of intuitive decision making, some libraries are attempting to provide training on how to become more intuitive.

QUESTION 15
How Should Conflicts among Staff Members Be Resolved?

The historical view of organizational conflict has been that it is something bad—conflict should not exist in healthy organizations. Today, management theorists recognize that some conflict is helpful in the library environment. If there is no conflict, things never change. On the other hand, if there is too much conflict, energy is spent on winning arguments rather than pursuing library objectives. Thus, there is an optimal middle ground—between monotony and open warfare—where conflict is functional and desired.

There are many benefits associated with appropriate levels of conflict. Foremost, there is the potential for innovation and change when staff members are free to express their diverse opinions about ways to meet organizational goals. From an assortment of ideas, new ways of communicating information, allocating resources, and providing services may emerge. Also, in an environment of functional conflict, issues and goals can be easily clarified, resulting in increased teamwork.[6]

When conflict exceeds appropriate limits, it usually means that staff members' disagreements no longer focus on library issues but rather on personal agendas. Instead of concentrating on better solutions, staff members become involved in an emotional tug-of-war which they strive to win. Unfortunately, the library becomes the loser—as its goals become secondary to the personal goals of those involved in the conflict.[7]

There are five different conflict resolution styles that can be discriminately used by library managers. In emergencies, the use of a *dominating* style may be the best technique for library managers. Here, the manager uses his or her power to take quick decisive action. An *accommodating* style is useful if there is much more at stake for the staff member than for the supervisor. Here, the library manager satisfies the staff member's needs as a goodwill gesture. An *avoiding* style is used when the matter is of little importance to the supervisor. A fourth technique, *compromising,* allows the staff member and supervisor to find a middle ground. It can be used if the issue is not worth the effort involved in collaborating. *Collaborating* is the best conflict management method to use when the issue is very important to both parties—and when there is sufficient time to come up with an optimum solution. With this resolution technique, the supervisor and staff member jointly address the issue to find a creative and mutually satisfying solution.

QUESTION 16
How Can Library Managers Foster Creativity?

Recognizing that some constructive conflict is desirable, the library manager can use groups for creative decision making when complex problems require a variety of opinions. High quality group decision making is typically accompanied by free expression of ideas, diversity, and flexibility. There are three group techniques that can be used to involve staff members in a creative decision-making process. These techniques are brainstorming, nominal grouping, and Delphi.

Brainstorming is a group approach that enhances the creativity of alternatives by allowing for an open discussion and exchange of ideas. Quantity of ideas, rather than an evaluation of feasibility, is encouraged. Members are made aware that no idea is too weird and that building upon unusual suggestions is perfectly appropriate. As this technique is useful for formulating a number of potential alternatives, criticism of members' suggestions is strictly prohibited.

The nominal group technique is in many ways opposite to brainstorming, as the free discussion of ideas is restricted. With this approach, members silently record ideas about possible alternatives and then present them to the group. No discussion or criticism is allowed while participants present their suggestions—only points of clarification are permitted. Members then silently rank all alternatives presented by the group. Since nominal grouping prohibits open discussion about the merits of suggestions, peer pressure is avoided.

The Delphi technique is procedurally similar to nominal grouping, except that the group members are geographically separate and their identities remain anonymous. Potential alternatives are generated by each individual and forwarded to a central location where a coordinator summarizes the information and redistributes it back to all members. Based on other members' inputs, the individual ranks the suggestions and sends the rankings back to the coordinator. This process continues until there is a general consensus about an appropriate alternative. Although the Delphi technique is somewhat slow, it reduces the need for travel, it can deal with sensitive issues, it allows for outsider participation, and it avoids political alignments and peer pressure.

QUESTION 17
What Happens When Groups Are So Cohesive That Even Constructive Conflict Is Avoided?

Despite the many advantages associated with group decision making, there can be inherent problems with groups—particularly when there is insufficient conflict. One of these difficulties is overconformity, which can result in "groupthink."[8] Groupthink occurs in overly cohesive groups where there is so much pressure for consensus that individual members lose their capacity to evaluate alternatives realistically. This push for agreement reduces critical thinking and impedes comprehensive development of options.

Groupthink can be identified based on the following symptoms: (a) illusions of invulnerability: overemphasis of the group's strengths; (b) illusions of unanimity: a lack of overt dissension is perceived as complete approval; (c) illusions of group morality: members of the group feel their position is totally just and ethical; (d) perceptions that the enemy is inferior: the opposition is regarded as weak, dumb, or bad; (e) self-censorship: members avoid verbalizing dissenting opinions; (f) mind guarding: self-appointed members actively try to eliminate any negative feedback; and (g) direct pressure: if members express negative opinions, they are controlled through overt coercion.

In addition to groupthink, there is another potential problem associated with using group decision making. This problem is polarization—defined as the tendency for members' opinions to be more extreme after group interaction. Rather than having a moderating effect, group discussion seems to push members to select more extreme solutions. For example, if members are generally leaning toward a somewhat risky solution before meeting, a "risky shift" may occur in which the group encourages a more precarious decision than the average premeeting opinion. If the premeeting opinion is somewhat conservative, a "cautious shift" occurs in which the group supports greater wariness. Even after the meeting, members cling to their polarized opinions developed through the group interaction.

One possible cause of polarization is social comparison. Group members compare themselves to others. Those who find that others have more extreme positions than they do may feel unsure about the appropriateness of their opinion. These members may shift to extreme positions to align with others and reduce their feelings of uncertainty.

Instead of striving for the agreement and consensus associated with groupthink and polarization, groups should attempt to achieve harmonies of difference, in which the diverse opinions of members are reconciled and integrated into a common solution. To encourage creative and high quality solutions, the library manager can facilitate true disagreement, argumentation, confrontation, scrutiny, and criticism. This can be accomplished by intentionally composing decision groups of individuals who have diverse perspectives and who question the perspectives of other members.

Library Management Tip

There are a number of techniques a manager can use to avoid overconformity in group decision making. First, the manager can encourage programmed conflict. Here, the "devil's advocate" role can be assigned to a member who takes the position of identifying potential problems inherent in a proposed course of action. Second, the library manager can mandate use of the dialectic method, in which there is a structured debate between opposing views in which even basic assumptions are questioned. Here, group members are asked to present information on why the popular alternative is not viable or why other alternatives are also viable. Third, library managers should avoid stating their preferences as members may be easily influenced by their formal position. Instead, the manager can serve as a coordinator and facilitator for the group. Finally, the manager can invite outsiders to participate in the decision-making process. Individuals not directly involved in the decision may offer unique ideas not previously considered by the staff.

REFERENCES

1. Adams, J. S. (1965). Injustice in social exchange, in L. Berkowitz (ed.), *Advances in experimental social psychology* (vol. 2; pp. 283–96). New York: Academic Press.

2. Pettas, W., and S. L. Gilliland (1992). Conflict in the large academic library: Friend or foe? *Journal of Academic Librarianship,* 18(1), 24–9.

3. Squires, D., H. K. Hoopes, and G. P. Gillum (Fall 1992). Librarians: A thinking and learning styles portrait. *Library Administration & Management,* 173–9.

4. Webb, B. (June 15, 1990). Type-casting life with Myers-Briggs. *Library Journal,* 32–7.

5. Behling, O., and N. L. Eckel (1991). Making sense out of intuition. *Academy of Management Executive,* 5, 46–54.

6. Kathman, J. M., and M. D. Kathman (1990). Conflict management in the academic library. *Journal of Academic Librarianship,* 16(3), 145–9.

7. Fisher, W., and G. Koue (Summer 1991). Conflict management. *Library Administration & Management,* 145–50.

8. Janis, I. L. (1982). *Groupthink: Psychological studies of policy decisions and fiascoes,* 2nd ed. Boston: Houghton Mifflin.

CHAPTER 4
Power Use and Abuse

What Does "Power" Have to Do with Library Management?

Simply stated, power is what managers use to influence others. When employees are cooperative, influence is easily accomplished. At other times, however, a manager may need staff members to do things against their will. It is in these cases that the use of power must be carefully considered. Philosophers and social theorists from Plato to Aristotle through Machiavelli and Weber have struggled with the phenomenon of power. It is a concept that is difficult to fully comprehend because while power is central to the accomplishment of library goals, it has a tendency to be abused. Unfortunately, the axioms "power breeds power" and "absolute power corrupts absolutely" do in fact have some merit. The challenge facing the library manager is to effectively use power in a manner that minimizes resentment, hostility, and vengeful reactions.

Borrowing from the seminal works of social psychologists Wendell French and John Raven, five different types or "bases" of power can be defined:[1]

1. *Legitimate power,* derived from the authority inherent in a managerial position.

2. *Reward power,* derived from the library manager's ability to allocate rewards.

3. *Coercive power,* derived from the library manager's ability to mediate punishments.

4. *Referent power,* which results when staff members identify with and are attracted to the library manager.

5. *Expert power*, which results when staff members perceive the library manager possesses special knowledge, unique expertise, or rare skills.

Legitimate, reward, and coercive powers are collectively known as "positional" bases, for they emanate from the job held by the manager rather than from any individual characteristics or attributes of the manager. Alternatively, referent and expert powers are "personal" bases, as they are earned by the manager rather than bestowed with a promotion or appointment to the management team.

QUESTION 19
Which Power Base Should the Library Manager Use?

The answer to this question is a definitive "it depends!"—it is contingent upon what outcome is desired in response to the use of power. Managers most typically exercise power to facilitate the execution of a request. Hence, the best outcome of an influence attempt is *commitment,* wherein a staff member enthusiastically follows a leader's wishes. Commitment typically results only when the personal power bases are utilized. A less acceptable outcome is *compliance,* meaning that a staff member will obey but with minimal effort exertion. Compliance usually follows requests made on the legitimate and reward power bases. A third, undesirable, outcome is *resistance,* in which staff members oppose a request either overtly or through more subtle means such as excuse making or delaying action. Resistance will be the typical outcome following use of coercive power.[2]

Given that staff members are likely to resist requests based on coercion, one might logically question whether this power base offers any benefit at all. But under some circumstances—such as emergency, times of crises, and severe economic constraints—coercion may be the most effective power base upon which to rely. Under such circumstances, coercive acts will be tolerated, and perhaps even expected, by staff members.[3]

Library Management Tip

Observation of individuals employed in service occupations such as librarianship has led to identification of the "mirror effect." The mirror effect results when staff members' treatment of patrons mirrors management's treatment of staff members. That is, if the personal needs of staff members are ignored by management, staff members will in turn disregard the needs of patrons.

In addition to examining the effectiveness of the power bases, it may also be important to recognize the consequences of power usage on attitudes and performance. Results from a meta-analysis conducted on these relationships are summarized in figure 1.[3] As shown, legitimate power usage neither enhances nor diminishes attitudes and performance. While reward power only influences performance, coercive power surprisingly has no effect on performance. Instead, coercion creates negative attitudes. And while referent power usage does indeed exert positive effects, expert power seems most conducive to improving satisfaction and heightening performance.

QUESTION 20
How Can the Library Manager Determine Which Power Base Is Being Used?

Power is often perceived differently by managers and staff members. For example, while a library manager may believe that subordinates are executing requests because of expert power, they may really be doing so to avoid coercion. As a consequence of this confusion, the library manager may be puzzled by staff member resistance to instructions. To gain insight into what power bases are predominantly utilized, the library manager might administer the "Library Manager Power Profile" questionnaire to staff members (*see* figure 2).

To encourage staff member cooperation in this exercise, the library manager might explain that input is being sought to improve the manager's leadership style. Given such an explanation, staff members will likely feel a greater sense of empowerment in their workplace. The exercise should only require about ten minutes of each staff member's time.

Figure 1. The Effect of Power Base Usage on Attitudes and Performance

	Outcomes		
Power Base	Satisfaction with Supervision	Job Satisfaction	Performance
Legitimate	No effect	No effect	No effect
Reward	No effect	No effect	Moderate positive effect
Coercive	Strong negative effect	Moderate negative effect	No effect
Referent	Strong positive effect	Weak positive effect	Weak positive effect
Expert	Strong positive effect	Strong positive effect	Strong positive effect

Figure 2. Library Manager Power Profile

Use the following responses to answer the fifteen questions:

    1 = Strongly Agree
    2 = Agree
    3 = Slightly Agree
    4 = Disagree
    5 = Strongly Disagree

_____ 1. I do what my supervisor asks because she or he has a right to direct my work.

_____ 2. I carry out my supervisor's wishes because she or he can reward me if I do.

_____ 3. If I don't do what is asked of me, I can expect my supervisor to make life more difficult around here for me.

_____ 4. Since I like my manager on a personal level, I try to do what she or he wants me to do.

_____ 5. I do what my manager asks because she or he usually knows what is best.

_____ 6. My manager occupies a position of authority, so I do what she or he wants me to do.

_____ 7. If I do what my manager wants, I can expect some extra compensation in return.

_____ 8. I do what my manager asks because I am afraid of the consequences if I don't.

_____ 9. I consider myself to have work values very similar to those held by my manager.

_____ 10. I consider my supervisor to be an expert in the field of librarianship.

_____ 11. I comply with requests made by my supervisor because a person in his or her position should be respected.

_____ 12. Compliance with my supervisor's requests often results in greater recognition and reward.

_____ 13. Not complying with my supervisor's requests will certainly bring about some reprisal.

_____ 14. I do what is asked by my supervisor because I respect him or her as an individual.

_____ 15. If I comply with the requests of my manager, I know things will be done right.

Scoring Key:

    Questions 1, 6, and 11 assess legitimate power.
    Questions 2, 7, and 12 assess reward power.
    Questions 3, 8, and 13 assess coercive power.
    Questions 4, 9, and 14 assess referent power.
    Questions 5, 10, and 15 assess expert power.

A score of 3 to 6 signifies a weak power base.
A score of 7 to 11 signifies a moderate power base.
A score of 11 to 15 signifies a strong power base.

QUESTION 21

How Can Using the Reward Power Base Backfire?

It is a well-established finding that recognizing and rewarding staff members for desirable behaviors can motivate them to repeat those behaviors. In fact, B. F. Skinner, the celebrated psychologist, developed his entire "reinforcement" theory around this idea. In the field of librarianship, empirical research has found that managers spend a large portion of their time making decisions about reward allocations.[4]

But notably, (over)reliance on reward power can produce some unintended adverse consequences. For example, when reward power is used to ensure compliance with requests, flirtations with impropriety would not be surprising. That is, some employees may go to inappropriate or even unethical lengths to gain the reward. Such undesirable acts may involve falsifying records, taking credit for coworkers' accomplishments, or ignoring all other job responsibilities except fulfilling the request.

Additionally, when employees begin focusing on earning extrinsic rewards, the joy of performing their work may be diminished. That is, intrinsic motivation may be inadvertently undermined. This is known as the *overjustification effect*. When overjustification is operative, any job enrichment efforts will likely be futile.

Next, if an individual comes to expect a reward each time a task is performed, the reward may be perceived as a right rather than as a discretionary bonus. As a corollary, withholding the reward may be interpreted as an act of coercion.

Finally, a reward may be perceived as a bribe, leading to perceptions that the library manager is manipulative. Despite these cautionary words, leaders not possessing personal power may have to rely upon reward power, since it is the positional base most strongly related to performance.

QUESTION 22
What Factors Diminish or Enhance the "Personal" Power Bases of Expertise and Reward?

Expert power is quirky; while it is the base that seems most useful under normal conditions, it is also the base that is most difficult to develop and most susceptible to erosion. As library managers share their specialized knowledge and unique skills with others, dependence upon the leader is reduced and expert power diminished. Because of this, some power holders attempt to protect their expertise by exaggerating the complexity of tasks and removing alternative sources of information. But as Brooke Sheldon—a recognized library leader[5]—observes, "the basic formula for success belongs to the [librarian] who . . . understands that the value of power is sharing it."[6] This is certainly true in the case of expert power. Fortunately, less subversive methods, such as keeping informed, are available for maintaining and even enhancing expert power. Notably though, for library managers to maintain expert power, they must possess knowledge in both the information science and the administrative domains.

History tells us the field of librarianship has benefited from the expertise of many, including Panizzi who developed cataloguing rules, Dewey who developed narrow subject classifications, and Jewett who structured subject headings.[7] But amassing expert power does not depend solely on the development of such innovations. Instead, expertise is incrementally built through continuing professional development, reading of professional literature, and personal efforts at maintaining sharp skills. Expert power results from being consistently approachable by staff members with questions, a willingness to share information, and a desire to help staff members solve work-related problems.[8]

Referent power positively influences both attitudes and performance, but it is most strongly related to satisfaction with the leader. Enhancing one's referent power base also facilitates employee loyalty— a topic which has received very little attention in the librarianship literature.[9] When relationships are based on referent power, staff members tend to imitate the supervisor's behaviors and adopt the supervisor's attitudes—which can eliminate workplace conflicts and facilitate efficient services. Since referent power is slow to develop, the process can be hastened by selecting employees similar to the library manager.

Library Management Tip ————————————————————————

While selecting a staff that holds values similar to those of the library manager may enhance referent power, such homogeneity can also diminish the creativity needed in the library. The benefits of a multicultural staff who posses divergent values are well known. Furthermore, library managers have both an ethical and a legal mandate to assemble a diverse staff. Thus a basic dilemma is created. Individuals of different backgrounds will have a difficult time identifying with the library manager, but simultaneously benefits will accrue to the patrons. One way to overcome this dilemma is for the library manager to decrease status differentials between the staff and him- or herself, increasing feelings of identification and reference.

Below are some guidelines for enhancing both the personal and the positional power bases.

Base of Power	*Guidelines for Use*
Legitimate	Make requests in a cordial, confident, and clear manner; follow up to verify understanding of requests; ensure requests are appropriate; enforce compliance with requests.

Base of Power	Guidelines for Use
Reward	Ensure that requests are work related, ethical, appropriate, and feasible; verify compliance with requests; offer rewards desired by staff members; ensure that reward follows compliance.
Coercive	Verify that staff members understand requests and the penalties associated with not executing requests; punish consistently and without bias; ensure that a punishment is appropriate to an infraction; discipline in private.
Expert	Maintain and protect credibility through personal and professional development; promote image of expertise; act confident and decisive when queried; recognize staff members' informational needs; avoid threatening employees' self-esteem.
Referent	Be sensitive to staff members' needs; treat staff fairly; defend the interests of the staff; emphasize value congruence with staff members; engage in role-modeling and mentoring.

Requests based on legitimate power should be made in a polite, rational, clear, and confident manner. Compliance should be enforced, as employees must believe that the library manager has the authority to expect obedience. Given the potential adverse consequences associated with the use of rewards, caution should be taken when exercising this power base. Requests should be appropriate, and rewards should be desired by the staff. Furthermore, rewards should be noneconomic as well as monetary. To minimize dissatisfaction when using coercive power, appropriate discipline should be administered. This requires that employees understand expectations, receive warnings before punishment, and perceive fair and consistent treatment. Appropriate use of progressive discipline and due process can promote compliance with rather than resistance to leader directives.

As expert power is susceptible to erosion, efforts should be taken to protect this power base. This can be accomplished by keeping up to date with new information. It can also be preserved through impression management; that is, by acting confidently and decisively. But power holders should avoid threatening employees' self-esteem when exercising expert power. Finally, referent power can be increased through treating staff fairly while being sensitive to their individual needs. Referent power is also enhanced when the library manager serves as a role model, protector, counselor, and friend to the staff members.

REFERENCES

1. French, J. R. P., and B. Raven (1959). The bases of social power, in D. Cartwright (ed.), *Studies in social power* (pp. 150–67). Ann Arbor: University of Michigan.

2. Yukl, G. A. (1994). *Leadership in organizations.* Englewood Cliffs, N.J.: Prentice-Hall.

3. Carson, P. (Phillips), K. D. Carson, and C. W. Roe (1993). Social power bases: A meta-analytic examination of interrelationships and outcomes. *Journal of Applied Social Psychology,* 23, 1150–69.

4. Mech, T. F. (September 1990). Academic library directors: A managerial role profile. *College & Research Libraries.* 415–28.

5. Gertzog, A. (July 1990). Library leaders: who and why? *Library Journal,* 45–51.

6. Sheldon, B. E. (1992). Library leaders: Attributes compared to corporate leaders. *Library Trends,* 40(3), 391–401.

7. Kilgour, F. G. (1992). Entrepreneurial leadership. *Library Trends,* 40(3), 457–74.

8. Hulbert, D. (1990). Assertive management in libraries. *Journal of Academic Librarianship,* 16(1), 158–62.

9. Lawson, V. L., and L. Dorrell (Fall 1992). Library directors: Leadership and staff loyalty. *Library Administration & Management,* 187–91.

CHAPTER 5
Letting Professionals Be Just That

QUESTION 23
Exactly Who Is a "Librarian"?

> *A recently published poster from ALA reads "Ask a Professional—Ask a Librarian." The question is, does a patron entering a library know who the professional "librarian" is?*
>
> Shannon L. Hoffman
> *Library Mosaics* (July/August 1993), 8

The answer to the above query is "probably not." To many patrons, everyone who works in a library—from those staffing the reference desk, to those shelving books, to those behind the circulation counter—is a "librarian." So how is a patron to know if she or he is asking a *professional*? And furthermore, does it really matter?

Many believe that it does. The client of a lawyer doesn't want advice from a paralegal. And patients don't visit physicians' offices to receive treatment from a paramedic. So why should patrons have to rely upon assistance from a paralibrarian? This is the argument advanced by those who advocate strict hierarchial segregation of library staff members.

When patrons don't receive opportunities for individualized interaction with professional librarians, the patron may not be the only one to suffer. In fact, the paraprofessional support staff members may experience increased stress. It can be argued that these individuals shouldn't be expected to possess the knowledge of a highly trained professional librarian. They are placed under great pressure if they are asked to handle assignments for which they have not been formally prepared.

Given that the library manager is persuaded by these arguments and seeks to distinguish among library staff members, how does he or she go about accomplishing this? One suggestion is to encourage support staff members to seek the assistance of professional librarians when they do not feel they can adequately respond to a patron's query. Of course, this suggestion is not achievable without the full cooperation of the professional librarians. Another is to include position titles on name tags clearly identifying professional staff members while simultaneously making known to patrons what informational assistance each level can be expected to provide.

Library Management Tip ─────────────────────────────

While the above suggestions are designed to highlight rank and status differentials among library staff members, many management theorists are proposing that just the opposite be done. To take advantage of the intellectual capital of all staff members, traditional divisions between hierarchial levels are becoming blurred in many industries.[1] When organizational members with less experience and formal education are intimidated by the qualifications of those higher up in the hierarchy, they may be deterred from offering valued input. To circumvent this problem, many efforts are being undertaken to remove overt symbols of hierarchial position.

A final suggestion that has been offered is to require patrons to make appointments to see librarians—especially reference librarians. Unlike those in the legal and medical occupations, proponents argue, professional librarians may be too easily accessible. They can be found "out in the open" scrutinizing the stacks and sitting at carrels housing computer terminals. It is thought by some that "isolating" librarians would not only make them more accountable, but would also increase the value of librarian assistance in the eyes of the patron.

QUESTION 24
Can Professionals Be Dually Committed to Both Their Employing Library and the Library Field?

There is an ongoing controversy and debate as to whether librarians can be committed to *both* their profession and their employing organizations. Many contend that such dual loyalties cannot be accomplished, pointing out that librarians will hold one of two incompatible commitments. Rather than being loyal to a specific organization, those who are "cosmopolitan" are primarily committed to their professional group. Since cosmopolitans have a stronger attachment to their profession than to their workplace, they tend to be mobile, moving from library to library in the course of their careers. "Local" workers, in contrast, are primarily committed to their employing libraries. Hence, they typically remain employed in one organization, resisting opportunities for professional advancement at other libraries.

Acceptance of this local/cosmopolitan dichotomy—which has received support from the social scientific research community—leads to the conclusion that professional commitment and organizational commitment might be incompatible. Staff members are typically more aligned with either the library or the profession. Furthermore, research suggests that orientations develop relatively early in a career. And once developed, orientations are difficult to alter.

The question that inevitably arises for library managers is, Which orientation is preferable? The answer is "both." Libraries that employ a mix of locals and cosmopolitans can benefit from the presence of both orientations. The cosmopolitans will bring to the library innovative and creative ideas implemented by other institutions, preventing organizational stagnation. They are also likely to engage in professional service and scholarly activities which will keep the library in public view. Alternatively, locals will introduce a degree of stability and permanence into the library's labor force.[2] Locals can also facilitate relationships with community supporters.

Realizing that both locals and cosmopolitans have a place in the library creates an obligation on the part of library managers to avoid undermining the orientations of staff members. Particularly problematic is the attempt of some administrators to "convert" cosmopolitans to locals. Such attempts tend to create internal conflict in cosmopolitans, which can eventually dilute morale, increase turnover, and hinder productivity. To ensure that the orientation of cosmopolitans is respected, managers should expose all new job applicants to the library's value system during the hiring phase—thus allowing them to withdraw from consideration if they detect incongruence. But once professionals are employed, managers should avoid placing them in situations where they must choose between the values of the profession of librarianship and those of the employing organization.[3] To do so would threaten their professional identity.

QUESTION 25

How Do Issues of Professionalism Influence Managerial Activity in the Library?

Some experts predict that the profession of librarianship is being "marginalized"; that is, its importance is slowly diminishing.[4] Much of the extant librarianship research has attempted to explain how and why this process is occurring. But from a managerial perspective the important question is, how does this process influence supervision and administration in the library setting? Summarizing the librarianship literature, a number of conclusions can be drawn about the state of professionalism and its impact on managerial activity in the library.

Librarianship is a "knowledge-based" profession, meaning that power accrues to librarians based on their informational expertise. In the current "information age," the rapid proliferation of technological advances is changing the nature of the librarian's job. Many complain, for example, that librarians are now spending more time instructing patrons in the mechanics of using CD-ROMs rather than serving as a resource for helping patrons define and satisfy their informational needs.[5] When a profession collectively becomes dispensable, the ability to demand financial resources is diminished. That is, when a profession is rendered less powerful, it becomes easier to overlook during budgeting cycles and funding allocations.

The field of librarianship seems to attract those who are willing to sacrifice themselves for the greater good. On the negative side, though, librarians tend to accept the lower pay and lower status that often accompanies employment in the profession. Rather than collectively taking action against such conditions, they tend to passively rationalize their plight. From a managerial perspective, pay and status are serving to dissuade job-seekers from entering the profession—making the recruitment and retention of qualified staff members difficult.

While there is certainly a place in the library for professionals who are not librarians (e.g., public relations specialists, systems analysts, and accountants), the appointment of nonlibrarians to positions of directorship should typically be protested. Often a director without an MLIS degree is appointed because of his or her fundraising or political skills. Such a figurehead may give the impression that "librarians" are not necessary to the smooth functioning of the library.[6] But even more problematic from a managerial standpoint is that the administrator may lack an intimate understanding of the operations of the library—leading to potentially inappropriate or dysfunctional decisions.[7]

The literature has reported that some librarians tend to downplay the importance of their postbaccalaureate education, referring to the MLIS degree as a "union card" that does little more than get librarians past the first day on the job.[8] But in reality, library education is designed not only to teach practical skills, but also to socialize students to the values and theories of the profession.[9] To minimize the importance of such an invaluable education is likely to promote resentment among the paraprofessional staff, who will see themselves as inequitably compensated just because they lack a piece of sheepskin. Instead, professionals should promote and utilize the intricate skills sharpened through their education. And they should proudly display their degrees, just as lawyers display their qualifications on office walls and physicians hang their diplomas in examining rooms.[10]

Librarians are often encouraged to become aligned with groups representing a variety of "nonprofessional" interests. Attempting to be socially responsible, many professionals join advocates fighting societal problems such as homophobia, homelessness, and latchkey children. While such causes may indeed be "noble" for pursuing on an individual's own time, there are several reasons why library managers should be cautious about offering institutional endorsements for "extra-library" causes. First, libraries often lack the requisite funding necessary just to pursue their basic mission.[11] Diverting funds to help cure larger social ills will likely result in the frustration of the library's mission. Second, such social activism transforms librarians into a strange hybrid of Peace Corps volunteer, social worker, and politician—potentially leading to professional role ambiguity. Third, since librarians come from a diversity of backgrounds, it is highly unlikely that any one issue can be identified as important to all staff members. When there is disagreement among staff members about social issues, organizational commitment will suffer and conflict will intensify. Fourth, library objectives will become blurred and subordinated to the personal goals of the activist librarians. When this happens, the library will flounder and lack direction. And finally, when librarians use their profession to advocate positions beyond their perceived realm of expertise, credibility is diminished and their service role is questioned.[12]

QUESTION 26
How Should a Library Be Designed to Best Accommodate Professionals?

Library design refers to how the organization is structured and jobs are grouped. Traditionally, libraries have been designed along "functional" lines (*see* figure 3), meaning that work groups are categorized by their distinct functions—the activities which are performed (e.g.,

Figure 3. Functional Design

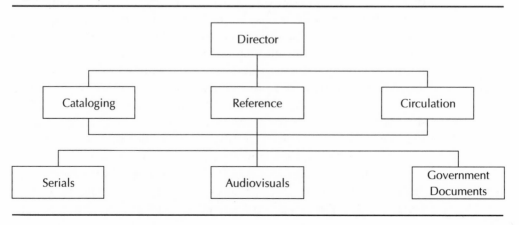

cataloging, reference, circulation). A primary advantage of functional departmentalization is that the training and socialization of newcomers is simplified, since they are grouped with other more experienced workers performing similar tasks. However, since functional managers are so focused on their own departments, they do not get the broader experience necessary to be promoted to director. Also problematic is that departments become so secluded that conflict, competition, and battles over turf are likely to ensue.

An alternative to functional design, first introduced into libraries during the 1950s, is loosely referred to as "product-line" departmentalization (*see* figure 4). Product-line departments can be organized around subject holdings (engineering, business), geographic locations (branches), patrons (children, adult), or types of material (serials, government documents).[13] The primary drawback of product departmentalization is the duplication of resources that results when each materials department needs, for example, a cataloger, a circulation clerk, and a reference librarian.

An organizational design that capitalizes on the advantages and minimizes the disadvantages of both the functional and product structures is the "matrix" design (*see* figure 5). In fact, the matrix design is a hybrid of these two approaches.[14] Under a matrix structure, staff members "specialize" in both a functional and in a product department. In this way, coordination is enhanced, duplication is eliminated, and technical expertise is maintained.

Figure 4. Product-line Design

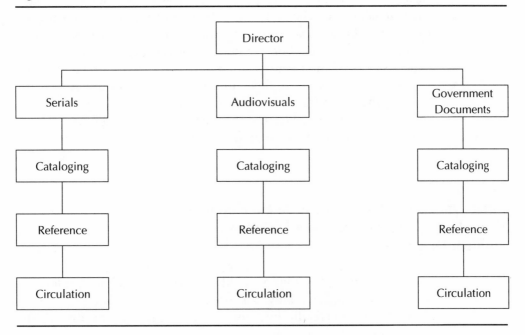

Figure 5. Matrix Design

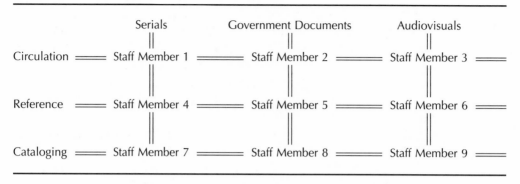

Despite its intuitive appeal, there are some obvious drawbacks associated with the matrix design. Most problematic is the dual line of authority to which staff members are subject. This violates the "unity of command" concept—a management principle suggesting that an employee should be responsible to one and only one manager. For example, "Staff Member 6" reports to both the head of "Audiovisuals" *and* the head of "Reference." When employees have two supervisors, stress is created by conflicting expectations, role overload, and ambiguity. Other disadvantages of matrix departmentalization include both the possibility of staff members playing the two supervisors against each other and personality problems between the two supervisors leading to the employee being stuck in the middle of power struggles.

Another important design consideration is *span-of-control,* which refers to the number of employees supervised by a single manager. Management researchers conclude there is not a universally ideal span-of-control. Rather, span-of-control should be determined based upon a number of factors. For example, a library department head can supervise a larger number of staff members if jobs are simple, jobs are similar, employees are highly motivated, employees are sufficiently trained, there is minimal geographical separation among employees, the environment is stable, and there are a number of policies, procedures, and rules in place to guide employee efforts.

QUESTION 27
What Types of Problems Might Be Encountered When Library Professionals Are Excluded from Problem Diagnosis?

In organizations that employ highly trained and qualified professionals, decisions made jointly will generally be more acceptable than those made unilaterally by administrators. Such is the case in the library setting. Professional librarians generally want and expect to be involved resolving administrative and operational problems. But they should also be included in the process of identifying problems. Correctly diagnosing a problem is critical to the success and quality of decision making by library professionals.

Accurate diagnosis is impeded, in many instances, by allowing available solutions to define the problem. If a decision maker is championing an idea or a "solution," the likelihood of defining a problem so that it will fit that preferred solution is increased. For example, a librarian may be personally interested in increasing the size of the staff, and hence may blame slow interlibrary loan turnaround time on an inadequate number of personnel. However, the actual reason for the delay might be inaccurate shelving which prevents ILL staff members from rapidly pulling items to be loaned. Though this shelving problem may be in need of attention, it will persist if the real underlying cause of the interlibrary loan problem is not investigated.

Defining a problem by how it can be most easily solved is also problematic. For example, assume a library manager perceives the staff is dissatisfied. Perhaps the real source of tension is a lack of sufficient space for the growing collection. Instead of committing to an expansion, the manager may attribute the dissatisfaction to a lack of support staff and therefore request additional student assistance. Rather than curing the problem, this solution will likely lead to further overcrowding. Such a course of action is selected not because a thorough diagnosis of the problem was undertaken, but rather because one solution was easier, cheaper, and more expedient than the alternatives.

Another error that can interfere with accurate problem diagnosis is defining a problem on the basis of its most obvious symptoms. Suppose a staff member refuses to sign his annual performance evaluation. When asked why, he replies that he doesn't agree with the substandard rating on item number seven, which pertains to tardiness. Perhaps he does think the rating is unfair. But he may in fact be protesting larger issues such as work scheduling, policies defining tardiness, or the unwillingness of his supervisor to consider his familial responsibilities which often cause him to be late.

Once a problem is defined accurately, there is no guarantee that the alternative selected to solve the problem will be appropriate. If the wrong alternative is chosen, the challenge facing library managers is to prevent the professional staff from engaging in "escalation of commitment"—becoming overcommitted to a losing course of action. Whether the decision be about purchasing a new on-line catalogue, hiring a new staff member, or implementing a large-scale bibliographic instruction program, there will be a strong tendency for professionals to persist once a decision is made. This tendency is perpetuated by the nature of librarianship work, which often precludes a lack of closure or completion—patrons continually need service; books are shelved only to circulate again; serials are processed just as new ones arrive in the mail.[15] To assist the library manager in determining when a professional staff member may be overcommitted to a decision, common characteristics of escalation of commitment are presented below.

Project setbacks are attributed to temporary problems, such as a back-order on additional equipment needed.

Successful completion of the project is likely to result in much prestige for the decision maker.

Previous commitments to similar projects resulted in positive outcomes.

Investments already incurred for the project cannot be recouped.

The decision maker has a strong need for "face-saving."

The decision maker feels personally responsible for the project.

The decision maker had a high degree of volition when entering into the project.

The decision maker fears for her or his job security.

The decision maker fears criticism from others.

The decision is publicly visible to patrons and co-workers.

The decision maker's social and professional identity is tied up in the project.

QUESTION 28
How Can Branch Managers Be Given the Autonomy They Need to Operate Effectively?

Managers of geographically separate library branches are most effective when they are both *autonomous,* able to exercise independent discretion and make decisions on their own, and *committed,* identified with the goals and values of the whole library organization. But not all branch managers will be effective. Instead, some will lack autonomy or commitment or both, resulting in dysfunctional managerial styles. To transform these managers into effective professional supervisors, the director can control the type and amount of information passed to branch managers through vertical communication linkages (up and down the hierarchy) and horizontal communication linkages (between peers). Appropriate communication strategies for each type of ineffective branch manager are discussed below.

Autonomy

Overly Independent Manager
(increase information in the
vertical linkage)

Effective Manager

Uncommitted ——————————————————— *Committed*

Isolated Manager
(increase information in both
the vertical and the horizontal
linkages)

Passive Manager
(increase information in the
horizontal linkage/decrease
in the vertical linkage)

Dependency

In the case of the *passive* manager (who is committed, but lacks
autonomy), the director should encourage information dissemination
through horizontal linkages while decreasing information communicated through the vertical linkage. Horizontal communication can be
increased by regular face-to-face meetings with other branch managers. The director should establish these meetings in order for the passive manager to learn coping strategies from colleagues. The director
might simultaneously decrease face-to-face interaction with the passive manager. Written communications create a greater psychological
distance between the two parties—an appropriate strategy for minimizing dependency.

The *overly independent* manager (who is autonomous but uncommitted) stands in sharp contrast to the passive manager. In this circumstance, the director must increase information disseminated through
the vertical linkage. Interaction with the director conveys interest and
caring, which may enhance organizational commitment. Personal meetings should take place both at the director's office and at the manager's branch. If the overly independent manager visits the central
location, there are greater opportunities to encounter other library
staff members—increasing the probability that the branch manager
will internalize organizational goals and values. In addition, the director should visit the branch, meeting with members of the support
staff, who are also likely to be alienated from the library organization.

Similarly, the director should visit the branch of the *isolated* manager (who is neither autonomous nor committed). Visits on the branch
manager's own turf may be less threatening than supervision at the
central location. This strategy may decrease the isolated manager's
sense of powerlessness. In addition to strengthening communication
in the vertical linkage, meetings with other branch managers are also
important for building feelings of *esprit de corps*.[16]

REFERENCES

1. Dyckman, A. A. (1992). Library assistants in the year 2000. *Journal of Library Administration, 17*(1), 77–90.

2. Rubin, R., and L. Buttlar (1992). A study of the organizational commitment of high school library media specialists in Ohio. *Library Quarterly, 62*(3), 306–24.

3. White, H. S. (May 15, 1991). The conflict between professional and organizational loyalty. *Library Journal,* 59–60.

4. Park, B. (October 1992). Libraries without walls; or, librarians without a profession. *American Libraries,* 746–7.

5. Campbell, J. D. (June 1993). Choosing to have a future. *American Libraries,* 560–6.

6. White, H. S. (January 1991). Professional librarians and professionals in libraries. *Library Journal,* 74–5.

7. White, H. S. (March 1990). Pseudo-libraries and semi-teachers. *American Libraries,* 262–5.

8. Anderson, A. J. (June 1, 1991). What makes a professional? *Library Journal,* 103–4.

9. Mitchell, W. B., and B. Morton (September 1992). On becoming faculty librarians: Acculturation problems and remedies. *College & Research Libraries,* 379–92.

10. White, H. S. (April 15, 1991). Librarianship—accept the status quo or leave it? *Library Journal,* 68–9.

11. White, H. S. (November 15, 1991). What should be our "professional" issues? *Library Journal,* 58–9.

12. Anderson, A. J. (September 1, 1991). An academic librarian with a cause. *Library Journal,* 167–9.

13. Hoadley, I. B., and J. Corbin (July/August 1990). Up the beanstalk: An evolutionary organizational structure for libraries. *American Libraries,* 676–8.

14. Johnson, P. (1990). Matrix management: An organizational alternative for libraries. *Journal of Academic Librarianship, 16*(4), 222–9.

15. Moreland, V. F., C. L. Robison, and J. M. Stephens (1993). Moving a library collection: Impact on staff morale. *Journal of Academic Librarianship, 19*(1), 8–11.

16. Carson, K. D., P. (Phillips) Carson, et al. (Summer 1993). Increasing the effectiveness of healthcare managers: Horizontal and vertical information linkages. *Hospital Topics,* 16–9.

CHAPTER 6
Supervising the Support Staff

QUESTION 29
Who Are "Paraprofessionals" and Why Are They Important in the Library Setting?

Theoretically speaking, the paraprofessional support staff exists to provide technical assistance to professional librarians. Hence, paraprofessionals should be delegated all the technical tasks that do not require the expertise of a MLIS degreed librarian.[1] In the contemporary library environment, paraprofessionals are becoming an increasingly significant component of the labor force. In fact, many libraries are expanding their hiring of paraprofessionals while simultaneously decreasing the hiring of professional librarians. Several explanations can be postulated for this trend.

Technological advances have resulted in the automation of many tasks that once required the expertise of a professional librarian. These advances created a need for workers who could operate the new productivity enhancing tools—work that does not necessarily require a master's degree.[2]

Increasingly restrictive budgets in both the private and public sectors are preventing the hiring of professionals and encouraging the employment of lower-paid library paraprofessionals.

The standardization of the field, brought about by such developments as national cataloging systems, tends to reduce the need for the professional expertise of librarians.

A shortage of qualified librarians who are able and willing to accept available jobs has encouraged some libraries to seek out paraprofessional applicants. In fact, the cognitive challenges and prestige inherent in library employment make paraprofessional jobs attractive to many college graduates.

Heightened demand for librarians (especially those in academic settings) to become involved in research, teaching, community service, and governance activities require that some tasks be shifted from the professional to the paraprofessional staff.

The collective effect of these environmental changes is an increased recognition of the importance and value of the support staff. Illustrative of their elevated status in the field, paraprofessionals are becoming increasingly involved in library association activities. Many library directors are seeking reclassification for library support staff members, who are sometimes paid even less than clerical assistants. And a new national journal, entitled *Library Mosaics,* is being published to explore the unique capabilities and concerns of this group. But one doesn't have to look to this journal to find research on the topic of managing the paraprofessional support staff. Dozens of library research articles have addressed this topic.[3]

QUESTION 30
How Should Library Employees Who Don't Possess an MLIS Degree Be Referred To?

Management researchers investigating the topic of compensation suggest that nonmonetary rewards, such as recognition, are just as effective at motivating high performance as are paychecks. One way in which employees can be recognized is through the "bestowing" of a position title that commands respect. While there is much debate and concern over the nomenclature used to refer to support staff members, there is general agreement that titles such as "nonprofessional" and "subprofessional" don't command anything but resentment by the position holder. Such titles seem to imply the work performed by support staff members is of inferior quality. And if the Pygmalion Effect is operative, the use of such unenlightened terms may, in fact, become a self-fulfilling prophecy.

Results from a survey recently published in *Library Mosaics* indicates the support staff titles most often utilized include "Library Assistant," "Library Clerk," "Library Technician," and "Library Technical Assistant."[4] Many others use the term "paraprofessional" while some even suggest the term "paralibrarian" be adapted from the legal profession.[5] No matter which term is chosen, library managers should realize that carefully considered titles might enhance the self-esteem and ultimately the productivity of the support staff. Given this, any resistance by professional librarians to changing outdated support staff titles may be symptomatic of underlying uncertainty about role responsibilities, obligations, and authority.

QUESTION 31

How Can Library "Professionals" Be Distinguished from "Paraprofessionals"?

Nearly 120 years ago Melvil Dewey observed, "the time has at last come when a librarian may, without assumption, speak of his [her] occupation as a profession."[6] But what characteristics of librarianship qualify it as a profession? The career management literature has outlined four criteria that distinguish professionals from other classes of workers. These criteria include: (1) technical knowledge in a highly specialized field, (2) advanced education and training required to enter the profession, (3) the presence of professional associations that attempt self-regulation and develop professional codes of conduct or ethics, and (4) commitment or sense of calling that binds one more to the profession than to the employing institution.

Applying these criteria, it becomes clear that MLIS librarians qualify as professionals. But what about members of the support staff—the so-called "paraprofessionals"? There is much consensus among those involved in the profession that not everyone who works in a library is a "librarian." But to what degree do support staff members exemplify the characteristics of professional librarians? To address this question, each professional criterion will be examined in turn.

The first criterion states that professionals possess technical knowledge in a highly specialized field. To a surprising extent, support staff members are expected to maintain technical competence in areas such as foreign language, computer usage, scholarly writing, and even administration/supervision to quality for "paraprofessional" jobs.[7] Furthermore, many libraries require their paraprofessional staff to have library experience as they are scheduled to work at the reference or information desk, conduct library tours, provide on-line catalog and CD-ROM instruction, and perform copy cataloging duties. Some libraries even permit paraprofessionals to engage in collection development, on-line searching, and original cataloging—tasks requiring substantial technical skills.

The second criterion requires professionals to obtain advanced education and training. Back in 1923, Charles C. Williamson proposed that postsecondary educational programs be established for library paraprofessionals. But it wasn't until 1969 that the ALA sanctioned such programs—a symptom of the general lack of acceptance and support granted to this educational track. While very few libraries today require their paraprofessionals to have earned a graduate degree (interestingly, nearly one-quarter of academic and research libraries do), many libraries do require support staff members to have a college degree. Thus some advanced training is deemed essential for many "paraprofessionals."

The third criterion requires the presence of professional associations. While there are currently no such associations that exist solely to support library paraprofessionals, support staff members are gaining increasing acceptance in regional, state, and even national library associations. In fact, a 1990 Association of College and Research Libraries (ACRL) task force recommended that paraprofessionals be encouraged to participate in such associations. And some far-sighted libraries are even allowing travel time and reimbursement for paraprofessionals to attend conferences. Although burdensome, this expense is justified by the fact that paraprofessionals often can benefit most from the information disseminated at professional association meetings.

The fourth and final criterion of professionalism dictates that individuals exhibit commitment or sense of calling to the field of librarianship. Extant research has adopted the stance that paraprofessionals are more loyal to their employing institution than to the field of librarianship because: (a) most paraprofessionals have worked in one and only one library, and (b) most paraprofessionals do not exhibit a strong desire to seek reemployment in other libraries in positions of increased responsibility.[8] However, the field is witnessing the emergence of an increasingly vocal cohort of paraprofessionals who are engaging in academic writing, fighting for a larger role in professional governance, and returning to school for MLIS degrees. Such actions do in fact exemplify a strong professional calling.

Thus, while paraprofessionals do not completely conform to these criteria as professional librarians do, the above discussion demonstrates the continual blurring of roles between librarians and support staff members. And in practice, there is a growing zone of overlap between the tasks being performed by these two groups. This blurring not only confuses patrons and threatens some professional librarians but also angers paraprofessionals who see themselves doing the work of librarians for less money, less prestige, and less respect.[9]

QUESTION 32
How Can Paraprofessionals Be Motivated in a Library Setting?

Whether public, academic, or special, most libraries operate as "professional bureaucracies." Although the term "bureaucracy," coined by German sociologist Max Weber (1864–1920), evokes visions of red tape and constraining overregulation, a professional bureaucratic structure simply implies that an organization employs two distinct classes of workers. In the case of libraries, these two classes are professional librarians and support staff members (paraprofessional and clerical/secretarial workers).

In a professional bureaucracy, professionals have much independent discretion and autonomy while fulfilling their professional obligations; that is, they have control over their work. Hence, professional bureaucracies are highly decentralized with power concentrated among the professionals, who have the expertise to provide complex services. In a professional bureaucracy such as a library, administrators most often involve the professionals in important operational and strategic decisions. This requires a democratic and participative management style.

In contrast to the professional librarians, support staff members typically have little or no collective power in libraries. Because of their lack of influence, they are often led less democratically than professionals. Thus, professional bureaucracies have two hierarchies. There is the democratic hierarchy for the professionals, and the traditional authority hierarchy for the less powerful support staff.

This "double standard" can lead to the alienation of support staff members. Such alienation can be costly to libraries. In fact, libraries spend slightly more than half of their total operating budgets on salaries. And allocations for support staff salaries are typically higher than for any other resource: higher than professional staff salaries, higher than serials acquisitions, higher than technology purchases. Yet it is paradoxical that the while the library support staff is the most expensive library resource, it is often the most mismanaged.

This mismanagement is manifested in short organizational tenure—the average tenure for a paraprofessional staff member is only two to five years. And turnover among paraprofessionals is three times as high as turnover among professionals. Furthermore, professional librarians are consistently more satisfied with their jobs than are paraprofessional staff members. One of the primary sources of job dissatisfaction among paraprofessionals is the dead-end nature of their jobs. Career ladders are generally absent, rendering paraprofessional promotions impossible. And without the possibility for promotion, paraprofessionals may quickly reach the top of their pay range. To compound these problems, professional librarians often expend more effort learning about new technologies than they do learning about the capabilities and requirements of the support staff.[10] But as Guy Lyle observed over two decades ago, "the [para]professionals form the backbone of the library staff and their morale and enthusiasm must be maintained if the library is to be successfully staffed."[11]

Library Management Tip

Interestingly, there is actually a legal mandate that requires differential treatment of the professional and the paraprofessional staff. A 1938 law known as the Fair Labor Standards Act (FLSA) distinguishes between the professional staff which is "exempt" from the protection of the law and the paraprofessional staff which is "nonexempt" or protected by the law. The FLSA, also called the "Wages and Hours" law, contains provisions regulating minimum wage and overtime payment. Nonexempt paraprofessionals must be guaranteed a minimum hourly wage rate. With regard to overtime, the FLSA mandates that any hours worked in excess of 40 per week (defined as seven consecutive 24-hour days, or a continuous 168-hour period) must be compensated at time-and-a-half (or 150 percent of the hourly wage). Those employees considered "exempt" (executives, administrators, managers, and professionals who are typically paid on a salary rather than an hourly wage basis) are not eligible for overtime pay.

So the challenge facing library managers is how to keep the paraprofessional staff motivated to perform in an environment where they may feel they are treated as second-class citizens. One approach which has proven successful under such conditions is application of the motivational theory of *goal setting*. This theory asserts that the conscious establishment of goals can dramatically improve performance, bolstering both library effectiveness and the paraprofessional's sense of value. Goal setting works because goals mobilize effort, direct attention, encourage persistence, and promote planning and strategy development.

The most consistent finding in the more than five hundred research studies on goal setting is that specific, challenging goals are more effective for increasing productivity than are easy goals, "do-your-best" goals, or no goals. Specific goals reduce performance variability, while challenging goals lead to higher performance. Frequent and specific feedback is also required for goal setting to be effective, since it allows individuals to compare their performance against the established standard.

Performance feedback, or knowledge of results, is defined as information about how well a staff member is meeting a goal. Feedback serves two primary functions—informational and motivational. It increases performance because it encourages staff members to work both smarter, by engaging in strategic task planning, and harder, by expending more effort. Staff members are motivated to the extent that there is a negative discrepancy between standards and actual performance. When such a discrepancy exists, staff members feel tension about their substandard performance. This tension motivates staff members to reduce the discrepancy.

Also, for goal setting to work, the individual must accept the goal and be committed to it. Goal commitment is fostered when the paraprofessional participates in the establishment of the goal(s) to be pursued. Unfortunately, it is more difficult for workers to stay committed to challenging goals than it is for them to stay committed to easy goals, which require less effort to attain. Easy goals result in low performance, but they are highly satisfying because they are reachable. On the other hand, if difficult goals are set, the individual will perform better but be less satisfied because standards are rarely reached.

To address this paradox, management experts suggest five techniques for increasing an individual's satisfaction while simultaneously attending to productivity: (1) set moderate goals; (2) establish two goals, one that is fully achievable and a second that is an ideal goal; (3) recognize partial success at meeting a difficult goal; (4) following attainment of an easier goal, incrementally raise the level of goal difficulty; and (5) define goal difficulty not on probability of success but on time and effort required.

When a goal-setting program is correctly implemented, it sets measurable quality—as well as quantity—goals. Quantity goals can improve quantity performance, and quality goals can improve quality performance. However, when goals are set for any single performance dimension (such as speed), other dimensions (such as accuracy) will be sacrificed. Although quantity goals are often easier for the library manager to establish and assess, research shows that absence of quality goals can induce poor quality performance. Thus, when the library manager feels that both quantity and quality performance are important, goals should be established with the paraprofessional for *both* dimensions.

QUESTION 33
How Might the Jobs of Paraprofessionals Be Enriched?

As far back as the time of the Industrial Revolution, management experts began searching for ways to make jobs more meaningful, more rewarding, and hence more motivating for the incumbent. It was quickly determined that specialization—in which workers performed narrow repetitive tasks—was demoralizing. One of the first redesign approaches adopted to combat specialization was "job enlargement" or "horizontal job loading." Enlargement involves workers completing multiple, rather than single, repetitive tasks. Because these additional tasks were very simple, boredom persisted.

As horizontal loading failed to achieve desired results, job rotation was implemented. Rotation involves shifting workers among various specialized tasks. And although rotation facilitates cross-training, worker motivation remained low. Even more problematic were the inefficiencies created by rotation: the workers required time to relearn tasks. The major fault of job enlargement and job rotation was that the nature or inherent characteristics of the job were not changed.

Then, in the 1960s, the concept of "job enrichment" emerged. To enrich a job, "vertical loading" is required. Vertical loading gives more depth and richness to a job. Job enrichment is best illustrated through the job characteristics model (JCM) shown in figure 6. The JCM suggests that jobs should possess five "core characteristics," which will result in the incumbent experiencing "critical psychological states," which ultimately translate into "positive outcomes." The five core job characteristics of the JCM include task identity, task significance, skill variety, feedback, and autonomy.

Task identity represents the degree to which a worker is able to complete a whole, identifiable piece of work. Highly specialized jobs, in which a worker completes only one small part of a finished job, would rate low in identity. For example, the paraprofessional who could pull, prepare, and mail an ILL request would experience greater identity than one who just prepared the request for mailing.

Task significance represents the degree to which a job possesses importance and value to society. A medical paralibrarian who assists physicians searching for articles about potential cures would likely experience high task significance.

Skill variety represents the degree to which an incumbent is able to utilize multiple abilities while performing a job. For example, a serials clerk who only processes mail would experience less variety than one who could also issue claims for missing journals.

Feedback refers to information on how well a worker is performing. *Intrinsic* feedback is derived from the job itself. *Extrinsic* feedback is provided by others. In the library setting, feedback might be provided from observing the empty book cart that was full just one hour ago

Figure 6. The Job Characteristics Model

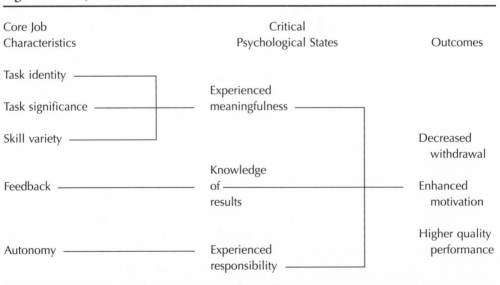

when shelving began (intrinsic). But it might also be provided by the library manager who comments on the speed and accuracy of a staff member's shelving (extrinsic). Extrinsic feedback can serve as a significant source of reinforcement; this may explain why reference department employees are often the most satisfied in the library. Their position affords them continual opportunities for interaction with and feedback from patrons.

Autonomy represents the degree to which workers are able to make independent decisions and use personal discretion while performing a job. Paraprofessionals who are too closely supervised may lack a perception of autonomy. On the other hand, the library manager may encounter a staff member who fears or doesn't want the responsibility associated with autonomy. It is true, in fact, that not every employee will seek out enriched work. Thus, before efforts are undertaken to redesign and enrich paraprofessional positions, the desires, needs, and capabilities of the incumbents must be considered.

QUESTION 34
How Should Library Volunteers Be Managed?

There is one important segment of the support staff which is often overlooked during redesign and other improvement efforts. This group is the volunteer pool, which typically saves the library substantial personnel expense by performing tasks without expecting a paycheck in return.

Library Management Tip

Many libraries want and desperately need volunteers, but have trouble with recruitment. Bonnie McCune, public relations manager for the Denver Public Library, observes that many libraries seem to be looking in the wrong places. Only about one in ten library volunteers is a "traditional" homemaker. Instead, many volunteers are now coming from the ranks of senior citizens not quite ready for retirement and students and unemployed workers seeking job experience. Other possible sources include people sentenced to do community service by the judicial system and corporate groups wishing to fulfill their social responsibilities. Finally, McCune advises that while minority groups and people with disabilities have been underrepresented among the volunteer ranks, they can bring unique expertise to the library.[12]

Although they are not on the payroll, volunteers should not be thought of as just a free source of labor. Their needs should be considered along with the needs of the paid staff members. All volunteers should be compensated for their services in forms such as recognition, experience, and personal satisfaction. The following recommendations can help the library provide volunteers with the "pay" they are typically seeking.

Develop challenging and rewarding jobs.

Don't underestimate the skill level or abilities of volunteers, but also ensure that staff members do not feel threatened or displaced when tasks are assigned to volunteers.

Provide continuing education to meet volunteers' self-development needs.

Volunteers typically seek opportunities for personal growth and development. They welcome opportunities to learn on the job and appreciate having the knowledge necessary for high performance.

Provide feedback.

All workers need to understand how well they are performing their jobs. Information about performance should be provided regularly on both an informal and formal basis.

Make volunteers feel appreciated.

Volunteers should be nurtured with support and recognition. Although an estimated 80 percent of volunteers find their work to be rewarding, 33 percent report their work to be extremely demanding, and 25 percent feel they are not adequately recognized for their contributions.

REFERENCES

1. Kathman, M. D., and L. Felix (Fall 1990). A library paraprofessional pay system. *Library Administration & Management,* 202–5.

2. Oberg, L. R. (May/June 1991). Paraprofessionals: Shaping the new reality. *Library Mosaics,* 11–12.

3. Jewell, C. H. (July/August 1993). Library support staff and paraprofessionals: A bibliography. *Library Mosaics,* 12–14.

4. Winkler, J. A. (November/December 1993). Support staff classification in academic libraries. *Library Mosaics,* 11–13.

5. Halsted, D. D., and D. M. Neely (March 1, 1990). The importance of the library technician. *Library Journal,* 62–3.

6. Dewey, M. (September 30, 1876). The profession. *American Library Journal,* 1, 5.

7. Oberg, L. R., et al. (May 1992). The role, status, and working conditions of paraprofessionals: A national survey of academic libraries. *College & Research Libraries,* 215–38.

8. Fitch, D. K. (July 1990). Job satisfaction among library support staff in Alabama academic libraries. *College & Research Libraries,* 313–20.

9. Oberg, L. R. (March 1992). The emergence of the paraprofessional in academic libraries: Perceptions and realities. *College & Research Libraries,* 99–112.

10. Turner, B. G. (1992). Nonprofessional staff in libraries: A mismanaged resource. *Journal of Library Administration,* 16(4), 57–66; Rais, S. (October 1993). Managing your support staff: An insider's view. *American Libraries,* 819–20.

11. Lyle, G. R. (1974). *The administration of the college library.* New York: H. W. Wilson.

12. McCune, B. F. (October 1993). The new volunteerism: Making it pay off for your library. *American Libraries,* 822–4.

CHAPTER 7
Career Management

Does Mentoring Help with Career Advancement?

Staff members typically strive to manage their careers successfully, as solid career management not only influences the nature of their work-life and income, but also affects broader personal issues such as life satisfaction and social standing. Library administrators are also concerned about career management issues, because staff members who are unhappy about their career progress can turn into liabilities through poor work performance or voluntary turnover. While administrators may have an obligation to smooth the employee's career path, it is the individual staff member who is ultimately responsible for his or her own career.[1]

In managing their careers, librarians often consider the use of mentors for facilitating their progression. Indeed, research has shown that a mentor can expedite advancement for some librarians. For example, among twenty-eight directors of major public libraries surveyed in one study, sixteen had been involved in a mentoring relationship.[2]

A mentor's age usually averages from the mid-forties to the early sixties with the protégé being considerably younger. Typically, there is a fifteen- to twenty-year age difference between the mentor and protégé. The alliance between the two is characterized by an intense relationship in which the mentor shares inside information with the protégé. Also, mentors are often in a position of power in a library or library association, and use their status to further the protégé's career. The alliance typically continues over a period of a few years until the protégé is promoted to a position of significant responsibility. Then the relationship ideally shifts from one of sponsorship to one of friendship.

Library Management Tip

Significantly more women in the library field report being helped by a mentor than do men—a logical finding since 80 percent of librarians are female and same-sex mentoring is the norm. While women librarians most often recognize their mentors for teaching them "tricks of the trade" and serving as competent role models, men librarians tend to acknowledge those who have encouraged them to enter the field of librarianship. Even though female librarians are more often privy to mentoring relationships than are males, they are much less likely to get promoted to directorates than their male counterparts.[3] Thus, while mentoring may influence promotion decisions, it does not necessarily present a straight path of advancement to the top. This may in part be due to those in power (who are typically male, even in the profession of librarianship) picking out successors who are very similar to themselves.

QUESTION 36
Why Do Supervisors Give Some Employees Exceptional Treatment?

While a mentor picks out special protégés to treat differently than others, supervisors, interestingly, do the same thing. Library managers do not generally treat all staff members the same. Rather, different expectations and controls are used depending upon whether staff members are (consciously or unconsciously) assigned to the "in-group" or to the "out-group."

If an employee is assigned to in-group membership, the "vertical-dyad linkage theory" asserts that the supervisor has high expectations and goals for the staff member. "In-groupers" are expected to help the supervisor run the library department. In turn, these favored staff members are included in the supervisor's communication and support network. They more often receive positive reinforcement, their accomplishments are made known to library administrators, and they are more likely to receive promotions.

However, if a staff member is relegated to the out-group, his or her relationship with the supervisor is formal and contractual in nature. The supervisor assigns the staff member certain tasks that are spelled out in the job description. The staff member is expected to complete these tasks and, in turn, receives a paycheck. But the supervisor does not go out of her or his way to provide support or act considerate. Rather, the supervisor only deals with the staff member if there is a negative deviation between expected and actual performance.

Library Management Tip

Out-group members are often assigned unchallenging work, because the supervisor lacks confidence in their ability to accomplish difficult tasks. As a result, most out-groupers resent their relegation to the out-group. They are frequently dissatisfied with their fate as compared to those with in-group status. The (often unconscious) splitting of staff into two groups results in decreased morale and reduced effectiveness in the department. To correct this problem, supervisors should be encouraged to expand the number of members in their in-group. This can be accomplished by allowing all staff members to participate in setting their own career and work goals.

QUESTION 37
What Are the Career Stages through Which Librarians Typically Progress?

Over a lifetime, individuals typically progress through distinct career phases. The first career stage experienced by an individual is *occupational choice*. When the occupational choice results in a good fit with one's personality, individuals are more satisfied, make fewer job changes, and achieve greater professional success than those who choose a vocation dissimilar from their interests. One career researcher, J. L. Holland, suggests that certain personalities are attracted to occupational groups he has labeled *realistic, investigative, artistic, social, enterprising,* and *conventional.*[4]

Holland's theory suggests that the shy, persistent, and stable person may choose, for example, to become a secretary in the library—an occupation in the realistic category. An analytical, curious, independent person may choose to become an interlibrary loan or systems librarian—occupations in the investigative category. The architect hired to design a library facility belongs to the artistic category— conducive to idealistic and imaginative personalities. And the cooperative, helpful, and understanding reference or children's librarian represents the social category. The attorney with whom the library administrator consults belongs to the enterprising category of ambitious, domineering, and self-confident personalities. Finally, the efficient, practical, conscientious circulation or cataloging librarian may represent the conventional category.

After choosing their careers, individuals invest in them through formal education and training. Significant amounts of time, money, and effort are required in preparing for demanding jobs in the library. During the educational process, an individual usually develops an attachment to the chosen occupation. While large investments are often required just to enter a field, motivated individuals continue to put forth a great deal of effort into their vocations during the *early-career stage*. During this phase, individuals become increasingly committed to their careers.

Career commitment, defined as the strength of one's motivation to work in a chosen occupation, has three facets. First, those who are committed to their chosen occupation in the library field are identified or emotionally attached to the vocation. However, to be fully committed to a career, the individual must engage in career planning, which involves identifying career goals and aspirations. The final component of career commitment is being persistent in the face of adversity, such as limited advancement or low pay. Unfortunately, this third aspect of career commitment, career adversity, is well known to the professional librarian.

By the *mid-career phase,* an individual's occupational identity has often become crystalized. Typically, individuals are highly involved in their careers during this stage. This involvement is reflected in reports of high career satisfaction. But while many are satisfied, others become bored. It is therefore becoming increasingly common to see individuals in this stage returning to school for training in another field. However, career change is only for risk takers; it's not for the faint hearted.

By the *late-career stage,* many are eager to retire; some library administrators see retirement as a desirable option during this phase. It seems that after decades of trying to keep up with constant changes in the field, they just get tired. Most of the current library administrators entered the field in simpler times. Today, they must fully understand such issues as budgeting, technology, personnel management, and risk management. To keep up, library managers must read relevant literature, attend library association meetings, and participate in training.

QUESTION 38
What Are Some Alternative Career Paths Available to Librarians?

A career path represents the particular work pattern individuals adopt in pursuing their career goals.[5] Those interested in traditional promotions are operating in a *linear* career path. Individuals in this path are achievers seeking to move upward through the ranks of the library hierarchy or through officer positions in a library association.

Instead of traditional linear career progression, many individuals choose a *steady-state* path. A person making this choice is concerned with stability in an occupational field. Once trained in a chosen vocation, those in a steady-state path maintain necessary skills for remaining in their vocation. They are not interested in advancement, but in remaining in a service role.[6]

Library Management Tip

A major problem in most libraries is that a professional can only advance by moving into management. However, there are many professional librarians who lack the desire to become administrators. And there are others who can contribute more to the library by performing their specialties rather than by assuming managerial roles. In response to this, some libraries have developed dual career ladders so that librarians can advance either through their specialty or through the management ranks. With a dual ladder, the specialist has the potential to earn more money and prestige without being forced into becoming a manager.

While the linear and steady-state paths are pursued by individuals who remain in a single vocational field, individuals who engage in vocational change may take a *spiral* career path. These individuals make occupational moves every five or ten years in pursuit of stimulation and personal growth. When they make a vocational change, however, it is likely that they will choose another career with the same anchor. A *career anchor* is a cluster of talents, ambitions, and ideals that form an individual's vocational self-concept.

Career anchors reflect the underlying personalities, ideals, and endeavors of individuals. The person who follows a spiral path will typically select a vocation that satisfies his or her one predominant motive. The five most common motives are *managerial,* a motive to influence others; *functional,* a motive to continuously develop a professional competency; *security,* a motive for stability in a particular company or geographical area; *creativity,* a motive to invent and create; and *autonomy,* a motive to be free of organizational expectations.[7]

A few people don't remain tied to a single career anchor. Consider, for example, the career change pursued by Rita Ormsby.[8] After earning a degree in journalism, she edited publications at the University of Iowa while teaching journalism at a community college for native Americans. She then was a VISTA worker at a center for rural affairs in Nebraska before going to law school for two years. Following this training, she spent more than ten years as a legal assistant for a Minneapolis firm. Becoming bored in this job, she returned to school and received her MLS degree at the University of Wisconsin–Madison in 1992. Today, she is employed in the Brighton Beach Branch of the Brooklyn Public Library, where she enjoys interacting with a "diverse public."

QUESTION 39
What Are the Common Coping Strategies Adopted by Plateaued Librarians?

Individuals pursuing a linear career path within their library or association are vulnerable to being impeded on their climb. And once frustrated in moving up, individuals become *plateaued,* or trapped in their job. Plateauing occurs when an individual becomes unlikely to receive job assignments of increased responsibility up the organizational chain. Social, economic, and demographic forces are combining in the current environment to cause the career plateauing of many library workers.

Plateauing is caused by several factors including fewer opportunities due to technological advancement, the elimination of mandatory retirement, limited positions available at the top of the hierarchy, retrenchment in public and education facilities, flattening of organizational hierarchies, increasing numbers of nontraditional labor-force entrants, and competition among baby boomers.

Currently, more than seventy-six million baby-boomers—those born between 1946 and 1964—are at midcareer. Those from the ages of thirty-five to forty-four now make up 15 percent of the labor force, while twenty years ago they represented only 11 percent. Members of this large group are becoming gridlocked in their jobs as they lack opportunities for promotion. And those who equate advancement with vocational success are finding themselves very frustrated.

For those plateaued in their jobs, frustration often intensifies with each passing day. But perceived career alternatives become increasingly limited as workers age. Further, age discrimination slams many career doors. Some libraries may block career advancement for older workers stereotyped as having lower performance and less capacity for development than those who are younger. Further, more than a few older individuals come to accept negative stereotyping about aging.

Career satisfaction is eroded by plateauing. When an individual experiences dissatisfaction, negative reactions such as anxiety, hostility, rumination, and despair may result. Boredom associated with overlearning a single job is also likely. And loneliness and stress are created when colleagues withdraw from plateaued workers because they are no longer part of the in-group. In the absence of constructive ways to deal with the isolation accompanying plateauing, entrapped employees may feel depressed.

As the duration and intensity of distress continues, an individual must engage in coping mechanisms to either eliminate or lessen its effect. *Coping* refers to an individual's efforts to handle stressors that are perceived as exceeding or straining the individual's available resources. Four coping mechanisms are frequently used to lessen career-related stress: exit, voice, loyalty, and neglect.[9]

Exit, or leaving an entrapping career, is often a very rational strategy. However, it is the mechanism least often used because of the huge investments often required and the losses associated with leaving. Also, many workers have responsibilities to others at home. For example, dual-career marriages may limit career mobility—an ever increasing issue as both spouses work in approximately four out of five marriages.

While leaving a dead-end career can be a rational response, personalities vary in their ability to tolerate such major changes. Because of need for social approval and fear of social rejection, employees with low self-esteem may be more susceptible to staying in a plateaued position than will those with high self-esteem. Relatedly, employees who are able to tolerate risk may be more likely to avoid career entrapment than those who are averse to risk. With lack of experience in an unfamiliar vocational field, career change may involve intensive efforts at learning, applying, and testing new skills. Because of the possibility of personal failure in changing careers, these individuals must embrace risk and have high self-esteem to tolerate potential setbacks.

Voice refers to actively and constructively trying to improve conditions through discussion of concerns. Such verbalization may alleviate distress either through catharsis or through motivating positive changes in the library. However, there are dangers in using one's voice as a coping mechanism. These include the possibility of retaliation from those higher up in the organization, the possible reputation of being a complainer, and the emotional upheaval of being confrontational with others.

The third possible coping strategy, *loyalty,* refers to passively but optimistically waiting for things to improve. Loyalty is used by those who feel that the costs associated with voice and exit are too high. As loyalty is a time-consuming and passive technique, skill atrophy and boredom may result.

The fourth and final coping strategy, *neglect,* involves intentionally allowing conditions to deteriorate. Neglect is manifested through reduced effort, withdrawal behaviors, lower quality work, and ineffective use of time. Essentially, neglect is a coping mechanism where the worker retires on the job.

Those who cope with plateauing through neglect are likely to focus their energy outside the workplace. Since administrative and collegial support may be withdrawn, the person may desire to spend more time with family and friends. Other likely diversions from work include traveling, joining civic organizations, and becoming more active in church. Fortunately, such leisure activities can be a major source of psychological satisfaction.

QUESTION 40
How Can Library Administrators Help Staff Members Deal with Burnout and Career Plateauing?

Some occupations—such as nursing, social work, teaching, law enforcement, and librarianship—are particularly vulnerable to career dissatisfaction and burnout. Nurses must face human suffering and death while lacking autonomy in performing their jobs. Social workers often must coordinate heavy caseloads while dealing with contradictions between court-ordered remedies and agency policies. Teachers must educate in overcrowded classrooms and deal with aggression and difficult discipline problems. Police officers must uphold the law in environments characterized by interpersonal confrontation, physical violence, and an ambivalent society. Librarians suffer from overload, as there is much work, little time, and inadequate support. Economic cutbacks have added to the prolonged stress, as librarians are increasingly feeling undervalued and underpaid.

In a survey of public librarians, it was reported that over half are experiencing medium to high levels of burnout.[10] A majority feel alienated from their patrons and feel unhappy with their jobs and themselves. Interestingly, the most highly educated feel higher levels of emotional exhaustion than the less educated—perhaps reflecting loftier and more idealistic goals that have been thwarted. Respondents indicated that they feel unfairly paid as there is no additional compensation for evening and weekend work. Further, their jobs have become too routine and clerical in nature, with an associated lack of opportunities for advancement.

To facilitate a plateaued employee's contributions to the overall effectiveness of the library, the manager can engage in several motivational techniques. But the library manager must understand that an employee's career can continue to grow despite the limited openings up the organizational ladder. However, growth is no longer focused on the next higher-level job, but is focused *within* the present job and *across* the organization.

While the employee may not acquire more organizational power, she or he can continue to grow personally, developing more expertise and a broader knowledge base. Examples of techniques available to the manager for plateaued workers include on-the-job training, lateral transfers, and job rotation or cross-utilization programs. Also, assignments to short-term project teams can be invigorating as the staff member learns new ways of perceiving the world from others with different backgrounds and perspectives. Opportunities for sabbaticals can also allow employees to pursue diverse experiences and training.[11]

Accurate information and feedback from supervisors is essential so that employees can develop realistic expectations about advancement in the library setting. The manager needs to be clear that while upward advancement is unlikely, the employee can still contribute to and be valued by the library. However, the manager cannot expect that this will be a conflict-free approach. For example, the employee may verbalize not only career dissatisfaction but also life dissatisfaction.

Beyond providing consideration to disaffected staff members, supervisors can help their employees assess alternative ways to deal with their individual situations. One choice staff members have is to assert themselves in the workplace. They can be encouraged to work actively and constructively at trying to improve conditions by verbalizing their concerns. Alternatively, supervisors may encourage staff members to engage in extra-role performance or "career citizenship" behaviors. Career citizenship behaviors are discretionary actions that are helpful to one's career field, but for which there is no direct compensation. Examples of important career citizenship behavior include mentoring younger staff members and actively engaging in activities of the library association.

REFERENCES

1. Greenhaus, J. H., and G. A. Callanan (1994). *Career management,* 2nd ed. Fort Worth, Tex.: Dryden.

2. Chatman, E. A. (1992). The role of mentorship in shaping public library leaders. *Library Trends,* 40(3), 492–512.

3. Harris, R. M. (October 15, 1993). The mentoring trap. *Library Journal,* 37–40.

4. Holland, J. L. (1985). *Manual for the vocational preference inventory.* Odessa, Fla.: Psychological Assessment Resources.

5. Driver, M. J. (1979). Career concepts and career management in organizations, in C. L. Cooper (ed.), *Behavioral problems in organizations* (pp. 79–139). Englewood Cliffs, N.J.: Prentice Hall.

6. White, H. S., and S. L. Mort (July 1990). The accredited library education program as preparation for professional library work. *Library Quarterly,* 60(3), 187–215.

7. Schein, E. H. (1985). *Career anchors: Discovering your real values.* San Diego: University Associates.

8. Berry, J. (October 15, 1993). Rita Ormsby: Career changer. *Library Journal,* 33.

9. Rusbult, C. E., et al. (1988). Impact of exchange variables on exit, voice, loyalty, and neglect: An integrative model of responses to declining job satisfaction. *Academy of Management Journal,* 31, 599–627.

10. Smith, N. M., N. E. Birch, and M. Marchant (1984). Stress, distress, and burnout: A survey of public reference librarians. *Public Libraries,* 23(3), 83–5.

11. Delon, B. A. (Winter 1993). Keeping plateaued performers motivated. *Library Administration & Management,* 13–6.

CHAPTER 8
Making the Roles Clear

QUESTION 41
What Information Should Be in a Job Description?

Job descriptions contain information about the duties and responsibilities of a job as well as the context in which a job is performed. Although documents will vary slightly by institution, a typical job description for a library position should include the following elements.

Position Title

Libraries use a variety of position titles, depending upon the mission, governance, and structure of the institution. Although administrators can exercise much discretion in choosing titles, the following caveats should be considered: (a) each different position should be granted its own unique title; (b) the fact that two different institutions utilize the same title does not mean that the jobs are necessarily comparable, as an "Assistant Librarian" at one library may have completely different responsibilities than an "Assistant Librarian" at another; and (c) titles should be meaningful and descriptive but should not alienate incumbents, such as the title "Nonprofessional Library Staff" might.

Department or Unit in Which the Job Is Located

This entry reflects the organizational structure, or divisionalization, of the library. The necessity of this information arises from the fact that in today's restricted budgetary environment, many library staff members receive dual assignments in which they report to two separate departments. Common examples include positions "shared" between reference and government documents and between serials and interlibrary loans.[1] In such cases, the job description must specify the percentage of time allocated to each department.

Incumbent Reports To

By specifying the position title of the incumbent's supervisor, the entire hierarchy of authority can be traced through the job description documents. To avoid violation of the unity-of-command concept, employees should ideally report to only one direct supervisor. But in the case of dual or shared assignments, it may be necessary to identify two or more supervisors.

Name of Incumbent (optional)

If the name of the incumbent is specified, caution must be taken not to adapt the job description to fulfill the abilities or needs of the position holder. There is often the tendency to overestimate the importance of duties that are performed particularly well by the incumbent. But when that incumbent leaves the position, a newcomer with different strengths will not have an accurate portrayal of the job she or he is expected to perform. Alternatively, specifying the incumbent may perpetuate a feeling of ownership of the job.

Name(s) of Job Analyst

Job descriptions can be developed using the input of several different sources, including the position supervisor, the library director, a human resource specialist, consultants, and even the incumbent. Yet caution should be taken in not depending too heavily on input provided by incumbents, as employees tend to inflate the importance and difficulty of their jobs. This is particularly the case when employees fear their jobs will be seen as unimportant, or when employees desire additional compensation. To avoid bias in developing job descriptions, several different information gathering techniques should be used—including observation of the incumbent, interviews with the incumbent, and questionnaires and activity logs completed by the incumbent.

Date of Job Analysis

Up-to-date job descriptions will be seen as more reliable and will be accepted more readily than those which are obsolete. To ensure that job descriptions depict a job accurately, they should be regularly reviewed and updated (at least yearly). In the library environment, rapid technological advances and personnel cutbacks brought about by budgetary constraints serve to make job descriptions rapidly obsolete.

Statement of Job Responsibility

Job descriptions should include a brief narrative summarizing the responsibilities inherent in a position. This summary, usually two to four sentences in length, should offer a concise overview of the position.

List of Job Tasks

Considered by many to be the essence of a job description, tasks should be listed in order of importance—with the most significant duty listed first. Typically, the number of duties entailed by a library job will range from eight to fifteen. Once the tasks are appropriately ordered, the frequency with which the tasks are performed (hourly, daily, monthly, annually, as needed) and the time required for completion (fifteen minutes, one hour, three days) should be noted.[2] The three pieces of information used to describe tasks (importance, frequency, and time) are mutually independent. For example, a very important task may be performed only once a year while a time-consuming task may be considered relatively unimportant.

Nature of Supervision Given

If the job holder assumes any supervisory duties (over any other staff member, student worker, or volunteer), they should be noted here.

Tools, Machinery, or Equipment Used to Perform Job

Entries may refer to computer hardware or software, typewriters, microfilm or fiche readers, bindery and book repair equipment, photocopy machines, demagnetizers, or any other aids used during the course of employment in the position.

Materials, Forms, or Documents Used to Perform Job

Entries may refer to informational or reference manuals, safety handbooks, book request forms, and any other paper or electronic documentation completed or used by the incumbent.

Degree of Interaction with Others

This entry should reflect the extent to which tasks are performed independently or interdependently. If the position requires close working relationships with coworkers in a team setting, or if the position requires interaction with patrons, requirements should be specified.

Physical Demands

With the recent passage of the Americans with Disabilities Act of 1990, this entry has assumed increasing importance in the job description document. The job description should specify the approximate percentage of time the incumbent is standing, sitting, and walking. Other physical requirements should also be noted, such as carrying (e.g., audiovisual equipment), pushing (e.g., bookcarts), loading (e.g., bookmobiles), and stretching and bending over (as is required with shelving).

Sensory Demands

Like physical demands, sensory demands must be carefully specified to avoid discriminating against individuals with disabilities. Sensory demands most likely to be found in the library setting include visual and auditory abilities. If included in the job description, sensory demands must be integrally tied to successful completion of tasks.

Working Conditions

Working conditions refer to environmental or contextual characteristics such as lighting, temperature, humidity, enclosure in cramped space, ventilation, and any hazards such as exposure to potentially harmful chemicals.

Other Duties As Required

This final "elastic" clause is often included in job descriptions to allow managers flexibility in reassigning duties when emergencies, unanticipated absences, or nonroutine events occur. Even if this clause is included, however, library managers should generally avoid asking employees to perform duties outside of their regular domain of responsibility. In "organized" workplaces, it is unlikely that labor union leaders will allow inclusion of this clause.[3]

Library Management Tip ——————————————————————

A "person specifications" document, which typically accompanies the job description, describes the skills (manual or physical and mental), knowledge (information or expertise needed), and abilities (reading, mathematical, reasoning, verbal, linguistic, interpersonal)—as well as the education, experience, characteristics, and personal attributes—which a successful job incumbent should possess.

QUESTION 42
How Can Job Descriptions Benefit Both Employees and Library Managers?

Job descriptions can be used for several purposes, including but not limited to the following:[4]

serving as a supervisory aid by providing library managers with a formal document outlining what they can expect staff members to accomplish;

communicating current performance expectations to job incumbents and future expectations should staff members seek promotion;

offering information about what aspects of performance will be evaluated during employee appraisals;

guiding training efforts by specifically detailing what behaviors incumbents should be able to perform proficiently;

informing job enrichment efforts by demonstrating the impoverished, routine, or mundane nature of some positions and the overchallenge inherent in others;

determining compensation levels;

identifying position redundancies, where two or more different jobs entail the same or overlapping duties or responsibilities;

clarifying to prospective employers exactly what duties were entailed in positions when asked to serve as a reference for former staff members;

aiding in the recruitment and selection process by outlining the skills, knowledge, and abilities an incumbent needs to successfully perform a job;

justifying disciplinary actions for failure to perform duties;

protecting the library against unfounded allegations of discrimination.

QUESTION 43
Why Is There Often Resistance on the Part of Library Employees to Completing and Using Job Descriptions?

Library managers are often resistant to completing or using job descriptions. This is because some supervisors perceive that the document serves as a rigid and inflexible barrier undermining their ability to delegate, make decisions, and exercise authority. However, for legal as well as practical purposes, it is important to make job descriptions complete, specific, and comprehensive.[5]

Other resistances and problem areas with job descriptions include:

Incumbents fear that if they reveal too much detail about their jobs, others will be able to perform them and the incumbent will become dispensable.

Incumbents don't have the time, motivation, memory, ability, or experience to participate in the development of job descriptions.

It is not in the incumbent's job description to help develop job descriptions!

Job descriptions are not kept up-to-date or adapted as positions evolve, rendering them antiquated and useless.

Job descriptions are tailored to the incumbent and hence do not provide an accurate portrayal of job requirements.

Job descriptions are completed, but are subsequently locked away and not shared with anyone.

Developing job descriptions is a time-consuming and expensive process. But they can be useful reference documents for both incumbents and library managers—if they are accessible and staff members feel uninhibited in consulting them. In fact, as part of the recruiting effort, candidates might be provided with descriptions of the jobs for which they are applying. And after being hired, newcomers should be provided with a copy of their job descriptions during orientation.

QUESTION 44

How Can the Development of Job Descriptions Assist the Library in Complying with the Americans with Disabilities Act (ADA) of 1990?

The ADA was signed into law by President George Bush to protect individuals who: (a) have a physical or mental impairment that limits one or more major life functions such as walking, breathing, learning, or seeing; or (b) have a record of impairment in the past; or (c) are regarded as having an impairment. The ADA is divided into three sections: one dealing with public access, one dealing with employment discrimination, and one dealing with communication and transportation availability.

Official estimates indicate there may be as many as forty-three million disabled Americans—but others believe the number is much greater (as many as 160 million Americans). Over the long term, the ADA is expected to affect over four million productive organizations and over five million buildings. There are over a thousand disabilities that can be identified as protected, including but certainly not limited to heart disease, high blood pressure, mental illness, diabetes, obesity, and in some cases, AIDS. Even recovering alcoholics and drug users are protected. Those who are not protected include homosexuals, bisexuals, individuals with gender-identity disorders, kleptomaniacs, pyromaniacs, active drug users, and compulsive gamblers.

Outlined in the ADA are requirements for public access which are enforced by the Department of Justice. Since 20 percent of a library's clientele is likely to be legally disabled, certain accommodations should be made including the installation of circulation desks that are, in some sections, no higher than thirty-six inches above the floor; periodical shelving no higher than fifty-four inches from the floor; curb ramps which rise only one foot for every twelve feet of distance; aisles that are at least thirty-six inches wide; and accessible parking spaces that are at least thirteen feet wide.[6]

Another title of the ADA prohibits employment discrimination based on mental or physical handicap. To facilitate the hiring of those disabled, employers are required to make "reasonable accommodations" (which might include altering the work schedule or modifying equipment and facilities) unless doing so would cause "undue hardship." Three factors are considered in determining undue hardship: the size of the organization in terms of number of employees, the budget of the organization, and the nature and cost of the accommodation required.

Library Management Tip ————————————————————

To minimize absenteeism and organizational expenditures on life, disability, and medical insurance, many libraries have subjected employees to physical examinations. The purpose of such exams was to ensure a healthy, fit workforce was selected. However, the 1990 passage of the Americans with Disabilities Act prevents preemployment physical exams. Currently, employers can ask candidates to take physical exams only after employment has been offered, when there is necessary reason, if the organization pays for the exam, and when all employees are subject to being examined. Furthermore, on application blanks and in interviews, employers may only inquire about an individual's ability to perform a specific task either with or without accommodation. Interviewers may not inquire about past worker's compensation claims.

The ADA is considered to be the most sweeping piece of employment legislation passed since the 1964 Civil Rights Act. Yet the ambiguous wording of the law offers libraries little guidance in determining when accommodations will cause undue hardship or when the nature of a position truly does prevent incumbency by an individual with a specific disability. This is why job descriptions are crucial. Valid descriptions that accurately specify position requirements can be used to demonstrate that discrimination against a certain class of disabled individuals is inherently unavoidable.

QUESTION 45

How Can the Development of Job Descriptions Assist the Library in Complying with Other Important Employment Legislation?

While job descriptions can help a library comply with the requirements of the ADA, they can also facilitate compliance with a number of other pieces of federal legislation. These include:

Fair Labor Standards Act of 1938

This tripartite law regulates: (1) minimum wage standards, (2) overtime hours and compensation—any hours worked over forty in one week must be compensated at time-and-a-half, and (3) child labor. However, the minimum wage and overtime provisions protect only those who are "nonexempt" from the law—that is, those who are not managerial, supervisory, technical, or professional staff members. To determine which workers are covered by the law and which are excluded, enforcement officials often consult job descriptions.

Equal Pay Act of 1963

This law mandates that male and female staff members must be paid equally if they perform work that is substantially equal in terms of effort, responsibility, skill, and working conditions. If the library is charged with pay discrimination, job descriptions can demonstrate that the work involved in different positions is substantially unequal and thus should be compensated at different rates.

Occupational Safety and Health Act of 1970

If the job description forewarns employees about dangerous or distasteful aspects of their positions—that is, aspects which may jeopardize their health or safety—staff members will have a more difficult time bringing lawsuits against the library for exposure to hazards. Also, in 1986, OSHA began enforcement of its "hazard communication" rules, commonly referred to as right-to-know rules. These rules require that employers inform staff members about the more than a thousand possible hazardous substances they may encounter on the job.

Civil Rights Act of 1964 (Title VII)

This landmark piece of legislation protects against discrimination in all aspects of employment based on race, color, sex, creed, or national origin. If charges of discrimination are brought against the library, job descriptions can be used to show, for example, that a person was denied a promotion because of lack of qualifications and not because of discriminatory intent.

REFERENCES

1. Moeckel, L. E. (Summer 1993). Managing staff with dual assignments: Challenge for the 1990s. *Library Administration & Management,* 181–4.

2. Dewey, B. I. (March 1990). A practical methodology for the study of job components and staffing needs. *College & Research Libraries,* 107–12.

3. Anderson, A. J. (April 1, 1991). It's not in my job description. *Library Journal,* 90–1.

4. Birdsall, D. G. (1991). Recruiting academic librarians: How to find and hire the best candidates. *Journal of Academic Librarianship,* 17(5), 276–83.

5. Cummins, T. R. (Fall 1992). Developing personnel and staffing standards. *Library Administration & Management,* 182–6.

6. Gunde, M. (December 1991). Working with the Americans with Disabilities Act. *Library Journal,* 99–100.

CHAPTER 9
Hiring the Right Person for the Job

What Activities Should Take Place before Screening Job Applicants?

Before the actual selection process begins, library managers must engage in human resource planning—the process of determining the needed quantity and quality of staff members. Staffing requirements will generally be dictated by the size of the collection, the types of programming offered, and the number of patrons served. Specific factors that may impact library staffing requirements include:[1]

Technology such as local area networks, personal computers, automated circulation, online public access computers, and CD-ROMs. While technology is often intended to reduce the number of staff members needed, technicians and support personnel will be essential. Thus, the effect of technology on staffing patterns is that it changes the type rather than the number of workers needed.

Degree of centralization of such support services as collection development, technical services, programming, and phone reference.

Service Points: the number of entrances, exits, reference desks, and circulation desks that must be staffed.

Service Hours: the number of hours per day and the number of days per week the library is open.

Levels of service, such as the depth (e.g., telephone) and type (e.g., directional or informational) of research and reference assistance.

Physical design and layout, such as whether stacks are open or closed.

Scheduling needs, allowing for vacation and sick leave, breaks, and mealtimes.

Circulation: the numbers and types of materials that are allowed to be checked out.

Types of special services, such as film and video, outreach, literacy, and home-bound.

Attrition Rates: voluntary and involuntary turnover.

Managerial Competence: the supervisory skill of the library director and other managers.

Level of usage, such as the number of patrons served per hour by the reference department. Some libraries have developed staffing formulas to help determine the number of staff members needed. For example, if the average reference question takes 5.3 minutes to answer, and approximately 30 reference questions are asked per hour, three reference librarians would be required (5.3 minutes × 30 questions = 159 minutes ÷ 60 minutes in an hour = 2.65 librarians needed).

Expertise of the staff, including education, ability, knowledge, skills, and experience.

Many times, the library manager may find that needed skills are already possessed by current staff members. When this is the case, administrators may consider promoting from within. There are many advantages associated with this method of "internal recruitment": the candidate is already familiar with organizational culture and norms, the performance capabilities of the candidate are already known, and it serves to motivate employees who want to move up through the organizational hierarchy. However, the library director should also recognize potential problems associated with internal promotions, including: (a) the candidate may not desire the additional responsibility, workload, or possible geographical relocation that accompanies promotion; (b) the candidate may be more valuable in his or her present position; (c) the candidate may accept an undesired promotion fearing organizational retaliation for turning it down; and (d) the candidate may be uncomfortable supervising employees who were formerly peers or colleagues.

Library Management Tip ───────────────────────────

The purpose of recruiting is to develop a qualified applicant pool from which the most appropriate candidate can be chosen. By definition then, not everyone recruited will be offered a job. In order to minimize disappointment, all nonhired applicants should be rejected with tact. A detailed explanation of the hiring decision is not necessary, yet diplomacy involves sending a timely personalized letter to each applicant with a correct salutation; indicating the hiring choice was very difficult due to the large number of qualified applicants; and briefly identifying the qualifications or experience of the individual chosen.

QUESTION 47
What Questions Should Not Be Asked of Candidates Applying for Positions in the Library?

Given legal and ethical mandates to avoid discrimination, certain questions commonly asked by application forms and interviewers should either be avoided, modified, or justified to applicants. Examples of such inquiries can be found in figure 7.[2] A review of this listing highlights the fact that many, if not most, commonly asked questions are not legally defensible.

In addition to avoiding unfair and possibly discriminatory inquiries, the following issues should also be considered during the information gathering process preceding selection.

The value of information provided by applicants depends upon its veracity and accuracy. Candidates too often fabricate or distort information to enhance their probability of being hired. While it is within the library's purview to terminate employees who have falsified information, it is in the organization's best interest to uncover fabrications before employment is offered.

Many libraries are beginning to require candidates to complete application forms on the premises and in the presence of an organizational representative. This is because between three and forty million (depending upon the definition adopted) functionally illiterate individuals are in the labor force. To be literate, one must possess not only reading ability, but also writing, math, and critical thinking skills—in short, those skills minimally necessary to succeed in the library environment.[3] By simply requiring applicants to compete forms on site, the organization will be offered some evidence of literacy.

Candidates often attach (unsolicited) prepared resumes to application blanks and other employment forms. While decision makers may value this additional information, caution must be exercised in not considering irrelevant or discriminatory data they may contain—such as sex, age, or marital status.

Employment forms can be "scored" (e.g., one point for each year of experience) to facilitate comparison across applicants. Furthermore, some questions may be weighted as more important or relevant to the job than others (e.g., two points for each year of supervisory experience and one point for each year of public service experience.

Figure 7. Fair and Unfair Preemployment Inquiries

Inquiry Subject	Examples of Fair Inquiries	Examples of Unfair Inquiries
Age	Are you under 18? If so, can require consent of guardian. Can require birth certificate after hiring.	How old are you? When were you born? Are you over 40? When is your birthday?
Arrests	None.	All.
Citizenship	Are you legally allowed to live and work in the United States? Can require proof of eligibility after hiring.	Are you a U.S. citizen? Where were you born? Where are your parents from? What is your mother tongue?
Convictions	Information about specific convictions within past seven years that relate to fitness to perform job.	Have you ever been convicted of a felony?
Credit rating	None.	Any direct or indirect inquiries to applicant or external agency. Do you own your car? Do you own or rent your residency?
Disabilities	Would you be able to perform, either with or without assistance or accommodation, the specific job tasks listed below?	Do you have any mental or physical handicaps? Are you healthy? Do you have any visual or auditory limitations? Have you ever received worker's compensation insurance? Do you smoke?
Education	How much education have you had? Did you graduate from high school or college? Favorite subjects of study.	When did you graduate? Name of school(s).
Experience	What relevant background have you had? May we contact your former supervisor?	Why did you leave your previous job?
Family	Do you have any obligations which might prevent you from fulfilling work obligations and commitments? Do any of your family members work for this organization?	Are you married? Do you have children? Where does your spouse work? Are your children in school? Have you ever been divorced? Do you use birth control? Are you pregnant? Do you have any plans to become pregnant?

(continued)

Figure 7. Fair and Unfair Preemployment Inquiries *(continued)*

Inquiry Subject	Examples of Fair Inquiries	Examples of Unfair Inquiries
Gender	None.	All.
Height/Weight	None.	All.
Memberships	Do you or have you ever belonged to any organization that may relate to the job you are applying for?	What organizations, societies, clubs, or fraternities do you belong to?
Military	Inquiries about relevant training, experience, or education in Armed Forces.	Nature of discharge. Any non–U.S. military experience?
Name	Have you worked for this company under another name? Will your references know you by this name?	Are you Mr., Miss, Mrs., or Ms.? Have you ever gone by any name other than your present one? What nationality is your name?
Photographs	May be requested after hiring for identification purposes.	Request that applicant submit or pose for a photograph before hiring.
Race or color	None.	All, including questions about hair, skin, or eye color.
References	Can you list three individuals we may contact to verify information you have supplied us. Who may we contact in case of emergency?	Requiring religious or past supervisory references. Who is your closest relative?
Religion	None, but can inquire about problems with work scheduling due to religious holidays.	All, including requiring a religious reference.
Salary	Would you accept the prevailing salary for this job, which is x dollars?	How much would you expect to make at this job? What were you making at your former job?

QUESTION 48

Is It Legal to Require Candidates for a Professional Librarianship Position to Have Obtained an MLIS Degree?

The general answer to this question is that each and every job requirement or inquiry on employment forms must have relevance to the job or be predictive of job performance. If court battles over discrimination ensue, the legality of every requirement and inquiry will be examined. And the library cannot necessarily assume that some criteria will be accepted as valid at face value. To demonstrate this, consider the highly publicized Merwine Case (Merwine v. Mississippi State University). In this legal proceeding, a library director was sued for rejecting an applicant who lacked the required MLIS degree from an ALA–accredited institution. While the court eventually upheld the director's right to require the degree, it was necessary to demonstrate that this educational criterion was relevant and necessary to successful performance on the job.[4]

The library field is not the only one in which educational prerequisites have been challenged. In fact, it is becoming increasingly difficult to demonstrate that a certain degree or certification can ensure success on the job. As an alternative to educational requirements, some organizations are choosing to base selection decisions on employment test outcomes.

There are several types of employment testing, both written and physical. Written aptitude tests measure an individual's potential to learn and perform a task; general intelligence (IQ) and mathematical reasoning tests are examples. Written and physical achievement tests indicate the skills, knowledge, and abilities currently possessed by applicants. One type of physical achievement test is work sampling, in which individuals actually perform tasks that would be part of their job if they were hired. Work sampling has been found to be highly valid in the library field.[5]

Library Management Tip ————————————————————————

Written personality tests—which attempt to assess an individual's temperament—are unreliable since they can be influenced by factors other than stable personality structure, such as mood or time of day. Additionally, it is difficult to establish a relationship between certain types of personality and performance. Therefore, personality tests (or any other devices, such as graphology, that attempt to assess personality) should *not* be included in selection batteries.

QUESTION 49

What Can and Should a Library Manager Say When Serving as a Reference for a Previous Employee?

Reference inquiries may take two forms—letters and telephone calls. Information provided in reference letters should generally be discounted because applicants self-select references to write recommendation letters for them and often have access to the letters that have been written. Given these circumstances, it is improbable that any negative information would be reported in reference letters. Telephoning references may provide a more balanced view of individual applicants. Unfortunately, very few library managers actually contact applicant references by telephone, instead relying upon the letters provided.[6]

The library manager who receives a reference call must be cautious when answering queries about the personal character of past employees. Legal liability can be prevented in the following ways:

Verify that the caller is who he or she purports to be and ensure that the caller has a need for the requested information.

Answer questions only about work-related behaviors—not about personality or attitude.

Do not use ambiguous words such as "average," which may have several interpretations. Instead, be precise and clear, providing specific examples of behavior.

Do not answer entrapping questions such as "would your organization rehire this individual?"

Do not volunteer unsolicited information or answer questions "off the record."

If possible, obtain written consent from the employee before answering queries.

Library Management Tip ────────────────────────

In many libraries, especially those in the academic domain, "search committees" assume responsibility for identifying and hiring the most appropriate candidate. When search committees are utilized, benefits such as collegiality, enhanced communication, and participation in decision making may accrue. But to realize these benefits, libraries should recruit search committee members who: (a) will be working with the new hire, (b) are cooperative group members, (c) have an in-depth understanding of the library's staffing needs, and (d) are willing to work irregular hours during the search process.[7] Those who are opposed to the use of search committees cite their high costs (about $1,500 in direct and $13,000 in opportunity costs per candidate), their overwhelmingly mediocre results (since a "compromise" candidate is often the only one upon whom members can be agree), the high turnover of committee hires (39 percent in the first year), and the inability of many librarians to conduct interviews effectively.[8]

QUESTION 50

What Is "Discrimination" and How Can It Be Avoided during the Selection Process?

Discrimination occurs when candidates are not considered for positions because of factors unrelated to their qualifications. The major anti-discriminatory laws with which library managers should be familiar are summarized below.

Civil Rights Act of 1964 (Title VII)

The Civil Rights Act prohibits discrimination against any applicant or employee based on race, color, religion, sex, or national origin. The Equal Employment Opportunity Commission enforces compliance.

Pregnancy Discrimination Act of 1978

This law states that a female applicant or employee may not be treated differently than a male because of pregnancy, capacity to become pregnant, or illness resulting from childbirth.

Age Discrimination in Employment Act of 1967

This act outlaws discrimination against persons over forty years old. It also eliminates mandatory retirement ages in most industries.

Executive Order 11246 of 1965

EO 11246 eliminated discrimination based on race, color, religion, sex, or national origin in public workplaces. Executive orders are issued by the President and apply only to federal employees.

Americans with Disabilities Act of 1990

Title 1 prohibits discrimination based on mental or physical handicap. To facilitate the employment of disabled persons, employers are required to make "reasonable accommodations" (which might include altering the work schedule or modifying equipment and facilities) unless doing so would cause "undue hardship."

These laws were designed to eliminate workplace discrimination, which can be manifested as either *disparate treatment* (discrimination against an individual) or *adverse impact* (discrimination against an entire classification or grouping of workers).

To establish disparate treatment, an individual claiming discrimination (the plaintiff) must prove the following four conditions:

1. The individual was a member of a protected class.

2. The individual applied when candidates were being sought.

3. The individual was qualified but was not offered the job.

4. The library continued to seek applicants after the individual was rejected.

The second form of discrimination, adverse impact, can be established by applying the Rule of Four-Fifths (or the 80 Percent Rule). This rule states that if the selection ratio of a protected group (computed by dividing the number of those hired by the number of applicants) is less than 80 percent of the highest selection ratio, discrimination has occurred. To illustrate, consider the following example given in figure 8.

In this case, the group with the highest selection ratio is the white females (selection ratio of 86% = 6 hired ÷ 7 applicants). There is not adverse impact against the African-American males as that group's selection ratio (75%) divided by the white females selection ratio (86%) is greater than 80 percent. However, there is adverse impact against the Hispanic females as their selection ratio (33%) divided by the white females selection ratio (86%) is less than 80 percent.

The four-fifths rule can also be used to determine how many of the Hispanic females would have to be hired to avoid adverse impact. Consider the following formula:

Number of protected group members (Hispanic females) **that need to be hired** (given that 6 of the 7 white female applicants were hired) =

$$\frac{\text{number of unprotected hired}}{\text{number of unprotected applicants}} \times 80\% \times \text{number of protected applicants} =$$

$$\frac{6}{7} \times 80\% \times 3 = 2 \text{ Hispanic females should be hired to avoid adverse impact}$$

Figure 8. Application of the Rule of Four-Fifths

Applicants	Number Hired	Selection Ratio	Selection Ratio ÷ White Female Ratio	Adverse Impact
African-American Males (4)	3	3/4 = 75%	75% ÷ 86% = 87%	NO 87% > 80%
Hispanic Females (3)	1	1/3 = 33%	33% ÷ 86% = 38%	YES 38% < 80%
White Females (7)	6	6/7 = 86%		

Despite the existence of antidiscrimination statutes, there are cases in which "discrimination" is legally defensible—that is, discrimination occurs but is not a violation of the law. The best defense to a discrimination charge is to establish "job relatedness" by statistically demonstrating that a selection criterion (e.g., five years previous experience) is valid or related to high performance on the job.

REFERENCES

1. Cummins, T. R. (Fall 1992). Developing personnel and staffing standards. *Library Administration & Management,* 182–6.

2. Carson, K. D., P. P. Carson, and C. W. Roe. (1995). *Management of healthcare organizations.* Cincinnati, Ohio: Southwestern.

3. Workplace literacy (May 1994). *Information Management Forum,* 4.

4. Robbins, J. (February 1, 1990). "Yes, Virginia, you can require an accredited master's degree for that job." *Library Journal,* 40–4.

5. Hiatt, P. (1992). Identifying and encouraging leadership potential: Assessment technology and the library profession. *Library Trends,* 40(3), 513–42.

6. Mika, J. J., and Shuman, B. A. (March 1988). Legal issues affecting libraries and librarians: Hiring, firing, and collective bargaining. *American Libraries,* 214.

7. Birdsall, D. G. (1991). Recruiting academic librarians: How to find and hire the best candidates. *Journal of Academic Librarianship,* 17(5), 276–83.

8. Fietzer, W. (1993). World enough, and time: Using search and screen committees to select personnel in academic libraries. *Journal of Academic Librarianship,* 19(3), 149–53.

CHAPTER 10
Complying with "Implied Contracts"

QUESTION 51
Given That Employee Manuals May Be Interpreted as "Implied Contracts," What Information Should They Contain?

To clarify newcomer expectations, many libraries issue employee manuals outlining organizational expectations and procedures. Notably, though, some courts have interpreted these manuals as "implied contracts" between the library and the staff member. Given this, careful attention should be paid to compiling, disseminating, communicating, and enforcing the contents of employee handbooks.

An employee handbook is a compendium of rules, regulations, and policies of the library. Many effective handbooks begin by describing the history, culture, organizational structure, and goals of the library.[1] Following these generalities, specific items addressed should include:

Issues Relating to Legal Mandates

    An equal opportunity statement of intent not to discriminate

    Guidelines defining, prohibiting, and outlining responses to allegations of sexual harassment

    Employee access to individual personnel files

Issues Relating to Professional Expectations

    Dress codes and appearance expectations[2]

    Conflicts of interest arising from multiple employment or accepting vendor gratuities

    Accepting gifts from patrons

    Patron confidentiality

    Employment outside the library

    Nepotism and office romances

Issues Relating to Employee Health and Safety
> Actions to be taken in case of emergencies such as fires, chemical leaks, or natural disasters
>
> Reporting on-the-job accidents
>
> The desire to maintain a drug- and alcohol-free workplace
>
> Instructions for handling security problems
>
> Safety and security procedures
>
> Smoking policies and designated locations for smoking

Issues Relating to Compensation and Benefits
> Employee status ("exempt" or "nonexempt," which influences time-keeping procedures and overtime payment computations)
>
> Worker's compensation insurance program
>
> Signing in or clocking in with time cards
>
> Expense and travel reimbursements for professional leave
>
> Leave for bereavement, voting, jury duty, and military service
>
> Sick leave or personal leave allotments (as well as procedures for requesting time off)[3]
>
> Tuition assistance for those seeking continuing education
>
> Borrowing privileges of staff members
>
> Policies on how overtime payment is accrued
>
> Performance appraisal procedures

Issues Relating to Discipline and Discharge
> Explanation and specification of probationary periods
>
> Rule infractions that lead to disciplinary action
>
> The progressive disciplinary process
>
> Absenteeism and tardiness policies
>
> Grievance procedures
>
> Exit interviews

Issues Relating to General Administration and Management
> Use of telephone for personal calls
>
> Parking availability and requirements
>
> Use of library equipment and supplies for personal purposes
>
> Rehiring former employees
>
> Solicitation and loitering during nonwork times
>
> Staff meeting schedules

A definition of the work week, including time off for meals and breaks

A holiday schedule indicating when the library will be closed

Bringing dependent children into the work environment

Library Management Tip —————————————————————

Some communication experts contend that positive, rather than negative, wording should be used when writing rules for employee manuals. For example, instead of saying "do not leave lights on at night," try "turn off lights when you leave." Others recommend that use of the word "should" be minimized or eliminated to whatever extent possible to avoid perceptions of being over-controlling.[4]

Since employee handbooks may be legally binding, they must be carefully worded, frequently updated, and inclusive in terms of content. Furthermore, manuals should not contain any rules that are not enforced consistently.

QUESTION 52
How Should the Contents of Employee Manuals Be Communicated to Employees?

Once employees are selected to become members of the library staff, they must be oriented to their new jobs and environments. Effective orientation programs usually begin by exposing newcomers to the importance of the organization to society, to their place in the organizational structure, and to how their job contributes to the success of the organization. Newly hired personnel should also be provided with a job description, a copy of the evaluation form that will be used to assess performance, and a copy of the employee manual or handbook.

But the simple provision of a handbook does not ensure that its contents will be read or understood. In fact, it may be desirable for the library manager to read through the manual with newcomers, allowing ample opportunity for questions and ambiguities to be addressed. Newcomers with disabilities may need the handbook available on audio or closed-captioned video cassette. Such actions must be taken to ensure that all employees are exposed to and understand the handbook. Failure to ensure comprehension may limit the library manager's ability to discipline employees for rule infractions.

Effective communication of the contents of handbooks also requires consideration of the following issues:

Handbooks should be updated frequently, deleting any unenforced rules and adding new rules that are to be enforced. When such modifications are made, changes must be clearly communicated to staff members.

Policies should be written in appropriate detail, such that structure is provided but management does not limit its flexibility. However, handbooks that are overly technical may not be understood by staff members.

Throughout the manual, beware of any wording that may imply continued employment—such as "permanent staff," "job security," "career path," or "just cause." Such phrases may limit the manager's ability to terminate staff members.

Include a statement to the effect that the manual is not intended to represent a contract.

Have employees sign a document attesting to the fact that they have been provided with a copy of the manual, have been afforded the opportunity to ask questions about its contents, and understand and agree to abide by its provisions.

Acceptance of the contents of an employee handbook can signal the beginning of the socialization process. *Socialization*—"breaking in" or "teaching the ropes" to newcomers—is often a slow process. However, indoctrinating newcomers into the library's culture can be expedited by orienting new employees in formal groups, setting an order and time frame in which job tasks should be learned, having new jobholders work together with previous incumbents, and ensuring that other staff members show support for the newly hired workers. Socialization is also easier when the newcomer chose the job above other employment options, the organizational value system is compatible with the newcomer's personal values, and the job is societally valued.

Library Management Tip —————————————————————————————

An organizational value emerging in importance at many libraries is the need to reduce, reuse, and recycle. Despite the automation and computerization of the library environment, paper usage continues to grow at a rate of about 4 percent per year. One law librarian discovered that the typical attorney generated one ton of paper each year—and that recycling one ton of paper could save seventeen trees. Through her research, she discovered that more than 60 percent of law libraries are now recycling. To encourage newcomers to participate in recycling programs, orientation programs should stress how much the library values such activities. This may be accomplished by explaining the benefits of recycling to the library, to the environment, and to the economy (more than one-fourth of all U.S. outbound cargo is used paper).[5]

QUESTION 53
What Should the Library Manager Do If the Rules in an Employee Manual Are Broken?

For a variety of legal, ethical, and social reasons, discipline should only be administered when there is "just cause." Just cause is demonstrated only when all of the following conditions are met: (a) rules are reasonable and clearly written; (b) employees are exposed to rules and penalties for violation of those rules; (c) rules are consistently enforced; (d) there are no mitigating circumstances inciting rule breaking; and (e) evidence from a disciplinary investigation is documented, credible, and obtained in a fair and objective manner.

Once just cause can be determined, progressive discipline should be followed, where possible. This can help ensure that the disciplinary penalty is fitting to the offense and appropriate given the offender's record of service with the library. For example, termination may be an acceptable penalty for theft but not for one incident of tardiness. Finally, due process should be followed. Due process asserts that even if guilt is admitted or clearly established, violators have certain rights including the right to expect the disciplinary procedure to follow reasonable time limits, the right to defend oneself or respond to allegations, and the right to be notified about the disciplinary process in writing.

In many cases, just cause is difficult to establish because rules included in employee manuals are subject to differing interpretations. A rule such as "no gambling," for example, is too ambiguous to be enforceable. Certainly it prohibits high-stakes poker games in the supply closet. But does it also apply to selling raffle tickets to fund a library scholarship or participating in a lottery pool? In addition to being clear, just cause requires that rules be "reasonable"—that is, they must relate to the safe, orderly, efficient operation of the enterprise. A rule requiring employees with long hair to wear hair nets may be reasonable in a cafeteria. But the same rule would be unreasonable if applied to librarians.

Once clear, reasonable rules are developed and communicated, they must be enforced consistently, fairly, and without discriminatory intent. That is, library managers should discipline staff members the way a hot stove burns those who touch it. The red-hot burners warn potential offenders about the consequences of touching the stove. If the stove is touched, the resulting burn is immediate and the cause obvious. The stove burns consistently, for all who touch it are burned every time they touch. Finally, the stove is blind, in that it burns everyone who touches it in an unbiased manner.

Having explicated the "hot-stove" rule, it is important to identify its exceptions. When mitigating circumstances surround a rule infraction, disciplinary action may not be warranted. For example, it may be inappropriate to censure staff members for verbal abuse when they are provoked by an antagonistic supervisor. Similarly, penalties should not be administered when supervisors encourage staff members to break rules or when staff members follow a bad example set by the supervisor.

QUESTION 54

What Are the Most Common Steps in Progressive Discipline?

If no mitigating circumstances can be identified, the progressive discipline procedure should be initiated following the breaking of a rule. *Progressive discipline* refers to the administration of increasingly severe penalties for identical repeated offenses. The first step in progressive discipline is normally an oral warning, which should be recorded in the employee's personnel file immediately following its administration. A written warning typically follows the oral warning. Employees should be asked to sign the written warning acknowledging its receipt. However, a signature does not equate to an admission of guilt. If the staff member does not agree that a warning is appropriate, he or she should be allowed to file a grievance. The third step in progressive discipline is often suspension or a disciplinary layoff without pay. Suspensions typically last one to three days. The final stage is termination or discharge.

QUESTION 55

Can a Library Manager Be Charged with Wrongful Termination for Discharging a Staff Member "at Will"?

Employment-at-will is a legal concept based on Horace G. Wood's 1877 treatise on "Master and Servant."[6] This doctrine assumes that unless a specific period of service is specified in a contract, either party can sever an employment relationship at any time—for good cause, bad cause, or no cause at all. However, employers should be cognizant of the three exceptions to the employment-at-will doctrine:

1. *Public Policy.* Wrongful termination occurs when an employee is discharged for refusing to break a law or for engaging in acts

to comply with the law (such as reporting a safety violation to OSHA).

2. *Good Faith and Fair Dealing/Implied Covenant.* Wrongful termination occurs when an employee is discharged as a result of a lack of fair dealing on the part of the employer.

3. *Implied Contract.* Wrongful termination occurs when an employee is discharged as a result of the employer not living up to promises or following policies (as outlined in a handbook or communicated in an employment interview).

Many library administrators are hesitant to discharge staff members because involuntary termination both limits an employee's ability to earn a livelihood and reduces the possibility of an employee finding alternative employment. But when the library manager sees no alternative to termination, she or he should do so only for just cause. Staff members who believe they have been inappropriately discharged from a library have the right to file a "wrongful termination" suit. And once in the courtroom, the library may not necessarily be privileged to blind justice. In wrongful termination cases heard by a jury, the defendant (the library being sued) faces a 70 percent chance of losing. The average award in suits decided in favor of a wrongfully terminated employee is $600,000. Such harsh penalties result because juries often base decisions on their personal perceptions of moral fairness rather than on strict adherence to the law.

QUESTION 56

What Are the Legal Limitations on Attempts to Ensure Contractual Compliance through Electronic Surveillance or Monitoring?

Nationwide, the performance of over ten million employees is monitored electronically by employers concerned about loafing, misconduct, and theft. Suspicious managers are bugging and taping workers on the phone and spying on employees with hidden video cameras linked to closed-circuit televisions. Devices are even available to measure computer uptime and keyboard usage, and sensitized chairs can determine the amount of a worker's "wiggling" (which is believed to be incompatible with working). Not even transport (or bookmobile) drivers are immune from electronic monitoring. Computer terminals can be installed in vehicles to track speed, oil pressure, engine RPMs, frequency and length of stops, and location.

While keeping such close tabs on workers may be perceived as an invasion of privacy, this is not likely the legal case. In fact, the courts have indicated that workers' rights to privacy are limited by normal employer practices—for example, if it is customary for a manager to open desk drawers or file cabinets to find needed information, these areas are not protected by privacy laws. Employers may also retain control over lockers assigned to employees and computer files. And in many cases, they also have the right to monitor employees electronically at work.

Notably, electronic monitoring is used not only to control rule-compliance and performance, but also to control theft. Examples of organizational theft range from pilfering pencils *to* making personal long distance calls from work *to* not charging for services rendered *to* diverting organizational funds into personal accounts. There are three common types of organizational theft: *larceny,* the simple taking of something; *embezzlement,* theft of something with which one has been entrusted; and *fraud,* theft of something through false pretenses, such as altering reimbursement accounts or time cards. "Time theft" (lengthy coffee breaks or packing up early to leave work) is also common, costing U.S. industry nearly $170 billion annually.

Many believe that electronic monitoring to prevent theft is "overkill," but consider the following facts that highlight the pervasiveness and devastating effects of this problem. Estimates of annual losses from employee theft range from $40 billion to $200 billion. Seventy-five percent of employees steal at least once, half steal at least twice, and 10 percent steal in volume. Thirty percent of all business failures are caused by employee dishonesty. Employees are often "taught" pilfering techniques by other employees. Internal employee theft is increasing at 15 percent per year. And more than 90 percent of all crimes occur inside business rather than out on the street.

Computer crime is perhaps the most elusive and expensive form of professional while-collar theft. Computer crimes include offenses such as illegally transferring funds or pirating software. The U.S. Army estimates the chance of a computer criminal being caught is only 1 in 100; and of being prosecuted, 1 in 22,000. While 65 percent of noncomputer thefts involve less than $150, the average loss from a computer crime is $500,000.

Unlike street crimes, only one-third of all employee thefts are committed because the perpetrator has financial need. Instead, they are typically motivated by a desire to retaliate against an employing organization perceived to be unfair and unjust. Interestingly, most dishonest employees are not sociopathic in other aspects of their lives and consider their work crime to be an aberration in their life history.

A library can protect itself against being victimized by "thieves at work" through several simple avenues. First, screen all job applicants thoroughly. Second, attempt to increase employee commitment to and identification with the library, as people do not steal from themselves.

Third, reduce theft opportunities through *physical* controls (such as sensitizers) and *social* controls (define honest and dishonest behaviors). Finally, though employee crimes may embarrass library managers, let staff members know about the crime and prosecute the criminal. Currently, only two in five employee thieves are prosecuted.

REFERENCES

1. Novak, C. (Fall 1992). Writing a handbook. *Outlook,* 56.

2. Anderson, A. J. (December 1992). Should the library have a dress code? *Library Journal,* 98–9.

3. Anderson, A. J. (October 1, 1992). I'm planning to be sick this weekend. *Library Journal,* 60–1.

4. Cubberley, C. W. (September 15, 1991). Write procedures that work. *Library Journal,* 42–5.

5. Briscoe, G. (October 15, 1991). Reuse, reduce, recycle. *Library Journal,* 43–4.

6. Mika, J. J., and B. A. Shuman (March 1988). Hiring, firing, and collective bargaining. *American Libraries,* 214.

CHAPTER 11
Work Scheduling That Works

QUESTION 57
How Can the Library Manager Schedule So That Employees Have the Flexibility Needed to Fulfill Nonwork Obligations?

Throughout the past decade, the labor force has experienced dramatic shifts in employment arrangements. The five-day, forty-hour, 8:00 A.M. to 5:00 P.M. work week is increasingly being replaced by atypical work arrangements. These shifts are being motivated by demographic changes in the labor force (such as the entrance of more women), and an increased emphasis on leisure activities (especially among the post baby-boom generation). Examples of atypical scheduling include "compressed work weeks," "flextime," "telecommuting," and "permanent part-time" employment. Each of these arrangements will be discussed in further detail.

Compressed work weeks allow employees to work a traditional forty-hour week in fewer than five days. The most common arrangement is four ten-hour days. Substantial organizational savings can be realized from reduced start-up time and lowered absenteeism. Staff members' advantages include lessened commuting time and more flexibility for completing personal business. The disadvantages associated with compressed work weeks—increased worker fatigue and scheduling problems—are generally trivial compared to the benefits of this atypical schedule.

Library Management Tip

Some organizations have chosen to adopt four-day/forty-eight-hour schedules, resulting in twelve-hour workdays. If such a compressed work week fits the needs of the library, it is important to remember that the Fair Labor Standards Act of 1938 requires overtime compensation for any hours worked in excess of forty in a single week (with a week being defined as 168 consecutive hours) by "nonexempt" employees (those who are not professional, technical, or managerial). Minimum overtime pay is one and one-half times the standard hourly rate of pay.

Under flextime arrangements, employees are required to be present during "core" bands of time (those time periods in which the library is busiest), but are free to work the balance of their shift during any of the remaining opening hours. To illustrate, consider scheduling at an urban public library which is open from 8:00 A.M. until 9:30 P.M. Observation of traffic patterns reveals the busiest times during the day are 11:30 A.M. to 1:30 P.M. (lunch hours) and 3:00 P.M. to 4:30 P.M. (after school hours). These three and one-half hours may thus be designated as core times. While all must be present during these hours, staff members may individually choose when they desire to work the remaining four and one-half hours of their required eight-hour shift.

The primary organizational benefit of such a discretionary schedule is a dramatic reduction in tardiness and voluntary turnover for the library. But for the individual staff members, this type of scheduling provides more flexibility in caring for children, reducing commuting time (as employees can avoid rush-hour traffic congestion), lessening physical fatigue, and heightening job satisfaction. Challenges inherent in flextime scheduling include overcoming communication difficulties, ensuring that at least some staff members are available during all opening hours, and coordinating interdependent tasks. Thus, libraries may find that those whose work is generally independent (e.g., catalogers, systems librarians, and interlibrary loan librarians) may be best suited to a flextime schedule.

Another, though less frequently used, atypical work arrangement is telecommuting. Telecommuting—which allows employees to work out of their homes—has been greatly facilitated by the advent of technological innovations such as fax machines, electronic mail, and modems. Although not possible for all workers, those who perform data entry and computer operations may prefer to work in the privacy of their own homes. This is verified by the fact that productivity often increases when workers are not exposed to the constant interruptions and conflictual demands made upon them in the workplace. Although social contacts are reduced, libraries may find telecommuters save office space, supervisory expenditures, and utility costs.

A final atypical arrangement—and one that is growing in popularity—is part-time employment. The number of part-time workers, defined as individuals working fewer than thirty-five hours per week, currently represents nearly 25 percent of the total labor force. Part-timers enter the labor force for two primary reasons: to supplement household income and to fulfill social and affiliative needs. Thus part-timers often come from the ranks of parents and retirees.

From an organizational perspective, part-timers can be a source of stable, dedicated, and relatively inexpensive labor, as most part-timers do not receive benefits. Part-timers may also be allowed to "share" or "split" jobs—where two permanent employees divide up a single job as well as the associated pay and benefits. In such cases, the library can get two employees (with different talents, perspectives, and strengths) for the price of one. Finally, developing a pool of permanent part-timers can reduce overtime pay (as they can be called in to fill a temporary vacancy or to work during peak service hours) as well as dependence upon temporary help.[1]

Library Management Tip ———————————————————————

Traditionally, temporary help has been limited to performing clerical tasks. But in the contemporary labor market, it is possible to temporarily hire a worker with nearly any type of skill—including accountants, computer programmers, and even information specialists. While many libraries depend upon temporary help to fill unexpected vacancies or to provide skills absent among the staff, the decision to use temporary help should be carefully analyzed. To assist in the decision, consider the following advantages and disadvantages of temporary help. On the positive side, temporary help can be quickly accessed and may serve as a recruiting source, providing the library an opportunity to review the work habits of an individual before offering them permanent employment. On the negative side, temporary help can be expensive (as the library must not only pay the employee, but must also pay a fee to the temporary help agency); temporary incumbents, who work for many firms, may have difficulty adapting to the library's culture and norms; and the library may realize decreases in productivity as the temporary incumbent will require time to learn a new job. To avoid this final problem, a library employing temporary help should carefully delineate the qualifications to be possessed by a referred worker.

QUESTION 58
What Dysfunctional Outcomes Are Associated with Ineffective Scheduling?

Ineffective scheduling can induce a variety of withdrawal behaviors. The progression of withdrawal behaviors typically begins with tardiness, intensifies to absenteeism, and culminates in voluntary turnover. Incidences of tardiness (which is typically defined as reporting six or more minutes late for duty) are usually handled through the progressive discipline process. Care should be taken to carefully define tardiness in the employee rules and regulations manual.

Minimizing absenteeism is typically addressed by providing employees only a fixed number of paid days off. Absences beyond that allocation become unpaid time away from work. On average, any given library worker will be absent four out of one hundred days. For each day an employee is absent from work, the organization loses 1.75 to 2.5 times the daily average salary of that employee. These costs result from payment of sick time to the absent employee; the cost of hiring a replacement or paying overtime to cover the vacancy; accrual of fringe benefits, which continues even when an employee is absent; and the cost of supervisory time devoted to handling the (unscheduled) absenteeism.

The technique found to be most effective at controlling absenteeism is the "paid-leave bank." Under this system, each employee is allocated a fixed number of days for absences. Distinctions are not made between sick leave days and vacation days. The program rewards employees by "buying back" unused time off. The negative aspect of the program is that the amount of sick time in the bank is less than traditionally granted. An employee who abuses time becomes forced to use vacation or personal days for real sicknesses.

QUESTION 59
What Are the Positive and Negative Aspects of Employee Turnover?

Most severe in the progression of withdrawal behaviors is turnover. Although turnover can be very costly to a library, there are some instances in which the organizational effects can be positive. Consider the following four interactions between performance and withdrawal:

Functional retention results when good performers stay on the job. This should be rewarded—through extrinsic and intrinsic compensation which demonstrate the employee's value to the library.

Dysfunctional turnover results when good performers leave the job. This should be eliminated—through identifying why it is occurring in exit interviews and initiating appropriate responses. Notably, though, some staff members will withdraw for reasons beyond the library's control, such as the relocation of a spouse (nearly 60 percent of librarians are married and many are involved in dual career situations) or staying home to raise a family.

Dysfunctional retention results when poor performers stay on the job. This shouldn't be tolerated. Assisting ineffective employees in identifying other opportunities that better match their capabilities may reduce organizational "deadwood." Another alternative is to invoke progressive disciplinary procedures to terminate the employee for poor performance.

Functional turnover results when poor performers leave the job. This should be encouraged, despite the cost involved in recruiting, hiring, and training a new worker.

QUESTION 60
Should the Library Manager Attempt to Control "Moonlighting" by Staff Members?

Moonlighters are defined as employees who hold wage or salaried jobs with two or more employers. Official estimates indicate that moonlighters represent between 5 and 6 percent of the labor force. Yet, empirical research suggests that moonlighting may be much more common than reported in the statistics, due to the hesitancy of some workers to reveal dual employment in fear of retaliation by one employer. In fact, the actual number of moonlighters likely approaches 20 percent of the labor force. Some even speculate that multiple job holding will increase in the future, especially in the white-collar sector.

Consistent with this prediction, substantial numbers of librarians are taking on additional employment in areas such as information brokering, document delivery, information systems analysis, indexing, abstracting, writing, editing, publishing, consulting, library association work, storytelling, records management, vending, database management, training, and free-lance librarianship. Given this trend, professional organizations such as the Independent Librarians' Exchange Round Table of the American Library Association (ILERT/ALA) and the Association of Independent Information Professionals (AIIP) have emerged.

Theorists have long asked why moonlighters hold down a second job. One answer is provided by proponents of the "deprivation/constraint" perspective. They contend that moonlighters are generally economically pressured and motivated by financial need (after all, moonlighters do select a second job for which they are compensated rather than a charitable or voluntary position). However, recent research suggests that a second answer, the "energetic/opportunity" perspective, is better supported.

This perspective asserts that moonlighters are a special breed of worker exhibiting extraordinary effort and energy to achieve personal and career expectations. Moonlighters tend to have a strong work ethic as well as a zest for life and are willing to bear discomforts associated with holding multiple jobs. Furthermore, research shows moonlighters tend to be well educated, often having unused skills and experience not required by their primary jobs. This underemployment has been found to be a strong motivation for moonlighting.

Based on the empirical research, then, library managers might want to avoid a knee-jerk reaction discouraging moonlighting. In fact, some benefits may accrue to the library employing staff who moonlight. Consider the case of the academic reference librarian who took an evening job at a bookstore one Christmas season. Attracted by what libraries might learn from retail bookstores, he accepted an entry-level job. At first he was uncomfortable with handling a cash register instead of a catalog, having access to only 25,000 books as compared to 250,000, and operating based on a "catalog of the mind" instead of on an OPAC. But what he discovered during his tenure at the bookstore gave him valuable experience that he carried back to his library. Working in the private sector gave him a fresh perspective on issues such as commitment to customer service, user-friendly operating hours, the importance of convenient patron access, and the superiority of personal assistance.[2]

While such insights may ultimately benefit the employing library, some staff members may have reservations about moonlighting colleagues. For example, a moonlighter's "divided loyalty" may be questioned. Even more basic is the question of whether any individual possesses the physical and cognitive resources necessary to successfully pursue multiple employment. And, ethical questions about conflicts of interest may arise. Conflicts are especially likely when the individual provides the same or comparable services in which she or he is engaged during library employment.

Library Management Tip

To raise awareness about potential conflicts of interest associated with moonlighting, the employing library may annually ask staff members to complete a form listing "Outside Professional Activities." This form could contain inquiries about the types of professional activities which were engaged in throughout the year, whether or not they were compensable, the names of other organizations that were involved, the nature of the work relationship, and the number of days engaged per year. Finally, staff members may be asked to explain if any reported activities may perceivably give rise to questions of conflicts of interest. While such disclosure may help "clear the air," it is important that the forms not be interpreted as an attempt to limit professionals' outside activities.[3]

QUESTION 61
Should a Library Give Special Attention to the Child-Care Needs of Staff Members?

With each passing year, more and more women are entering the world of work. Currently, women constitute about half of the labor force. In the library setting, however, the proportion of female workers tends to be even higher than average (about 80 percent of librarians are female). With the increase in female labor force participation, libraries are recognizing that fringe benefits are needed to help employees balance their careers and family lives.[4] Consider the following statistics:

More than 75 percent of women between the ages of twenty-five and forty-nine—prime child-bearing years—are employed.

Nearly 70 percent of new workers entering the labor force this century will be women, and three-fourths of these will become pregnant while employed.

Fifty-eight percent of women who have children under the age of six are working—a figure that has quadrupled since 1950.

Thirty-eight percent of working female librarians and 44 percent of working male librarians have children.

Nearly 35 percent of MLIS female librarians have withdrawn from the labor force at one time or another for child-rearing reasons.[5]

In response to these trends, child care is the fastest growing employee benefit. And libraries that do not offer some type of reimbursement and/or referral service may find their applicant pool reduced. It should be remembered, however, that standard provision of this benefit can create morale problems for workers who do not have children. Also worth remembering is that not all staff member dependents are offspring.

While many library employees have child-care obligations, some also have elder-care responsibilities (a duty to care for aging relatives in poor health). And some workers—particularly those in their forties—are burdened with intergenerational care (of *both* children and parents). Since 12 percent of individuals who take care of elderly relatives are forced to quit their jobs to do so, some libraries are beginning to offer geriatric day-care benefits in addition to child care.

REFERENCES

1. Contingency workers: Not a quick fix (April 1994). *Finance Forum,* 1.

2. Strickler, D. (June 15, 1992). What I learned working in a bookstore. *Library Journal,* 47–8.

3. Bjorner, S. N. (Fall 1991). "Which hat are you wearing today?": Ethical challenges in dual employment. *Library Trends,* 40(2), 321–7.

4. Greenhaus, J. H., and G. A. Callanan (1994). *Career management,* 2nd ed. Fort Worth, Tex.: Dryden.

5. Detlefsen, E. G., J. E. Olson, and I. H. Frieze (March 15, 1991). Women and librarians: Still too far behind. *Library Journal,* 36–42.

CHAPTER 12
Potential Pitfalls in Performance Evaluations

QUESTION 62
Why Are Performance Appraisals So Often Met with Resistance?

Although it is statistically impossible, four out of five library staff members believe their performance is "above average," and 90 percent think they outperform their peers. Given the natural tendency to overestimate individual performance, employees who receive negative appraisals are likely to grow defensive and resentful. But employees are not the only ones who don't like performance evaluations; library managers don't like them either. Nearly three-quarters of all supervisors question the usefulness of evaluating subordinate performance.[1]

Although appraisals are often met with opposition and cynicism, the evaluation of work-related behaviors dates back several centuries. For example, in the 1600s, the Chinese Civil Service employed an "Imperial Rater" to assess the Royal Family's performance. The first industrial appraisal system was devised around 1800 by Robert Owens, a Scottish industrialist, who would place color-coded blocks at each worker's station indicating the previous day's performance.

Surveying the librarianship literature, one finds that writings on performance appraisals date back to an article in the September 1887 issue of the *Library Journal.* A 1914 monograph on the Oxford University Libraries demonstrates the simplicity of early library evaluations. It states that the library director "who was to be in the Holy Orders, should once a year hand over to the Chancellor and Procters the keys of the library: If after visitation he was found to be fit in morals, fidelity, and ability, he received them back." Despite historical precedent, performance appraisal continues to be the subject of much research, study, and debate. Since the early 1900s, more than 250 library science articles have been written on this topic.

QUESTION 63
Why Should Performance Appraisals
Be Conducted at All?

Contemporary literature agrees that performance appraisals are conducted for two main purposes: (a) developmental: to identify areas of deficiency that might be improved through training; and (b) evaluative: to gather data for making personnel decisions about promotions, pay increases, discipline, or discharge. It is the contradiction between these two purposes that creates resistance to performance evaluations: the former purpose is aimed at helping, while the latter is aimed at judging the worker.[2] Hence, how can an evaluator be perceived as helpful when he or she may jeopardize the worker's future employment? Or, how can a staff member admit to needing training when that admission may lead to disciplinary action? And how can appraisers give accurate ratings if they will diminish trust between the supervisor and the worker? These inherent conflicts can only be resolved through the development of a procedurally fair performance evaluation system.

QUESTION 64
Who Should Evaluate Staff Member Performance?

One critical consideration in designing a fair performance appraisal system is selecting the evaluator(s). Two conditions must be met before an individual can appraise another's performance. First, the evaluator must understand the job requirements of the specific position. Second, the evaluator must have ample opportunity to observe the worker's on-the-job performance.

In over 75 percent of all libraries, a staff member's direct supervisor will be the one and only evaluator. This may, however, be problematic—especially if the supervisor oversees the work of many subordinates or if the supervisor is geographically separated from her or his subordinates. Furthermore, many library managers do not have the requisite skills, knowledge, ability, or desire to evaluate staff performance. Therefore, other appraisers should also be considered.

For example, intradepartmental peer evaluations may be used. However, peers who are employed in different positions may not fully understand the requirements of a coworker's job. Further, peer evaluation may result in deflated ratings (if employees are competing for advancement to the same position) or inflated ratings (if employees feel a need to "cover" for one another). Therefore, peer ratings may be more suitable for training than for evaluation purposes.[3] One notable exception is that peer review is typically used to assess the performance of professional librarians, as administrators without library science training would not be qualified to serve as evaluators of professional activities.

A third option is self-rating by the worker who is being evaluated. Inviting self-ratings gives staff members the opportunity to identify problems of which others may be unaware (such as outdated technology that prevents maximum performance). Self-ratings may also provide a nonconfrontational opportunity for staff members to disagree with library managers. Like peer evaluations, though, self-ratings may be most suitable for developmental or training purposes. If employees trust that honest evaluations will be used only to help improve their performance and not to penalize them, they are more likely to provide accurate assessments of their deficiencies.

While supervisory and self-ratings are most often used to evaluate the performance of nonmanagerial staff, subordinate evaluations are increasingly being used to assess the performance of library managers. Subordinates may be asked to evaluate their supervisors since they are in a unique position to provide constructive feedback on management styles and methods. To prevent fear of retaliation or artificially inflated evaluations, subordinate evaluators should be anonymous. Concealing the identity of evaluators may, however, encourage subordinates to use performance appraisals to vent hostility and frustration—especially if there is no other outlet for reporting supervisory misconduct.[4]

Finally, librarians have a unique opportunity to solicit performance feedback from patrons.[5] Consistent with the "total quality management" philosophy (*see* chapter 19), customer input can be a valuable source of information. However, three caveats are in order. First, patrons are likely to report only incidents of extremely good or extremely poor behaviors. Second, some staff members have only minimal contact with patrons, while others have none. In the absence of such contact, patrons do not observe all library staff members in action. And third, patrons often focus only on the personality of the employee (such as friendliness and helpfulness) rather than on more objective measures of performance. This is particularly problematic since a 1970 ruling from the Supreme Court in the case of Griggs v. Duke Power Company indicated that performance appraisals should be tied to job requirements rather than to individual traits.

QUESTION 65
What Aspects of Staff Member Performance Should Be Evaluated?

Many performance appraisal techniques, instruments, and formats currently exist. To simplify the confusing choice of which method to use, libraries too often select the one that appears to be the simplest, fastest, or cheapest. However, this encourages the development of arbitrary, unlawful, and ineffective performance appraisal systems. Alternatively, the following four criteria must be considered.

Validity	If a performance appraisal instrument evaluates any aspect of behavior or personality that is not included in the job description, the evaluation is "contaminated." If an instrument fails to evaluate any behavior included in the job description, the evaluation is "deficient." Only when there is perfect overlap between the instrument and the job description is the evaluation valid.
Reliability	Reliability refers to consistency. That is, if two evaluators observe the performance of the same employee, both should provide similar ratings. Such consistency can only result when performance appraisal inquiries are specific and job related.
Acceptability	A performance appraisal instrument must be understandable and tolerable by both evaluators and employees. That is, both parties must perceive the evaluation as being fair and beneficial.
Usefulness	The appraisal instrument should provide guidance and direction for performance improvement. That is, the employee should be able to examine a suboptimal rating and understand what behaviors must be engaged in to improve performance in subsequent evaluation periods.

Unfortunately, most performance appraisal systems currently used in libraries fail to satisfy these criteria. This is particularly true of the all-too-common "graphic rating scale" format that assesses staff members' personality (as when evaluators are asked to rate the "cooperativeness" of a staff member on a scale ranging from "unacceptable" to "outstanding"). Although simple to construct and use, graphic rating scales always pose two insurmountable problems (even if inquiries about personality are avoided). First, these scales are not reliable, as anchors such as "outstanding" may mean different things to different raters. Second, these scales do not suggest strategies for performance improvement.

Given the deficiencies surrounding the graphic rating scale, behaviorally based performance appraisal systems are recommended by personnel experts in the librarianship field. One of the most commonly used behavioral techniques is the "behaviorally anchored rating scale" or "BARS." As the name implies, scale levels under a BARS system are anchored with concrete behavioral descriptions—not with vague labels such as "outstanding" or with arbitrary numerical ratings such as "1" to "5." A BARS is constructed in accordance with the following steps.

First, relevant performance dimensions are identified for each position using the job description. In the library setting, most jobs involve between ten and fifteen major performance dimensions.

Second, each relevant performance dimension identified must be defined. For example, the performance dimension of "provide reference assistance" may be defined as "assisting patrons in locating appropriate information to fulfill their needs."

Third, for each relevant performance dimension, behavioral anchors representing superior, average, and unacceptable performance must be generated. For example, the behavioral anchor representing unacceptable performance may read: "The librarian often replies he or she simply doesn't know the answer to a patron's question." The behavioral anchor representing average performance may read: "The librarian usually just points to the appropriate area of the library in response to a patron's inquiry." And the behavioral anchor representing superior performance may read: "The librarian walks with the patron to the appropriate location, pulls a book that satisfies a patron's request, and hands the book to the patron." Usually, seven to nine behavioral anchors are used for each dimension, representing the entire range of possible performance.

Finally, the evaluator compares and matches the performance of the employee to the performance described in the anchors. An employee whose behavior matches that which is deemed "unacceptable" may be referred to the "superior" performance anchor as a guideline for improvement.

QUESTION 66
How Can Personal Bias on the Part of the Evaluator Be Minimized during the Appraisal Process?

Human nature dictates that appraisers will always be tempted—either consciously or unconsciously—to bias ratings. The best method for minimizing biases, however, is to be aware of their existence and adverse effects. One common bias that can distort performance evaluations is "central tendency error," which occurs when appraisers evaluate all staff members as average. "Leniency error" occurs when everyone is evaluated as above average, and "severity error" when everyone is evaluated as below average. With each of these biases, range restriction is evident; that is, evaluators use only portions of the rating scale as opposed to the entire range. Specifically, raters suffering from either leniency or severity bias use only anchors on the ends of the scale, while raters with central tendency bias use only the middle anchors.

Leniency results from artificial inflation of performance ratings, while severity results from artificial deflation. Some common reasons for systematically biasing evaluations either upward or downward are listed below:

Causes of Lenient Ratings

Hesitancy to create a negative document that will be permanently placed in the evaluatee's personnel file

Fear of reducing employee motivation and performance

A desire to avoid publicizing any information that would reflect poorly on the supervisor or other members of the department or library

The need to protect a good performer who had an "off" period or an employee whose productivity has suffered due to personal problems

A desire to reward effort or improvement even though performance was low

Fear of damaging interpersonal relationships and being placed in a confrontational situation

Causes of Severe Ratings

A desire to scare or punish a rebellious employee

The need to show an employee who is boss

A desire to create a record that will justify termination

The hope of encouraging an employee to quit or request a transfer

Many problems are created by range-restriction biases. For example, when only portions of the scale are utilized, there will appear to be only small performance differentials among staff members. Also, subordinates of a supervisor with severity bias will compare unfavorably to subordinates of a supervisor with leniency bias—even though actual performance may be very similar.

In addition to biases from range restriction, the order in which performance appraisals are completed may introduce bias. "Contrast error" results when an employee is inadvertently compared to the employee previously evaluated rather than to an absolute standard. Contrast error is manifested in two ways: (1) when an average performer is evaluated after an exceptional performer, the average performer will be rated as below average; and (2) when an average performer is evaluated after an inferior performer, the average performer will be rated as above average.

Other timing biases include "recency error" (the tendency for performance just prior to evaluation time to be most salient) and "primacy error" (the tendency for performance at the beginning of the evaluation period to be most salient). Employees hope to capitalize on their appraiser's recency error when productivity improves, tardiness ceases, and coffee breaks shorten just prior to their evaluation. Primacy error is most likely to occur when a supervisor— frustrated by an inability to recall employees' performance—makes a concerted attempt at the beginning of the next evaluation period to monitor and document work-related behaviors. But as time passes, attention is diverted, and less effort is placed on observing performance . . . until the next evaluation period approaches.

In addition to range restriction and timing biases, there are also perceptual biases. For example, human beings have a strong tendency to form quick first impressions about others. Once formed, perceptions are difficult to alter. This is the underlying rationale of the "anchoring and adjustment" bias—once first impressions are "anchored" in our minds, it takes robust contradictory evidence to cause us to "adjust" them. Unfortunately, biases based on first impressions can distort performance evaluations far into the future—as employee behavior which is inconsistent with the evaluator's expectation is simply rationalized or excused away.

If the evaluator was responsible for hiring a particular employee, first impressions (and performance appraisals) are likely to be persistently favorable. Even if the employee's performance is substandard, submitting negative evaluations may reflect poorly on the supervisor's judgment and credibility. Such a bias is reflected in "escalation of commitment"—that is, the tendency to favorably judge an individual in whom the evaluator has an investment.

Library Management Tip

First impressions are also likely to be favorable when the appraiser and the appraisee are similar in terms of age, personality, sex, or national origin. The "similar-to-me bias" is manifested as evaluators believe any staff member like themselves must be valuable to the library.

Another perceptual bias is the "halo effect," which occurs when exceptional performance on one dimension positively influences performance ratings on all other dimensions. A "horns effect"—the converse of halo—occurs when extremely poor performance on one dimension negatively influences ratings on all other dimensions.

REFERENCES

1. Kaehr, R. E. (March 1990). Personnel appraisal, who needs it? *Journal of Academic Librarianship,* 16(1), 35–6.

2. Cummins, T. R. (1990). Personnel management in libraries. *Public Library Quarterly,* 10(1), 25–43.

3. Arthur, G. (July 1990). Peer coaching in a university reference department. *College & Research Libraries,* 367–73.

4. Perkins, G. H. (Fall 1992). Enhancement of organizational structure through upward evaluation. *Library Administration & Management,* 198–202.

5. Anderson, A. J. (November 1, 1990). Can store service policy fit a library? *Library Journal,* 64–5.

CHAPTER 13
Finding Value in Performance Evaluations

QUESTION 67
Should Pay Be Based on Performance Evaluations?

Pay-for-performance is an appealing concept to both employers (who believe that employees will work harder if they expect the increased effort will result in higher pay) and employees (who believe that doing a job well will be recognized and rewarded).

Library Management Tip —————————————————————————————

When members of the labor force are questioned about criteria that should be used to determine compensation increases, performance emerges as number one. In rank order (from most to least important), other criteria include: (2) nature of job; (3) amount of effort expended; (4) cost of living; (5) training and experience; (6) increases outside organization; (7) budgetary considerations; (8) increases within organization; and (9) length of service, tenure, or seniority.

___

But before committing to performance-based pay, the library manager should consider the following prerequisites to a successful compensation program. First, employees must believe that enhanced effort and improved performance will definitely result in increased pay. Second, employees must value money and view it positively (as a reward), not negatively (as a bribe to improve performance). Third, there must be in place a systematic, fair mechanism for evaluating performance. And finally, other motivators besides money must also be used to shape behavior and performance.

If the above conditions are not met, a pay-for-performance system is sure to fail. The success of performance-based pay will also depend on effectively communicating the program and ensuring that employees clearly understand how it is administered. Other caveats to remember when administering pay-for-performance include:

Merit pay differentials between superior and average performers must be sizeable enough to motivate excellence.

Some staff members (particularly those with long tenure) would prefer that compensation be based on seniority rather than on performance.

The individual focus of merit pay plans may spur intraorganizational competition.

QUESTION 68
What Laws Should the Library Manager Be Aware of When Determining Compensation?

One important piece of compensation legislation is the Equal Pay Act (EPA) of 1963, which prohibits gender discrimination. This law requires equal pay for "substantially equal" work—in terms of skill (knowledge, ability, training), effort (physical and mental), and responsibility (decision making and control of resources) under similar working conditions. The EPA has attempted to eliminate male-female pay inequities—but, on average, women still earn only $.70 to a man's $1.00.

In the library profession, the average pay differential between males (who constitute 20 percent of the library work force) and females (who constitute 80 percent of the library workforce) performing the same job is $3,000. A closer examination of library compensation practices reveals the following statistics. The average salary for a male university librarian is $45,336, compared with an average salary of $41,777 for females. Among the ranks of university library directors, the average salary of females ($100,272) is 3 percent lower than the average salary of males ($103,987).[1] In general, female librarians are paid 12 percent less than their male counterparts with similar education and experience.[2] The desire to minimize knowledge about gender-based pay inequities has perpetuated the practice of pay secrecy. Although considered to be proper etiquette (less than 20 percent of employees wish to have their pay level exposed), not publicizing compensation structures can lead to gross overestimation of others' salaries and can perpetuate feelings of unfairness.

Like the EPA, the doctrine of "comparable worth" has also drawn attention to male-female pay gaps. Comparable worth is based on the notion that while the true value of jobs may be similar, some jobs (typically held by women) are often paid at lower rates than other jobs (typically held by men). To illustrate, assume the "true" value of a maintenance job is the same as the value of an administrative assistant position (each worth $10 per hour). If the maintenance worker (usually male) is paid $10 but the administrative assistant (usually female) only $7, the female-dominated job is being paid at only 70 percent of its value.

Comparable worth has been applied to ask why medical librarians receive less than men with jobs requiring less than an eighth-grade education; why female Ph.D. lab scientists earn less than street sweepers and gardeners; why nurses earn less than painters, tree trimmers, and parking lot attendants; and why stenographers earn less than male toll collectors. Supporters of the comparable-worth doctrine often sport red handbags, symbolizing that the lower rates of pay often put women "in the red."

QUESTION 69
How Can Performance Evaluations Direct Training Initiatives?

Library staff members fail to perform effectively for three reasons: (1) they are impeded from performing as they know they should, (2) they are not motivated to perform, or (3) they do not know how or when to perform. Training can resolve only the third problem—and only when the first two obstacles are removed. That is, staff members must be allowed to use their skills, knowledge, and abilities to satisfy their professional obligations. And they must be intrinsically and extrinsically motivated toward superior performance.

But just as important, developmental performance appraisals must accurately diagnose areas of deficiency—for only valid performance appraisals can suggest training content and design. One important design consideration is the selection of the training site. Work-related instruction can take place on the job (e.g., training in technical skills); on site, but off the job; or off site (e.g., communication skills learned in a classroom setting).

Employees generally enter the library setting with some formal training. However, becoming familiar with specific equipment, techniques, and procedures used in the library may require on-the-job instruction. Although on-the-job training is generally inexpensive (in that it does not require any new or additional facilities or staff), it can be risky. For example, an employee learning to do literature searches on the job may cause a patron to become frustrated and lose confidence in the expertise of the library staff (not to mention the cost!!).

On-the-job training most commonly takes the form of supervisory instruction, in which a library manager teaches a staff member.

Although supervisors should be familiar with jobs performed by subordinates, they may not possess enough specific, detailed knowledge to instruct them. Furthermore, learning from one's boss may create apprehension in a novice struggling to master new skills. An alternative is peer modeling, where a coworker coaches a novice in the requirements of a position. However, this form of training poses the hazard of accumulating error; that is, if a staff member who performs a job incorrectly trains others in the same techniques, errors will be perpetuated. And even an employee who performs a job correctly may not possess the educational skills or motivation necessary to instruct others.

QUESTION 70
What Educational Programming Should Supplement On-the-Job Training?

The most common form of on-site/off-the-job training in the librarianship field is the formal lecture. Lectures are most useful for transmitting detailed information to a large audience. However, several problems can minimize the effectiveness of this training technique. First, since information flows only one way, the trainee is a passive participant in the process. This passivity can minimize recall and restrict the application of lecture material to real workplace situations. However, postlecture discussions may reinforce learning. Mass lectures also ignore individual differences in trainee ability and capability to comprehend information.

A form of off-site training particularly applicable for continuing professional education is attendance at library association conferences. At these meetings, colleagues have the opportunity to share research discoveries, insights for improving service, and suggestions for enhancing productivity. Library managers who value continuing education will typically reimburse professionals for conference attendance.

Another form of off-site training is the assessment center approach. Assessment centers—which are really more of a concept than a place—were originally developed by AT&T in the 1960s to serve two purposes: to identify candidates for promotion to positions of increased responsibility and to identify skill deficiencies and training or developmental needs. Typically, a team of three to five evaluators (senior library managers, human resource specialists, and organizational psychologists) rate candidates who perform the following exercises:

In-basket simulations, which require participants to process a collection of memos, reports, letters, and phone messages within a prespecified amount of time. Participants must elect either to personally handle, to ignore, or to delegate responsibility for the correspondence. This exercise reflects the participants' ability to prioritize, use logic, and act decisively.

Case analyses, which are usually interpersonal in nature (e.g., a participant might be asked how he or she would handle a patron who complains about limited library holdings). Case analyses reflect a participant's personal interaction abilities.

Role play, which forces participants to assume the role of another—for example, a library director—while a second participant may play the role of a parent angry about the adult content of books her child has been allowed to check out. Role play demonstrates a participant's ability to remain calm under stressful situations, think objectively, solve problems, and communicate.

Leaderless group discussions, which involve presenting a problem to a group of participants who are asked to come up with a solution (e.g., a budget and resource allocation problem). These discussions demonstrate teamwork ability, leadership and followership skills, and consensus-building capacity.

Once the assessment center experience—which usually lasts three to five days—is complete, participants receive confidential feedback about their individual performance. Results and feedback seem to be quite valid, as it has been found that assessment centers can identify and nurture leadership in the library and information science profession.[3]

QUESTION 71
How Can the Library Manager Determine If Training Initiatives Are Successful?

It is important, in this era of increasingly restricted budgets, to ensure that training dollars are being well spent. To assess the value of monies spent on instruction, the following three evaluation criteria might be considered:

1. *Knowledge acquisition,* the degree to which instructional programming is understood by the trainee.

2. *Knowledge retention,* the degree to which information presented during instructional programming is remembered and recalled.

3. *Knowledge transfer,* the degree to which information presented during instructional programming relates to, or can be directly applied to, the position held by the trainee.

Each of these three criteria can be measured through a variety of techniques, including: (a) evaluating changes in behavior or productivity; (b) surveying employees about their reactions or attitudes toward the training; and (c) testing how much learning occurred during training (which requires comparing results on a pretraining test to results on a posttraining test).

Training tends to be more successful when trainees actively participate in instructional programming—as opposed to being passive recipients of information. Further, learning and knowledge transfer result only when trainees accept the techniques being taught as appropriate and the information being disseminated as factual. Finally, learning is reinforced through practice. Repeated practice, which results in overlearning, may be necessary until certain reactions become innate and reflexive. Overlearning also increases information retention and the probability that quality decisions will be made during times of stress and emergencies.

Tom Peters, coauthor of the best-seller *In Search of Excellence,* identifies ten additional elements that characterize successful training programs.[4]

1. Extensive entry-level training should focus on exactly those skills in which the organization wishes to be distinctive. For example, if the library wants to be recognized for superior service, staff members should be initially trained in how to please irate patrons. And, if the library wants to be recognized for efficiency, staff members should be initially trained in quick turnaround time.

2. All staff members should be treated as career employees. When a newcomer enters the library setting, managers should assume that the staff member will be employed in the library until he or she retires. Approaching personnel management from this perspective will encourage investment in human resources. And investment in people will yield increased loyalty as well as heightened effectiveness.

3. Regular retraining is required. Library managers cannot assume that one training session will be sufficient for guaranteeing desired work behaviors. Training must be scheduled on an ongoing basis at regular intervals.

4. Both time and money must be generously expended. Staff members must be allowed time away from their positions to attend training sessions—which should be conducted by experts. In addition, libraries should encourage continuing education through the provision of tuition reimbursements.

5. On-the-job training is important. Many skills cannot be learned in a lecture hall; they must be learned on the library floor or in the

stacks. To the extent possible, the library should be transformed into a living classroom.

6. There are no limits on the skills that can be profitably taught to everyone. Library training should expand beyond just the information science field. All staff members would probably profit from instruction in statistics, psychology, management, and computer science.

7. Training is used to herald a commitment to a new strategic thrust. When the library wishes to pursue a different direction or capitalize on a new niche, training can help staff members understand the need for and accept the change.

8. Training is emphasized during times of crisis. During times of fiscal crisis or budgetary constraints, the training budget is often the first line-item to be slashed. Such a response is, however, short sighted. Training—technically defined as the systematic acquisition of skills, rules, concepts, and attitudes that result in improved performance in the work environment—is particularly necessary for improving efficiency and effectiveness when resources are limited.

9. Training content is participant driven. The types of training offered must be dictated by the needs and deficiencies of the staff, rather than by the expertise of the trainer.

10. Training is used to teach the organization's vision and values. Training can expedite the acculturation process and help staff members understand and become aligned with the values of the library.

QUESTION 72
What Effect Might Library School Closings Have on the Profession?

Planned workplace learning costs U.S. organizations over $200 billion annually—a figure similar to the amount spent on elementary, secondary, and higher education combined. But as Will Rogers observed, "the schools ain't what they used to be and never was." When institutions of higher education fail, employers must pick up the slack, encouraging and providing for continuing staff development. This is particularly true in the library setting, where opportunities for academic education are increasingly dwindling.

In 1978, the University of Oregon became the first to shut down its Graduate School of Librarianship. By the mid-1990s, the number of library school closings has reached well into the double digits. In response to this alarming trend, two questions beg answers. First, what are the reasons for the closings? And second, what can libraries do to prevent additional closings that shift the burden of educating librarians from the university setting to the library itself?

Several reasons—both political and practical—have been advanced to explain why library schools are failing at such a dramatic rate when society is in the midst of the information age. These include declining student enrollments, underemployment of graduates, weak curriculums and nonproductive faculty, interpersonal isolation of the library school faculty from the remainder of the campus, curriculum overlap between library schools and business and computer science programs, the inability or unwillingness of library school graduates to contribute financially to alumni associations, and the low status of library science programs.[5]

Whatever the underlying reasons are, the closure of library schools will have dramatic long-term implications for the profession. For example, closings mean fewer schools and greater distance between schools. This is problematic since geographic convenience is the primary criterion students consider in determining whether to pursue graduate library education. Other criteria such as perceived quality, cost, and the availability of specialized courses are minimal in comparison.[6] Hence, when potential students must consider geographically relocating to attend library school, enthusiasm wanes. In fact, relocation is often impractical since most potential students are working full time and desire to attend school on a part-time commuter basis. The end result is fewer professionally trained library applicants. Also alarming is that many of the library schools offering doctoral programs are being closed, eliminating future replacements for current library science professors—whose average age is around fifty.[7]

If current trends continue, would-be librarians may have no choice but to seek training on the job. To avoid this undesirable circumstance, librarians must collectively emphasize the value of the profession. There is little debate as to the fact that librarians are currently undervalued—even in the university setting where they would appear to be critical to the success of the entire academic community. In fact, one survey found that university librarians were perceived to contribute less to the academic community than did track and assistant football coaches.[8]

Among the public, perceptions are even worse. As evidence, Americans spent $330 billion on legalized gambling in 1992. If those gambling expenditures were allocated to the nation's public libraries, that one-year total would fund such institutions for seventy-five years. If lottery proceeds were added into the pot, libraries could be funded for an additional five years.[9]

REFERENCES

1. Detlefsen, E. G., J. E. Olson, and I. H. Frieze (March 15, 1991). Women and librarians: Still too far behind. *Library Journal*, 36–42.

2. Academic salaries up 2%, 12,000 positions surveyed (April 25, 1994). *Library Hotline*, 4.

3. Hiatt, P. (1992). Identifying and encouraging leadership potential: Assessment technology and the library profession. *Library Trends*, 40(3), 513–42.

4. Peters, T. (Summer 1990). Train and retrain. *Library Administration & Management*, 127–30.

5. Paris, M. (October 1, 1990). Why library schools fail. *Library Journal*, 38–42.

6. Birdsall, W. F. (1992). Why don't more faculty love librarians? *Journal of Academic Librarianship*, 17(6), 375.

7. Futas, E., and F. Zipkowitz (September 1, 1991). The faculty vanishes. *Library Journal*, 148–52.

8. White, H. S. (October 15, 1990). The education and selection of librarians: A sequence of happenstances. *Library Journal*, 61–2.

9. One year of legal gambling equals 75 library years (April 25, 1994). *Library Hotline*, 5.

CHAPTER 14
Unionization

QUESTION 73
What Factors Encourage or Discourage Library Employees from Seeking Unionization?

Membership in unions—defined as organizations formed by employees who wish to act as a single unit when dealing with management about work-related issues—is currently maintained by less than 15 percent of the labor force. This meager figure is attributed to many factors including the sophistication of contemporary human resource managers; the proliferation of laws aimed at protecting workers' rights; and the entrance of nontraditional labor force members historically excluded from unions, such as women and minorities.

The first library union was formed in 1914. In response to administrative inadequacy, these workers mobilized to enter the "labor relations process": the process through which an exclusive collective bargaining agent representing the interests of workers jointly negotiates and administers the terms and conditions of employment with management. The labor relations process is typically initiated when discontented, dissatisfied employees contact and query organizers about the benefits of unionization. Attentive library supervisors can usually detect early interest in unionization by the following symptoms: (a) a decrease in communication between employees and supervisors or a reduction in employee complaints; (b) an increased interest in organizational policies, procedures, and governance; and (c) heightened concerns about job security.

Just as important as detecting an interest in unionization is understanding why library employees may seek to be represented by a collective bargaining agent. Like other workers, library employees join unions when they are dissatisfied with compensation and supervision, object to workplace conditions, perceive "safety in numbers," and believe the union can achieve more than they can individually. Additionally, some workers join unions because family members or coworkers persuade them to become members or because they perceive greater opportunities for social interaction with colleagues. Some who are employed in non-right-to-work states join because they are forced to do so. Others vote yes just because they philosophically believe in the concept of unionism. Still others join to receive benefits such as union-sponsored life, automobile, and homeowner's insurance.

Finally, a decision to unionize may be spurred by an isolated incident that evokes great mistrust and resentment among the staff. This was the case in Albany, New York, where public librarians voted for unionization after the library director docked the pay of four supervisors who closed the library one hour early on March 13, 1993— during what became known as the "blizzard of the century."[1]

Having identified motivations for seeking representation, reasons that library employees avoid unionization should also be identified. Some fear organizational retaliation. Others believe that the costs of joining a union (average initiation fee is $50 and average monthly dues are about equal to two hours of wages) are greater than the benefits the union can achieve. Still others—particularly young, educated professionals—identify strongly with their employing libraries and don't feel they need to be "protected." Some librarians—especially those employed in branches—are overlooked and never approached to join. Some decline to join because of religious convictions. And finally, some refuse because employees who are eligible to belong to unions but prefer not to join are afforded the same benefits unions obtain for their members—without paying union dues.

QUESTION 74
To What Extent Do Librarians Believe That Union Membership Is Incompatible with Professionalism?

Certainly there are some librarians who contend that union membership is "unprofessional" because librarians are highly trained and skilled information experts, not "laborers." Some advocates of this position even contend that union affiliation is inconsistent and incompatible with membership in professional library associations. Those who disagree claim that the reasons for joining these two organizations are vastly different.

Those who belong to both a professional association and a collective bargaining unit explain that unions are dedicated to increasing the level of institutional support (such as salary increments) provided to librarians, improving working conditions, and handling grievances against their employing organizations. Alternatively, union-supporting librarians suggest that individuals join professional organizations to improve their chances for tenure and promotion, to share research and network with others, to influence the direction of the profession, and to receive association publications that heighten their current awareness of professional issues.

Given these arguments, then, it is conceivable that union and professional organization membership may be compatible and even complementary. For example, unions may assist in increasing travel funding for librarians to attend professional conferences. The question then arises as to which institution possesses the primary loyalty of librarians who are members of both. In one study of academic librarians in California, nearly 50 percent of those who responded indicated that they would drop their professional memberships before their union affiliation, if forced to choose. Only 22 percent indicated they would retain their professional membership rather than their union affiliation. (The remaining 38 percent were noncommittal.) Such results may be disturbing to administrators who wonder why many librarians are more loyal to their union than to professional organizations.

One reason may be that librarians must actively renew professional memberships on an annual basis. This requires the initiative of completing forms, writing a check, and mailing them both. On the other hand, most dues are automatically deducted from paychecks ("dues check-off"—an arrangement that is usually mutually satisfactory to both library administrators and union leaders). Thus it is easier to disaffiliate from professional organizations that it is from unions. Second, many librarians perceive that they receive greater direct economic benefits from the union than from professional organizations. And, to a large extent, they still have access to library journals—and notice of professional events—through other organizational memberships and journal subscriptions.[2]

QUESTION 75
What Labor Relations Laws Should the Library Manager Facing Unionization Understand?

Hoping that labor would be the impetus for pulling the U.S. out of the Great Depression, the first piece of legislation aimed at protecting workers' rights to unionize in private organizations was passed in 1935. The National Labor Relations Act (NLRA; also known as the Wagner Act) contained three major provisions. First, the law *protected worker rights* to form and join labor unions, to engage in collective bargaining or negotiation, and to engage in selected forms of mutual aid and protection such as strikes, pickets, and boycotts. Second, the law *defined unfair labor practices* (ULPs) and restricted employers from activities such as interfering with employee rights to organize, sponsoring company unions, and discriminating on the basis of union membership. And third, the law *formed the National Labor Relations Board* (NLRB), a five-member panel appointed by the president to oversee the implementation of the act.

In 1947, an amendment to the NLRA was passed. This amendment, the Labor-Management Relations Act (LMRA; also known as the Taft-Hartley Act), was designed to rebalance the scales of power that had been tipped in the favor of unions by the Wagner Act. The LMRA contained several provisions. First, the amendment defined *union ULPs* and restricted unions from activities such as coercing individuals to join, causing an employer to pay for featherbedding (hiring unnecessary workers), and charging excessive or discriminatory dues or initiation fees. Second, the amendment provided a mechanism for states to pass *right-to-work* legislation, which prohibits forcing employees to join unions. Third, the amendment outlawed *closed-shop* provisions, which forced individuals to join a union before accepting an offer of employment. Fourth, the amendment established the *Federal Mediation and Conciliation Service* (FMCS)—a board that assists labor and management in resolving disputes. And fifth, the amendment allowed for *decertification* elections when unions no longer adequately represent the interests of their members. In the library setting, decertification is especially likely in academic libraries.

In 1959, a second amendment to the NLRA was passed. The Labor-Management Reporting and Disclosure Act (LMRDA; also known as the Landrum-Griffin Act) offered a "bill of rights" to union members. This law regulated the internal functioning of unions by imposing mandatory elections and term limits for union leaders and requiring financial disclosure to the Department of Labor.

QUESTION 76
What Rights Do Library Staff Members Have during a Union Organizing Campaign?

Library workers interested in representation enlist the aid of "organizers" who are typically professional, competent, and articulate union employees. The job of the organizer is to solicit widespread support for the union among eligible library employees. To achieve this goal, the organizer must persuade employees that collective action is supported by their peers and colleagues. The organizer will also conduct a cost/benefit analysis to determine whether it is financially feasible for a union to pursue the organization of a particular group of workers.

Support for the union is demonstrated when employees sign authorization cards, which are nonbinding, noncontractual statements certifying that the worker wishes to be represented by a named union. In the process of collecting these signatures, both unions and management must adhere to specific rules. Unless "No Solicitation" signs have been posted and enforced prior to the union campaign, organizers have the right to distribute literature and solicit authorization card signatures on library premises. Employees further have the right to solicit during nonworking times in nonworking areas of the library (such as an employee lounge).

While the union is collecting authorization card signatures, library managers typically engage in a campaign of their own. Management's objective is to maintain a union-free workplace, where supervisory decision-making power and authority are preserved. To persuade employees to oppose unionization, employers often conduct "captive-audience" speeches. Staff members are forced to attend these meetings, which are held during working hours. During captive-audience speeches, management can inform employees that the union cannot protect them from justifiable discharge, factually describe the character of the union and its leaders, remind employees of the dues they must pay to the union, and urge employees to give the organization a second chance.

However, during captive-audience speeches, management must avoid making threats about what will happen if the union wins, or promises about what will happen if the union loses. Furthermore, no captive-audience speech can be given within twenty-four hours of an election. Questioning employees about their individual attitudes toward the union or intent to vote for the union is prohibited, as is questioning them about the attitudes, beliefs, or intentions of their coworkers.

In order to be recognized, a union must demonstrate that employees are interested in being organized. Evidence of sufficient interest is documented when 30 percent of eligible employees sign authorization cards. Once these signatures are gathered, the organizer must file a representation petition with the NLRB. After verifying the authenticity of signatures on the authorization cards, an election date is set and bargaining units are specified.

The determination of appropriate bargaining units—the employees eligible to vote for and be represented by a particular union—is made by the NLRB. Bargaining units are usually determined based on the "community of interest" doctrine. This doctrine states that workers who share similar working conditions should be grouped together in the same bargaining unit. The community of interest criterion requires examination of factors such as level of professionalism, similarity of economic concerns, extent of job integration, forms of compensation received, physical locations, and nature of supervision.

However, any library employee with supervisory or managerial responsibilities is ineligible to vote for or be represented by a union. According to the NLRA, a "supervisor" is an individual who has the ability to autonomously authorize the hiring, transfer, suspension, promotion, or disciplinary action of another. In the library setting, any employee who spends more than 50 percent of his or her time engaged in such supervisory decisions is automatically excluded from the bargaining unit.[3] Although not explicitly defined by the NLRA, a "manager" is one who has the ability to formulate and effectuate library policy. Like supervisors, managers are excluded from union representation.

Once the date for voting arrives, secret-ballot elections are conducted by the NLRB on organizational premises—usually on a payday. However, the NLRB reserves the right to hold mail-ballot elections if voters are geographically disseminated among branches. The union wins if it earns a simple majority of votes. All other labor relations elections are then barred for at least one year (including decertification elections).

QUESTION 77
What Issues Have to Be Negotiated with Unions during Collective Bargaining?

Once a union is recognized, it will immediately begin the process of negotiating a contract on behalf of the represented employees. This process of contract negotiations is referred to as *collective bargaining*. The NLRA requires that both management and the union bargain "in good faith," which is defined as making an honest and concerted effort to reach agreement using reasonable positions, tactics, and strategies. Notably, bargaining in good faith does not mean that one party must agree to another's offer or proposal, nor does it require making concessions. But good-faith bargaining does require that both sides meet at reasonable times and places, make proposals and counterproposals, and not engage in stalling tactics or adopt a one-shot "take-it-or-leave-it" position.

Good faith also requires that only appropriate topics be considered during bargaining. There are some restrictions on what issues are to be negotiated. "Mandatory" bargaining issues relate to wages, hours, and other critical terms and conditions of employment. These issues must be discussed and settled before a contract can become effective. "Prohibited" issues are those that cannot legally be discussed, such as imposing a mandatory retirement age or eliminating overtime pay. "Permissive" issues are those which can be, but do not legally have to be, discussed (e.g., the library's operational hours). Failure to agree on permissive issues does not make a contract unenforceable.

Library Management Tip

During negotiations, labor representatives will typically insist on discussing union security provisions. Security clauses are designed to help unions recruit and retain members. Two common security provisions found in library contracts are union-shop clauses and agency-shop clauses. "Union-shop" clauses, allowable only in non-right-to-work states, require employees to become union members within thirty days of being hired in order to retain their jobs. "Agency-shop" clauses state that employees need not join a union, but if they are represented by the bargaining unit they must pay the union an amount equal to about 20 percent of union dues—to cover their share of collective bargaining expenses. In exchange for agreeing to these union security provisions, management will usually insist on including a "managerial rights form" outlining decisions that managers can make unilaterally.

QUESTION 78

In Case of Negotiation Breakdowns, What Techniques Can Be Used to Avert a Strike?

Even when both parties negotiate in good faith, there may be instances when agreement cannot be reached. In these cases, the parties have come to an *impasse*. To resolve impasses, a variety of techniques may be used. Mediation involves inviting a third party into the dispute to make nonbinding recommendations about settlement. When either party rejects the mediator's recommendation, arbitration may be used. Arbitrators are neutral third parties who make legally binding recommendations to resolve a dispute. The arbitrator may recommend that the union's or management's position be accepted in its entirety by the other party (final-offer selection), or the arbitrator may "split the difference" between the two parties' proposals (traditional-interest arbitration). Although final-offer selection is rare, it does encourage both sides to adopt a reasonable position. Finally, "med-arb" is a combination technique in which mediation is tried through a prespecified date after which an arbitrator makes a final decision. When a neutral third party is invited into a dispute, both union and management must agree on the individual selected to arbitrate—and both must compensate the arbitrator.

Another form of impasse resolution is a work stoppage, which can take the form of either an employer-initiated lockout or an employee-initiated strike. "Economic strikers" (i.e., those who engage in a work stoppage during contract negotiations) can legally be replaced unless the employing organization has committed an unfair labor practice. Similarly, wildcat strikers (who engage in work stoppages without union consent) can be replaced.

Although work stoppages should be avoided if at all possible (since they can result in patron dissatisfaction and long-term internal conflict within the library), the manager of a unionized library must be prepared to deal with a strike.[4] This requires "contingency strike planning," although the process should not be publicized. If union members are aware that managers are planning for a strike, they may perceive library management as being antagonistic. Important issues to be addressed during contingency strike planning are dictated by whether a strike will likely be engaged in by paraprofessional employees in the library, professionals in the library, or nonprofessionals who service the library (such as maintenance workers).

In general, plans must address such matters as who will be available to work if a strike occurs and what skills they have. Reassignments may be necessary so that the library can perform its essential functions during a strike. Essential services that must be provided on an ongoing basis—even if the library is only to be open restricted hours—include circulation, collection maintenance, reference, microform availability, interlibrary loans, mail processing, and delivery receiving. Lists of former workers, student assistants, and volunteers willing to work should be complied if positions vacated by strikers need to be temporarily filled.

If a strike is foreseen, preventive maintenance should be scheduled, given the possibility that repair personnel may not cross a picket line. Additionally, computers should be safeguarded against virus infection, and security should be tightened at entry and exit points and in open stacks. Library managers should request that employees return all facility keys, for the security of both the collection and striking personnel (who may be placed under suspicion should any damage occur to the library building or its contents). Finally, administrators should develop additional signage to direct users with simple queries and should keep the public and other libraries informed about the state of the impasse resolution.[5]

Once union leaders believe that management's offer is fair, they must present the proposed collective bargaining agreement to the membership for a vote of ratification before the strike will end. In 90 percent of cases, the membership will approve of and ratify the contract. Refusal to ratify a contract usually stems from member dissatisfaction with union leaders. If the contract is rejected, both parties must reenter into negotiations.

QUESTION 79

What Factors Encourage Employees to File Grievances against the Library and Its Management?

When employees protest the perceived violation of a negotiated contract, they file a grievance. Grievances may be filed for many reasons, including: (a) an employee truly believes management broke the contract, (b) ambiguous contractual language was interpreted differently by employees and management, (c) employees want to draw management's attention to a problem in the library, (d) employees have no other mechanism of upward communication, and (e) an employee knows the contract was not broken, but files anyway hoping management will just settle.

Each and every grievance filed by a bargaining unit member must be processed by management, regardless of its merit. Grievance proceedings are conducted during working hours, and participants are paid regular wages during their involvement in the process. Because of this, management should always insist that grievances be presented in writing. This practice may discourage some employees from filing grievances. An additional benefit is that written grievances initiate a paper trail of the proceedings.

The manner in which grievances are to be handled must be outlined in the contract. If the parties within the library are unable to resolve the grievance, a "rights" arbitrator should be invited to decide the issue. On average, arbitration of a single grievance takes nearly a year and can cost both sides several thousand dollars. Therefore, there is a strong incentive to settle prior to arbitration.

REFERENCES

1. Albany public library employees vote to unionize (January 1994). *Library Journal*, 30.

2. Anderson, R. N., J. D. D'Amicantonio, and H. DuBois (July 1992). Labor unions or professional organizations: Which have our first loyalty? *College & Research Libraries*, 331–40.

3. Gilardi, R. L. (January 1990). The representational rights of academic librarians: Their status as managerial employees and/or supervisors under the National Labor Relations Act. *College & Research Libraries*, 40–5.

4. Weber, M. (1992). Support staff unions in academic and public libraries: Some suggestions for managers. *Journal of Library Administration*, 17(3), 65–86.

5. Morton, B., and N. S. Alldredge (Summer 1991). Contingency strike planning in the academic library. *Library Administration & Management*, 130–9.

CHAPTER 15
Unethical Behavior

QUESTION 80
What Constitutes Sexual Harassment in the Library Setting?

Sexual harassment is legally defined as unwelcome sexual advances, requests for sexual favors, and other verbal or physical conduct that constitutes a hostile environment when:

submission to the conduct is either explicitly or implicitly a term or condition of employment;

submission to or rejection of such conduct by an individual is used as the basis for employment decisions;

such conduct has the purpose or effect of unreasonably interfering with an individual's performance or creating an intimidating or offensive work environment.

Examples of sexual harassment may include subtle pressure for sexual activity, unnecessary patting or pinching, constant brushing against another, "friendly" arms around the shoulder, sexual slurs and insults targeted at members of the opposite sex, and hanging pictures or cartoons of a sexual nature.

Nearly 80 percent of librarians report they have been harassed on the job—and 70 percent report they are victimized at least monthly.[1] As a result, an astounding 90 percent of library staff members feel they are at risk when at work.[1] In the library setting, 83 percent of those who are harassed report incidences of "visual harassment" (e.g., being leered at or being flashed), 83 percent report incidences of "verbal harassment" (e.g., being threatened or subjected to offensive language), and 40 percent report incidences of "physical harassment" (e.g., being touched or physically attacked).[2]

QUESTION 81

How Can a Manager Eliminate Sexual Harassment in the Library Environment?

To assist library directors in curtailing incidences of sexual harassment, six commonly accepted "myths" will be reviewed and dispelled.

Myth 1. Ignoring harassment will make it stop.

In the library setting, incidences of harassment are often perpetrated by the same offender. This knowledge has led some libraries to compile a "most wanted" list of harassers. By circulating descriptions and information about harassers, the library director may find many have been victimized by the same offender. When corroborating witnesses present testimony, courts are much more likely to arrive at a harassment conviction.

Library Management Tip ─────────────────────────────

While ignoring harassment will not make it stop, telling an offender to stop harassing will, quite often, curtail the problem. This is because many offenders do not realize that their behaviors are harassing in nature. However, it is not advisable for a library director to request that victims address the harasser and handle the problem on their own. Instead, the library must carefully formulate and disseminate a policy outlining the behaviors that constitute sexual harassment. To ensure that harassers understand what behaviors are prohibited, some libraries send offending employees to seminars on sexual harassment as part of their disciplinary protocol.

Myth 2. If the harassed individual doesn't ask the harasser to stop, the sexual attention must be desired.

Unfortunately, many librarians are hesitant to report incidences of sexual harassment. This hesitancy arises, in part, because librarians are often made to feel that sexual harassment is their own fault—brought about by their dress or body language. Others feel that harassment "comes with the territory" of being a librarian in a service role. Still others fear retaliation by supervisors, who are often ambivalent about investigating complaints of sexual harassment. Finally, it is difficult for some employees to determine whether a behavior is harassing or just annoying.

Myth 3. A sexually harassed man does not have the same rights as a sexually harassed woman.

While male harassment of females is most common, males can be victimized by females as well as by other males. In such cases, males are afforded the same legal rights to a hostile-free workplace as are female victims.

Myth 4. Lack of sexual harassment complaints is a good indication that harassment is not occurring.

Given emerging evidence, it is safe to assume that sexual harassment is currently occurring in nearly all libraries. If complaints are not being voiced, the library probably lacks appropriate mechanisms for employees to report their harassment experiences. Provision of a complaint mechanism—such as a grievance procedure—can assist employees in determining what actions they should take in response to harassment. Another recommended mechanism for assessing incidences of harassment is employee surveys. Specifically, employees should be asked if they know what constitutes sexual harassment, how often they have experienced harassment, what they did about the harassment, and how the harassment has affected their personal and work lives. Such inquiries can provide library directors with valuable insight into the extent and severity of the sexual harassment problem in their institutions.

Myth 5. An employer cannot be held liable for harassment unless the employer knows it is occurring.

It has been soundly established in the legal arena that employers can be held personally (and financially) responsible if employees are being harassed—whether or not the employers acknowledge they were aware of such harassment. In the library setting, this realization may be one of the most effective weapons for getting directors to intervene and address sexual harassment problems.

Unfortunately, may staff members believe library directors have not adequately responded to their complaints of harassment. Many explanations can be offered for this:[3]

Directors simply do not perceive the extent of the sexual harassment problem (employee surveys can easily remedy this problem).

Directors are more concerned with patron rights than with employee safety (an assumption believed true by many staff members).

Directors wish to avoid involvement in lengthy, expensive lawsuits (however, avoiding the problem of sexual harassment can bring about such an outcome).

Directors direct attention away from harassment to other problems that are easier to investigate and solve (it is true that determining the "facts" of a sexual harassment case can be challenging).

Library Management Tip ————————————————————————

Despite the desire of many directors to wish away the problem of sexual harassment in libraries, more proactive measures must be taken. As a first step, administrators must create awareness of the problem, develop policies prohibiting sexual harassment, and consistently enforce policies. Additional recommendations include reserving close parking places for those who lock up, inviting local police to provide seminars on self-defense, arming staff members with personal attack deterrents, withholding last names from badges, raising lighting levels, and installing surveillance cameras. Finally, it should be remembered that those who are required to enter the stacks to assist patrons and those who lock up in the evening are particularly susceptible to sexual harassment.[4]

Myth 6. A library director has little control over harassment by patrons.

In the library setting, harassment can occur between staff members, between patrons, or between staff members and patrons. While the extant library literature has begun to address the issue of employee harassment of coworkers, quite little has been written about harassment involving patrons.

It has long been clear that library directors would be held liable when one staff member harassed another. But a recent court case involving a Las Vegas blackjack dealer may broaden directors' responsibility. In that case, the dealer alleged she had been terminated for complaining about harassment by a player. The court agreed, citing the guideline that states, "an employer may be responsible for the acts of nonemployees, with respect to sexual harassment, where the employer knows, or should have known of the conduct and fails to take immediate and appropriate corrective actions." This court decision, in effect, assigns the library director responsibility for preventing patron harassment of staff members. But library administrators must be equally prompt to investigate patron complaints of harassment by staff members. Just as the library manager must provide a hostility-free environment for workers, she or he must also provide one for patrons.

QUESTION 82
What Moral Philosophies Are Used for Making Ethical Decisions and How Does Morality Develop?

As was suggested in the discussion of sexual harassment, ethical dilemmas are ever present in the library.[5] Determining what is ethical and what is not is a complicated issue, but there are several philosophies that offer moral guidance.[6] Among these philosophies are teleology, enlightened egoism, utilitarianism, deontology, and relativism. Each views ethical decision making from a different perspective. *Teleology* suggests that an act is moral if it produces the desired consequence. With *enlightened egoism,* an act is moral if it maximizes personal self-interest while allowing for others' well-being. Those advocating a *utilitarian* approach say that an act is moral if it has utility for the greatest number of people. *Deontology* asserts that an act is moral if it conforms with universal moral principles and equal respect is given to all people. And *relativism* contends that an act can only be judged as moral or immoral after considering the demands of the situation.

No matter which moral philosophy is adopted to define an ethical dilemma, outcomes are dependent, in part, upon the decision maker's personal development. The individual who is highly ethical has progressed through six stages of moral growth.[7] In stage one of moral development, children merely obey to avoid punishment. With maturation, they develop to stage two in which they follow the rules to get a fair deal. In stage three, individuals attempt to live up to important others' expectations. In stage four, individuals develop a sense of obligation. In stage five, individuals begin respecting others' personal rights. And in the final stage, individuals begin following internalized, mature ethical principles.

Unethical decisions are made by persons who have been morally stunted in their progression through these stages. Those low in moral development are self-centered and seem to lack understanding about justice and personal rights. Fortunately, many librarians are mature morally and attempt to take into consideration ethical principles. The moral propensity of these grounded individuals is further enhanced when the library culture also promotes ethical decision making.

QUESTION 83
How Can Library Managers Be Encouraged to Make Ethical Decisions?

Library managers are constantly making decisions that have ethical implications, whether they are aware of it or not. They set objectives for their units, determine how work is to be organized, evaluate the acceptability of performance, develop reward systems for their staff, and have responsibility for the efficient and effective use of resources. But like all humans, library managers vary in their propensity to make ethical decisions. There are a few who are immoral—they know right from wrong, but actively choose to do wrong. Conversely, there are many who are moral—they consistently choose to do the right thing.

However, some library managers can be categorized somewhere between these two extremes. They are neither immoral nor moral, but rather "amoral" in their judgments.[8]

While some library managers are intentionally amoral, others are unintentionally amoral. Intentionally amoral managers think that different rules apply to their decisions at work than to other parts of their life. Therefore, they do not consider ethics in their management decision making. As compared to the intentionally amoral, the unintentionally amoral managers are ethically lazy. They just don't consider the impact of their decisions on others in the library environment. However, ethical behavior cannot be achieved by those who don't think about moral issues or by those who play it safe by avoiding certain actions. Rather, library managers must actively choose to make ethical decisions.

Those less morally advanced might be encouraged to engage in ethical decision making . . . if the library fosters ethical behavior. To promote an ethical orientation in the library environment, three conditions should be present: (1) top administrators must support and emphasize ethical decision making; (2) ethical expectations must be backed up by written policies and guidelines; and (3) formal communication channels must be available for discussing ethical concerns and reporting infractions.

Communication channels are a must in the library environment. In their absence, the library administrator will be unable to predict how the observance of an unethical situation will be handled by employees. Possible reactions include anonymously, quietly, or publicly informing management. Other actions include anonymously informing the offending party, sabotaging the implementation of an unethical library activity, quietly ignoring the implementation of unethical library activities, or threatening management with telling external sources.

Library Management Tip

One of the most menacing behaviors that an employee can engage in from a management perspective is anonymously or publicly "blowing the whistle"— telling outside agencies about wrongdoings in the library. Estimates indicate that over 65 percent of U.S. employees observe acts of wrongdoing on the job. But most don't report such incidents, fearing the harm it will do to their careers and personal lives. Because whistle blowing puts both the employee and the library administrator in precarious positions, a better course is for libraries to set up formal communication channels for reporting unethical practices. With communication mechanisms in place, the administrator's authority is not threatened, and the concerned staff member is protected. And, most importantly, the questionable practices can be addressed.

QUESTION 84

How Does the Library's Professional Association Address the Problem of Unethical Behavior?

The American Library Association has developed a code of ethics for librarians. This 1981 code states:

1. Librarians must provide the highest level of service through appropriate and usefully organized collections, fair and equitable circulation and service policies, and skillful, accurate, unbiased, and courteous responses to all requests for assistance.

2. Librarians must resist all efforts by groups or individuals to censor library materials.

3. Librarians must protect each user's rights to privacy with respect to information sought or received, and materials consulted, borrowed, or acquired.

4. Librarians must adhere to the principles of due process and equality of opportunity in peer relationships and personnel actions.

5. Librarians must distinguish clearly in their actions and statements between their personal philosophies and attitudes and those of an institution or professional body.

6. Librarians must avoid situations in which personal interest might be served or financial benefits gained at the expense of library users, colleagues, or the employing agency. (Adopted 1981 by ALA Membership and Council)

While the library association warns against personally benefiting at the expense of other stakeholders, the library administrator would be well advised to formulate written policies for conflicts of interest. For example, employees need to understand guidelines about the acceptance of gifts from publishers and vendors. Of course, bribes would be considered a blatant violation of this policy, as the receipt of a "gift" should never be used as a basis for a management decision. But is it all right to accept lunches or passes to special events? And what if the value of a gift is small?

Sometimes the conflict of interest is emotionally and socially problematic. Consider, for example, former colleagues who have left the library setting to work for vendors. In their new job, they come back to their old place of employment to sell a service or an automated system. In these cases, it may be hard not taking care of an old friend, but the librarian must avoid giving them special information, privileges, or advantages because of the relationship.[9]

Other questions beyond receiving vendor favors should be covered by the conflicts of interest policy. Is it ethical for librarians to solicit monies from vendors for a fundraising event? What are the guidelines on accepting gifts from patrons? Is it ethical to buy a book for the library because of a personal interest in the topic? As a rule of thumb, the librarian should avoid even the suspicion that a conflict exists. Thus, the safest course of action is to avoid the appearance of entanglements.

One of the more important issues in the library association guidelines is librarian-patron confidentiality.[10] Historically, there have been a number of invasions into patrons' privacy. FBI agents have requested information on patrons borrowing books on making explosives. And other local, state, and federal government agents have similarly attempted to examine circulation patterns. For example, city officials monitor records to investigate the illegal manufacture of street drugs. In a recent case in the Northwest, a prosecutor used a library's circulation records to build his theory that a woman read books on cyanide and poisonous doses in her preparation to murder her husband by putting poison in his medication.

In response to attempts to track the readings of patrons, the American Library Association has successfully lobbied for legislative protection in several states as well as in the District of Columbia. But despite these accomplishments, there has been difficulty with the concepts of confidentiality and privileged communication. *Confidentiality* is an ethical obligation not to discuss information about a client, whereas *privileged communication* protects an individual from being legally required to give information. A librarian may refuse to have records reviewed by a law enforcement officer on grounds of confidentiality. Communication between librarians and patrons, however, is not considered to be privileged. If a subpoena is received from a court, a librarian can face potential contempt charges for refusing to reveal information even though it is considered confidential within the profession.

While the present code provides some general ethical guidelines for librarians, some have suggested that the code needs to address more clearly the ideals and responsibilities of librarians. One researcher has outlined ten categories that could be included in a new code of ethics.[11] These are: (1) the essence of the profession, to maximize the value of recorded information for humanity; (2) confidential information, to not disclose information unless compelled by law; (3) extravocational activities, to avoid off-duty conduct that would adversely affect on-the-job performance; (4) research, to seek out and share innovative practices; (5) career development, to dedicate oneself to the profession and assist junior practitioners in their development; (6) membership in an association, to interact with peers and attend professional meetings; (7) collegial control over conduct, to allow for peer group supervision of professionals; (8) continuing education, to maintain and enrich one's competence; (9) special issues, to address such concerns as intellectual freedom and material selection; and (10) a catch-all phrase, to capture behaviors that might discredit the profession.

REFERENCES

1. Manley, W. (January 1993). Will's World—no laughing matter this month. *American Libraries,* 68.

2. Manley, W. (July 1993). Will's World—sexual harassment by patrons: Part two. *American Libraries,* 652.

3. Manley, W. (September 1993). Will's World—sexual harassment by patrons: Part three. *American Libraries,* 756.

4. Manley, W. (October 1993). Will's World—sexual harassment by patrons: Part four. *American Libraries,* 828.

5. Smith, M. M. (1992). Infoethics for leaders: Models of moral agency in the information environment. *Library Trends,* 40(3), 553–70.

6. Du Mont, R. R. (1991). Ethics in librarianship: A management model. *Library Trends,* 40(2), 201–15.

7. Kohlberg, L., and D. Candee (1984). The relationship of moral judgment to moral action, in W. M. Kurtines and J. L. Gerwitz (eds.), *Morality, moral behavior and moral development* (pp. 52–73). New York: Wiley.

8. Carroll, A. B. (March–April 1987). In search of the moral manager. *Business Horizons,* 30, 7–15.

9. Epstein, S. B. (September 15, 1990). Ethical considerations in an automated environment. *Library Journal,* 59–60.

10. Garoogian, R. (1991). Librarian/patron confidentiality: An ethical challenge. *Library Trends,* 40(2), 216–33.

11. Finks, L. W. (January 1991). Librarianship needs a new code of professional ethics. *American Libraries,* 84–92.

CHAPTER 16
Managing Risk and Change

QUESTION 85
What Should a Library Manager Do in Preparation for a Natural Disaster?

On March 18, 1994, Robyn Bjoring, the new head librarian at Grand Canyon Community Library in Arizona, was faced with a disaster. Her library burned to the ground. In response to this crisis, a local modular structure company erected a temporary facility, and Ms. Bjoring began asking for donations of money and books. As is too often the case, the library was underinsured. Ms. Bjoring did, however, note one small bright spot in the recovery process. "Luckily we had a lot of overdue books, so we're asking people to return them now, because that's all we have left."[1]

While Ms. Bjoring experienced one major catastrophic event, librarians at the University of Guam have lived through two major natural disasters in recent years. On August 23, 1992, the library was flooded by Typhoon Omar. And just twelve months later, a 45-second earthquake measuring 8.1 on the Richter scale caused 90,000 volumes of material to fall off the shelves. Luckily, the earthquake occurred on Sunday evening after the library was closed, so no personal injuries occurred. However, the building sustained stress fractures, masonry crumbled, and ducts and lighting fixtures protruded through the suspended ceiling.[2]

In the central part of the United States in 1993, libraries and communities were covered with mud and water after the Mississippi River and its tributaries overflowed their banks. At Carter County Library in the Ozarks, librarians had no children's books to lend after thirty inches of water flowed into their facility. It is estimated that there was over $300,000 of water damage. To deal with the catastrophe, the library applied for Federal Emergency Management Assistance funds and appealed to book vendors for donations.[3]

The devastating winds of Hurricane Andrew in 1992 caused severe damage to the Miami-Dade County Public Library system, blowing down doors, uplifting roofs, and crashing windows. Four of the system's buildings had to be closed because of structural damage. The remaining facilities were overstaffed because there was no disaster plan for personnel allocation. Like many other types of U.S. organizations, libraries generally do not have a systematic, clear-cut catastrophe reaction plan. Only about 19 percent have one, and only an additional 17 percent are working on one.

Because of the lack of planning, many library staff members are unprepared to handle natural disasters.[4] But a readiness plan can ease the stress of such occurrences. When planning for natural disasters, there are four basic questions that need to be asked.[5] For what types of disaster should the organization prepare? How broad should the scope of the plans be for these disasters? Which potential crises can the library safely ignore? What is the rationale for including or excluding a potential crisis?

Once a readiness team answers these questions, it is faced with developing appropriate documentation. Certain essential items must be gathered, such as blueprints of the facilities showing fire alarms, extinguishers, and exits. Further, the team needs to prioritize the materials in the building and spell out procedures to follow in an emergency. The procedures for fire would include, for example, signaling the alarm, calling the fire department, and evacuating the building. In addition to the initial response, subsequent procedures such as removing burnt and wet materials, contacting the insurance company, and involving contractors in the rebuilding process should be made clear. Also, provisions should be made for relocation of staff and collections if temporary or permanent closing is required. Finally, it is important that these plans be revised annually and not allowed to gather dust on the shelf.

QUESTION 86

How Should a Library Manager Respond to Staff Members Who Have Experienced a Disaster?

In some cases, a crisis (e.g., fire) only affects a single facility. Here, library management must assess the overall damage to the facility and begin the process of restoration. However, in other cases of large-scale regional disasters (e.g., earthquakes, hurricanes, or floods), management must also determine the effect the disaster has had on the personal lives of the employees. Some staff members may need a week or more off to restore their personal lives and find housing. Management should regularly check on those who are unable to come to work to find out how the library might aid in their recovery.

In addition to contacting appropriate relief agencies for employees, management may want to assess how staff members are coping with the stress of this major trauma.[6] One common, but often unrecognized, response to a disaster is grief. Typically, grief is studied in relation to death and dying. But profound losses, such as those often associated with disasters, can elicit common grief reactions. In order of occurrence, reactions to grief include denial, anger, bargaining, depression, and acceptance.[7]

Denial results when staff members refuse to accept that changes are needed in response to the crises. Statements such as "our library must never be closed, even temporarily, because we are needed" may cue administrators that members are denying that changes need to take place. Next, *anger* is often manifested through accusations and finger-pointing. Statements such as "administration should have been more responsive to this situation" typify an anger reaction. *Bargaining* occurs when staff members negotiate for change to stop. Bargaining for stability may be exemplified through statements such as, "if the government would only give us more, we could be just the way we were." *Depression* follows the realization that things will never be as they were before. Finally, *acceptance* of change leads to the understanding that stability cannot be maintained. However, acceptance is not synonymous with resignation. Rather, acceptance implies recognition by the library staff that the change can be handled.

QUESTION 87
How Should Library Managers Deal with Risks Beyond Those of Natural Disasters?

Administrative activities designed to reduce unanticipated financial losses are collectively called risk management. Besides natural catastrophic events, risk management also focuses on such problems as preventing patron injuries, limiting exposure to hazardous materials, controlling liability for transportation accidents, eliminating embezzlement, protecting against lawsuits claiming breach of contract, and defending against defamation charges.

The control of risk can be divided into three categories: risk avoidance, risk shifting, and risk prevention. Risk *avoidance* means refraining from certain services in order to avert losses. For example, if a library has a special program of loaning work tools to community members, and a lawsuit is threatened by a patron because a power tool resulted in personal injury,[8] this nontraditional service may be terminated. While risk avoidance involves abstaining, risk *shifting* entails transferring responsibility away from the organization to others. For example, window cleaning may be subcontracted with the stipulation that the cleaning firm assumes all liability for accidents to its employees. The third control category, risk *prevention,* involves identifying why and how lawsuit claims occur and instituting action to prevent or minimize adverse events.

Library Management Tip

Risk prevention can take place before or after an incident occurs. Preoccurrence risk prevention activities include the establishment of appropriate policies or the sponsoring of educational programs to make library staff aware of problem areas. Postoccurrence risk prevention activities can occur either before or after litigation. Prelitigation activities occur immediately after an incident and are designed to avoid claims or lawsuits. Postlitigation activities involve attempts to lessen financial and reputational losses. Often postlitigation prevention requires using settlement techniques.

While libraries may be sued for normal business activities—as when patrons are injured on the premises or employees file charges of discrimination—they must also be concerned about the issue of professional liability. When citizens need answers to or information about particular problems, they will often head for the library. Because librarians are perceived as gatekeepers to important information, their advice and assistance is often sought. But when staff members aid in the search for solutions to patrons' problems, liability problems may be created. This is particularly likely in the medical and legal arenas, where library research may have a dramatic effect on the well-being of individuals.

More than two million articles dealing with biomedical issues are published annually. The database MEDLINE contains well over ten million references.[9] Because of this immense amount of information, practitioners cannot be expected to know all the answers. Therefore, computer-assisted literature searches are often one of the most important procedures performed in medical facilities—and these medical searches cannot be left to the underinformed. Medical librarians must be conversant in medical terminology and translate requests into database language. The subsequent information that medical librarians retrieve can influence treatment outcomes for patients. And while medical librarians are not responsible for the quality of the databases they search, they are responsible for using reasonable care and skill in retrieving information.

Though a physician is much more likely to be sued than is a medical librarian, practitioners rely on literature reports for making clinical decisions. Thus, there is the potential for a librarian to be held liable if there is a reasonably close connection between a negligent search and resulting bodily injury.[10] To demonstrate the critical importance of medical information located by librarians, consider the outreach job of Mary Jo Dwyer.[11] She makes monthly rounds among thirteen hospitals in the Lower Rio Grande Valley. Using her laptop computer, she performs online searches for practitioners at these medical facilities. Recently, a surgeon requested that she find information on how much tissue should be removed around a rare tumor. Within fifteen minutes, she produced an abstract with the requested information . . . and it's a good thing she was speedy, as the patient was on the operating table!

Paralleling the medical field, the lawyer is much more likely to be sued than is the law librarian. Yet the potential for liability exists because the delivery of information on outdated laws, for example, may preclude the patron from having a fair trial. While to date no legal librarian has been sued, the integrity of information librarians provide is subject to lawsuits—as discovered by a head librarian at a naval air station. In this case, the librarian was held responsible for a plane crashing, because of failure to replace an outdated maintenance manual.[12] While this liability was created because of incomplete information, liability can also result from the mere provision of information. Consider the following problem.

A case was presented in the *Library Journal* in which a troubled teenager checked out a book on suicide titled *Final Exit*, by Derek Humphrey.[13] The circulation librarian was aware of the teenager's emotional instability and expressed his fears to the director. The director cited the library's policy on the user's right to privacy, and the matter was dropped. Three days later, the teenager committed suicide. Next to her was the library's book. Subsequently, the father accused the library staff of "killing" his daughter. Analysts of this case differed in their responses. One suggested that the library sensitively defend its principles, not the book.[14] The other analyst suggested that the staff should have intervened by notifying school authorities such as a social worker or a counselor.[15]

In cases like this, rational arguments can be made on each side. Not doing anything protects the borrower's First Amendment rights. Intervention could save a life and reduce the library's liability. A risk preventive approach can also be used in circumstances such as these. At the St. Louis Public Library, management worked with parents on formulating a policy to determine which materials could be checked out to minors. According to the new policy, parents and legal guardians can decide whether their child under 18 will be issued a restricted card (limiting check-out to juvenile materials) or an unrestricted card (giving access to all materials except adult videos).[16]

QUESTION 88
What Are Some Fundamental Legal Issues That Library Managers Should Understand?

The Constitution of the United States delineates three branches of the federal government: executive, legislative, and judicial. Executive orders are legally enforceable Presidential decrees. These orders typically apply only to governmental institutions—affecting librarians at Department of Veterans Affairs hospitals, for example. An executive order may affect a library in the private sector if, for example, it is geographically located in a declared disaster area. The laws passed by Congress and state legislatures are called *statutes,* while laws passed by local governments are called *ordinances.* Most laws that influence the behavior of library managers have been enacted by the legislative branch. Finally, the judicial branch of the government—the court system—interprets the law.

Court opinions become important for translating statutes and clarifying ambiguities and conflicts within laws. As a result, laws are often derived from decisions made in courts. When interpreting statutes, the court will consider legislative intent, or what Congress was attempting to accomplish when it passed a law. The court will also take into account *precedents,* or decisions from earlier cases on the same or closely related disputes.

Library Management Tip

The court system was established to ensure that society abided by the laws passed by the legislative branch. However, some laws have mechanisms for assuring compliance outside of the court system. For example, there are a number of statutes that set up independent administrative and enforcement agencies of which the library manager must be aware. These include the *Occupational Safety and Health Act,* which protects the health and well-being of employees; the *Equal Employment Opportunity Act,* which prohibits discriminatory practices in hiring; and the *National Labor Relations Act,* which ensures that workers have the right to form unions and engage in collective bargaining.

Three areas of common law are especially important to library managers. These are the law of agency, tort law, and contract law. The *law of agency* involves the idea that organizations are legally responsible for the actions of their representatives. Developed in England, the agency law doctrine was based on the notion of "respondeat superior." Today, this common law states that organizations may be financially responsible for problems that arise because of staff member negligence.

Sometimes, however, it is the organization and not the employee that is potentially negligent. A former technical librarian for Caterpillar, Inc., testified that the company ordered the library to destroy documents that could be used against Caterpillar in litigation involving operator injury. This particular case, which is still in the appeal process, raises the question of liability for librarians. While there is no liability if the librarian is conforming to a document retention policy, what about the library manager—an agent of the company—who is carrying out a policy that is legally flawed? In some states, there are corporate criminal responsibility laws to punish managers who engage in covering up dangerous defects.[17]

Tort law is applied in cases where there has been an infliction of harm. To apply tort law, the complainant must establish that there was a breach of duty resulting in harm—inflicted either intentionally or unintentionally. Examples of intentional torts include wrongful termination, battery, and defamation. Unintentional negligent tort occurs when an individual either fails to do something a reasonable person would do or does something a reasonable person would not do.

Contract law involves legally binding agreements identifying rights and obligations of the parties involved. A breach of contract occurs when one party does not fulfill its obligations. When a breach occurs, there are three types of remedies available to the injured party: rescission, specific performance, and damages. *Rescission* renders a contract null and void. *Specific performance* requires the breaching party to fulfill the contractual agreement as written. *Damages* are monetary compensation paid to the injured party.

QUESTION 89

What Is the Nature of Organizational Change That Is Not Brought On by a Crisis?

Even in the absence of legal crises or natural disasters, organizations continually experience change. Change is inevitable and occurs even when staff members prefer stability. External forces in the environment—such as technological innovations, demographic factors, budget adjustments, and labor force attributes—demand changes in the way libraries operate. The challenge facing library managers is to anticipate, initiate, and manage change effectively.

The desired outcomes of planned change in a library include enhanced productivity, higher work satisfaction, increased workplace commitment, better quality of service, and heightened professionalism. To realize these benefits, planned change must be carefully managed, since the majority of staff members in any library are likely to be somewhat skeptical of change. Human nature is such that individuals generally object to change. Managers should anticipate such resistance and understand why it occurs. Some common sources of resistance to change are described below.

Source	Description
Habit	Once staff members master their jobs, they become comfortable with procedures and operations. To change requires active learning, energy, and effort. Change also introduces the fear that knowledge currently possessed will become obsolete.
Threatened Loss of Power and/or Status	Organizational change often requires restructuring. Such a change can threaten staff members' past accomplishments and achievements. Thus, some may fear their authority and power will be diminished. Others may fear monetary loss or job insecurity.
Fear of the Unknown	While staff members may be able to anticipate some losses as a result of change, they may also predict that other unidentifiable or unexpected losses are likely to occur. These ambiguities may arouse more resistance than the anticipated loss.
Comfort with Status Quo	Those who rock the boat are often viewed with suspicion. Employees tend to be skeptical of change because they cannot anticipate the outcomes. And in many cases, workers will prefer "the devil they know" to the one they don't.
Fear of Failure	Change requires the mastery of new skills and knowledge. Some may fear they lack the intellectual, physical, or emotional capacity to deal with change. Those who have low self-esteem may feel particularly vulnerable.
Misunderstanding	Objective information should be used to convince employees of the need for change. Rather than emotional appeals, staff members should be shown facts that point to a need for change. They could also be provided with information about the personal and organizational benefits to be derived from the proposed change. This tactic can help build commitment to the change initiative.

Since change is likely to be opposed by staff members, there are certain strategies that can be used for managing resistance. Participation and involvement are considered to be the most effective mechanisms for overcoming resistance, as they can build commitment to the program of change. These are particularly important techniques when those responsible for initiating change need the support of others having the power to stifle the change. Facilitation and support are helpful when resistance results from fear. Those having emotional difficulty adjusting to the change may be provided time off or counseling, for example. Negotiation and agreement can be used when there will be a clear loser as a result of the change. Here, something valued by resistors is exchanged for their support—a technique traditionally used to counter union resistance to managerially initiated change.

In addition to these three strategies, there are a couple of other approaches that are less popular among staff members. Manipulation and co-optation are deceptive tactics that can be implemented relatively quickly and cheaply. Specific techniques may include distorting relevant information about negative outcomes of change or seeking the endorsement of resistors through enticements. However, these tactics can alienate employees and raise ethical questions. Finally, implicit and explicit coercion involve threats and force and should be used only when change must be quickly introduced. Of course, coercion may elicit staff member compliance, but never commitment to the change process. Further, coercion can undermine trust between library administration and staff members.

REFERENCES

1. Fire at Grand Canyon library destroys building and contents (March 28, 1994). *Library Hotline*, 1.

2. Earthquake shakes Guam library (September 1993). *American Libraries*, 792.

3. Kristi, C. (January 1994). Flash flood causes $300,000 in damage to Missouri library. *American Libraries*, 15.

4. Kahn, M. (December 1993). Mastering disaster. *Library Journal*, 73.

5. Pearson, C. M., and I. I. Mitroff (1993). From crisis prone to crisis prepared: A framework for crisis management. *Academy of Management Executive*, 7, 48–59.

6. Wymen, N. (1993). The big one: Staff survival after a disaster. *Library Administration & Management*, 7(2), 103–5.

7. Kubler-Ross, E. (1969). *On death and dying*. New York: Macmillan.

8. Mersky, R. M., and B. L. Koneski-White (September 15, 1991). Law librarians: The trials ahead. *Library Journal*, 34–7.

9. Palmer, R. A. (Summer 1991). The hospital library is crucial to quality healthcare. *Hospital Topics,* 20–5.

10. Herin, N. J. (Summer 1991). The liability of the hospital librarian: Why you need a professional medical librarian. *Hospital Topics,* 26–9.

11. On rounds with Mary Jo Dwyer (June 1993). *American Libraries,* 469.

12. Protti, M. E. (1991). Dispensing law at the front lines: Ethical dilemmas in law librarianship. *Library Trends,* 40(2), 234–43.

13. Anderson, A. J. (May 1, 1992). "You killed my daughter!" *Library Journal,* 53–4.

14. Anderson, K. (May 1, 1992). Respond with compassion and sensitivity. *Library Journal,* 54–5.

15. Singer, Phyllis Z. (May 1, 1992). A missed human relations opportunity. *Library Journal,* 55.

16. St. Louis parents win right, can restrict YA borrowing (March 28, 1994). *Library Hotline,* 2.

17. St. Lifer, E., and M. Rogers (February 1, 1993). Jury rules corporate library willfully destroyed documents. *Library Journal,* 14.

CHAPTER 17
The Unhealthy Workplace

What Safety and Health Issues Are Most Problematic in the Library Setting?

The library manager has an ethical and a legal mandate to provide a safe and healthy workplace for staff members. Before this can be accomplished, however, potential hazards must be identified. One pervasive safety and health issue in libraries is the "sick" building phenomenon. Librarians typically spend more than 90 percent of their workday indoors—a matter of some concern, since the Environmental Protection Agency estimates that exposure to dangerous pollutants is two to five times greater indoors than it is outdoors. Libraries are certainly not the only institutions susceptible to becoming sick. In fact, it is estimated that about 30 percent of all workplace buildings are "sick," costing U.S. enterprises about $12 billion in lost productivity alone.[1] But the question arises as to why libraries are so particularly vulnerable. Several potential explanations can be advanced.

Libraries are designed to maximize energy efficiency; thus the entrance of outside air—which can help alleviate the sick-building syndrome—is minimized. Windows are sealed shut and insulation is thickly applied.

Air filters are typically designed to prevent the introduction of large particles that might damage mechanical and electronic equipment. Hence, it is the smaller particles—the ones that can enter and congest the human respiratory system—that are usually allowed to pass through filters.

Tall stacks and periodical shelving often prevent air from effectively being filtered through ceiling-mounted air vents. Thus, pockets of stagnated and potentially infectious air are trapped and recirculated in certain sections of the library.

Large volumes of paper housed in the library introduce much airborne dust, aggravating many human allergies.

Various toxic glues and solvents used to bind books introduce volatile organic gases, such as formaldehyde, into the library environment.

Photocopiers, electronic readers, and computers introduce ozone and heat into the environment (interestingly, each personal computer generates the equivalent of one person's body heat).

QUESTION 91
How Can a "Sick" Building Be Made Healthy?

Library administration has a threefold mandate to protect staff members, patrons, and the collection from dangerous indoor pollutants. Unfortunately, attempts to fulfill these obligations often result in a "Catch-22" situation. That is, measures to protect the collection may inflict harm on the patrons and vice versa. Acknowledging this conflict, the following suggestions and precautions are offered to keep both human and inanimate library occupants safe.

Ensure adequate ventilation by installing high quality air filters and preventing moisture from collecting in air handling systems, as moisture can promote the growth of microbes which are harmful to both humans and paper holdings.

Ensure that computer and photocopier rooms are equipped with proper ventilation systems, preferably ones that route exhaust directly outdoors.

Ensure proper temperatures. As the life of paper doubles with every degree decrease in room temperature, libraries are often tempted to keep the facility temperature too low. While 55 degrees Fahrenheit is optimal for the collection, such a low temperature would prove to be uncomfortable for human occupants of the library. Thus a compromise temperature of about 75 degrees should be maintained to protect the integrity of the holdings and the health of the workers and patrons.

Ensure a relative humidity range between 40 percent and 55 percent.

Ensure proper lighting and air circulation. Darkness, accompanied by humidity, stimulates the growth of bacteria, mold, and mildew. When circulation is good, moisture build-up will be reduced.

Those who are affected by the sick-building syndrome will manifest symptoms similar to those of colds, flu, and allergy. However, symptoms will disappear when inhabitants leave the sick building. Since the causes of such vague symptoms are hard to diagnose, many libraries unknowingly continue operations even though the building in which they are housed is "sick." To prevent symptoms from becoming too intense or widespread, library managers should be proactive in assessing the health of their buildings on an ongoing basis.

QUESTION 92
What Can Be Done to Avoid the Physical Hazards Posed by Working with Computers?

Excessive use of computers not only pollutes the indoor environment, but may also directly inflict a host of physiological problems on users. In fact, scientific investigation in the medical domain has revealed that prolonged computer usage seems to be related to

cataracts and other visual difficulties such as eyestrain, blurred vision, itching, burning, tearing, and red or irritated eyes;

increased likelihood of birth defects, spontaneous abortions, and miscarriages;

"terminal dermatitis," which produces a tingling sensation in one's face, skin blushing or redness, and cheek peeling;

the induction of seizures in epileptics;

prolonged headaches;

reduced mobility and heightened inactivity which leads to blood clots;

muscular-skeletal problems such as stiffness of the neck, back, and shoulders;

carpal tunnel syndrome and repetitive strain disorders.[2]

Carpal tunnel syndrome and related repetitive strain disorders, which are extremely problematic in the library environment, are induced by repeating a particular motion hundreds of times. Such motions cause swelling and inflammation of the tendons and ligaments which can lead to irritation of the median nerve in the wrist. Forty-eight percent of all job-related illnesses and injuries result from repetitive strain disorders. And treatment of carpal tunnel syndrome costs an average of $15,000 to $20,000 per case.[3]

To minimize the likelihood of repetitive motion disorders, several interventions should be implemented including job rotation, frequent breaks, and the installation of ergonomic furnishings. Ergonomic furnishings are biologically designed to minimize physical strain and exertion in the work environment. Library staff members working regularly with computers should be supplied with chairs equipped with adjustable seat pans, backs, and armrests. To realize benefit from expenditures on ergonomic furnishings, the library manager should offer instruction on adjusting chairs to comfortable positions—including leaning seatpans forward and removing armrests.

In addition to the provision of adjustable chairs, ergonomic workstations should include desks ranging from twenty-two inches to forty-five inches in height. Adjustable keyboard pans are also recommended, so that users can maintain a ninety-degree angle between their upper and lower arms. Finally, video display monitors should be positioned about twenty degrees lower than eye level—and never be positioned *above* eye level.

While ergonomic furnishings may avert many muscular-skeletal injuries, supervisors should be trained in detecting potential situations that may induce carpal tunnel syndrome. If caught early enough, repetitive motion disorders may be treated with therapy, wrist splints, and stretching exercise. If not, surgery may be required.

QUESTION 93
What Can Be Done to Minimize the Emotional Problems Associated with Computer Use?

In addition to the physiological problems arising from computer usage, there may also be some affective or emotional damage. Library managers must ensure that automated information systems don't alienate or create overwhelming amounts of tension among staff members. Whether labeled "compustress," "cyberphobia," or "computer anxiety," the fear of using computers is prevalent in many workplaces today. Although over 90 percent of all libraries utilize computers in their operations, over 30 percent of all workers fear them. Cyberphobia, manifested through symptoms ranging from nervous disorders to sweaty palms to dizziness, can result from fear of any or all of the following: change, status or power loss, interacting with electronics, the potential negative impact of computers on society, failure, isolation, job displacement, injury from posture changes or illness from emission of harmful rays, inability to communicate in "computerese," increased job complexity, and time pressures and shortened deadlines.

There are three common (and dysfunctional) reactions to computer anxiety:

Aggression	Disabling the computer through sabotage (e.g., dumping pencil shavings, coffee, or other foreign matter into the keyboard or planting "viruses" on the disk drives).
Projection	Blaming the computer for problems caused by other factors. Projection would be evidenced by remarks such as "How can I get any work done when I have to spend all my time fooling with this computer?" or "I would have had this project finished if that computer hadn't destroyed my data."
Avoidance	Withdrawing from, refusing to use, delegating use to others, or "forgetting" to use the computer. This defense mechanism is the most common reaction among cyberphobic library administrators.

Library Management Tip

Training can often help ease the negative side effects that arise from human resistance to computers. Library managers must find friendly ways to communicate with apprehensive users, particularly since manuals and instruction guides are often dense, cold, and incomprehensible. One method found to be effective is to allow staff members to "play" computer games on automated systems, allowing them time to get used to the mechanics of the hard- and software.

QUESTION 94
How Can Libraries Avoid Worker's Compensation Claims?

Worker's Compensation is a state-regulated insurance program designed to protect workers from loss of income due to injuries and illnesses contracted due to employment. Premiums are based on three factors: the size of the staff, the type of work performed, and past number and dollar amounts of claims. Premiums are distributed to injured or ill workers, who are often able to recover two thirds of the income lost due to missed work, plus total medical expenses. Lost wages comprise 60 percent of all expenditures, while medical spending comprises 40 percent.

In addition to premiums, libraries may also incur legal fees, as attorneys are involved in one of every five workers' compensation claims. Expressing a caring and concerned attitude toward all injured workers may minimize attorney involvement. But this may be difficult at times—particularly when the library manager believes a claim to be fraudulent. The attuned manager may be able to detect potentially fraudulent claims by paying attention to the following suspicious circumstances.[4]

Injuries that occur first thing on Monday morning or those that allegedly occurred on Friday afternoon but were not reported until Monday morning. It is possible that such injuries may have occurred at the employee's home over the weekend.

Injuries that occur just prior to a disciplinary hearing or layoff/termination.

Injuries that occur when a family member of the claimant has recently become ill.

The injured party or the claimant's lawyer has a history of filing fraudulent claims.

The claimant rejects formal medical treatment that may verify alleged injuries.

If the library is not self-insured, the manager should report any unusual or potentially suspicious circumstances to the insurance carrier. But meanwhile, the library manager should maintain continuous contact and guarantee the employee that she or he is welcome to return to work when healthy.

Of course, not all worker's compensation claims are fraudulent. Many injuries and illnesses do occur as a result of employment. To avoid legitimate claims, the library manager should regularly inspect the facility to identify known and potential hazards. Also, the manager should track all job-related injuries and illnesses to identify patterns. Managers who do so might be surprised to find the Pareto rule in application—that is, 80 percent of all problems are caused by only 20 percent of all hazards.

Library Management Tip ─────────────────────────

A common physiological ailment found in the library setting is back injury. As 80 percent of the American population suffers from back pain, lifting tasks should be designed carefully so as to avoid twisting movements of the torso. Back supports can also help eliminate strain and can be acquired for about $35 each.

When work injuries occur, it is advisable to have the injured party's physician(s) tour the facility. When medical care providers become familiar with the context and content of library jobs, they will be better able to prescribe a return-to-work date. If the physician is unable to visit the library in person, the manager may want to provide the physician with a detailed job description outlining responsibilities and working conditions and a videotape of the job.[5]

QUESTION 95
What Legal Obligations Does the Library Have to Protect the Safety and Health of Staff Members?

In 1970, Congress passed the Occupational Safety and Health Act—a law designed to protect workers in their places of employment. This piece of legislation was passed in response to the large number of employees who contracted illnesses and injuries while working. In fact, even today, one in eleven workers will experience a job-related health problem. To enforce the provisions of the act, an administrative body, the Occupational Safety and Health Administration (OSHA) was established to develop and regulate occupational safety and health standards.

OSHA deals with two distinct types of threats: (1) safety risks (such as cuts, burns, and broken limbs), which impair an employee's physical well-being and lead to occupational injuries; and (2) health hazards (such as exposure to chemicals, dust, and fumes, loud noises, and inappropriate lighting), which impair not only physical well-being, but also mental and emotional well-being. Health hazards lead to occupational illnesses—the symptoms of which may not be immediate, but instead may take a long time to manifest. OSHA classifies occupational illnesses into several categories, including

skin diseases, such as dermatitis, eczema, rashes, acne, inflammation, and ulcers;

lung diseases, such as asbestosis and pneumoconioses;

respiratory problems due to toxic agents, such as chemicals, dust, and fumes;

chemical poisoning from agents, such as lead, mercury, arsenic, formaldehyde, solvents, and insecticides;

disorders due to physical agents, such as extremely high and low temperatures, and ionizing (isotope) and nonionizing (microwave) radiation;

disorders associated with repeated trauma, such as noise-induced hearing loss and bursitis;

all other occupational illnesses, such as infectious hepatitis, anthrax, tumors, and food poisoning.

REFERENCES

1. Silberman, R. M. (Summer 1993). A mandate for change in the library environment. *Library Administration & Management*, 145–52.

2. King, R. M. (October 1991). Health effects of video display terminals. *Nursing Management*, 61–4.

3. Kusack, J. M. (July 1990). The light at the end of the carpal tunnel. *Library Journal*, 56–9.

4. The Lynch Ryan Report (1993). *Warning signs of fraud*. Westborough, Mass.: Lynch Ryan Foundation.

5. Hoyme, C. (October 1993). Help physicians diagnose injuries. *Laborwatch*, 4.

CHAPTER 18
Workplace Crime and Violence

QUESTION 96
Is Workplace Violence an Issue That Should Concern Library Managers?

A problem increasingly prominent in today's headlines is violence in the workplace. A recent survey suggests that one in four employees in the United States last year were attacked, threatened, or placed in a fearful position while on the job. Over half of all organizations have had major incidents and serious threats of violence in the 1990s. In fact, violence is the leading cause of death in the workplace among U.S. women: an average of fifteen people are killed on the job each week.[1]

Violence can be carried out by disgruntled workers, or it can result from domestic disputes that spill over into the workplace. However, employee injury and death most frequently result from patron violence. Librarians are not the workers most vulnerable to assault by patrons. Those most at risk are taxi drivers, law enforcement officers, hotel and motel clerks, gas station and convenience store workers, and security guards. These occupational groups are particularly susceptible to armed robbery, a crime that accounts for over half the workplace violence.

Despite the fact that librarians are not on this dubious list, violence in libraries is becoming an ever more salient workplace issue. Librarians are increasingly the targets of random acts of violence. This has become such a problem that the Library Administration and Management Association established a Library Safety/Security Discussion Group to brainstorm about ways to protect librarians in the workplace.[2] The concern of this professional organization seems entirely appropriate as some of the violent acts have been quite grizzly. Consider, for example, the December 1992 incident in a small community near Phoenix, Arizona, where the 45-year-old head librarian of the Buckeye Public Library was sexually assaulted and stabbed thirty times by a man who was wanted by police for parole violations. In April 1993, two reference librarians were killed in Sacramento when a man walked through the front door and opened fire.[3]

Despite increasing incidents such as these, few libraries have policies and procedures for dealing with workplace violence. Libraries need to have security plans in place to deal with violent episodes, and staff members should be periodically drilled in handling dangerous situations.

QUESTION 97
How Should Staff Respond to Workplace Violence?

An act of violence occurred in Utah in March 1994—but partly due to good management planning, the outcome was not so devastating as it might have been. In this incident, a man pulled a .45-caliber gun on nearly 100 people at a ceremony at the Salt Lake City Public Library, ordering librarians and patrons into a conference room. However, during the early chaos, a seventeen-year library veteran in the children's department, Gwen Page, managed to help several people escape while electing to remain a hostage herself. The gunman wound up capturing ten hostages, holding them at gunpoint with his semi-automatic weapon and an antipersonnel claymore mine. The five-hour ordeal ended when a police lieutenant seized upon an opportunity to shoot the gunman.[4] No staff member or patron was injured during this siege; and one week later, Ms. Page was presented with the Commendation of Bravery by the governor of Utah.[5]

This Salt Lake City incident serves as a training model for dealing with crises in the first critical minutes. First, the library staff called 911 and gave the police specific information about the nature of the incident. Second, the employees were able to remain composed enough to calm the perpetrator. Third, the librarians followed appropriate procedures for evacuating the building. Rather than sounding the general alarm as might happen with a fire, a phone tree system was used to alert the various departments so that the building could be cleared while panic was avoided. Next, the staff made a sweep of the building to make sure it was vacated. Finally, the staff was available to help police with floor plans of the building.[6]

Although it is difficult to prepare for all contingencies, staff training can help prepare employees for general responses needed to manage violent incidents. Training can provide information on crisis techniques, and practice sessions can be conducted that allow staff members to learn appropriate behaviors. Further, it is important to have a positive working relationship with the police so that there is an early response mechanism established with local authorities. These officers can also conduct classes on handling specific types of crises.

Library Management Tip ————————————————————

Employees should receive specific training on dealing with bomb threats. First, when a phone call comes directly to them, they should take the threat seriously, make notes during the conversation, inquire as to when the bomb is going explode, ask questions that would help locate the bomb, notice any background noises that might help identify the caller's location, and immediately upon hanging up inform the supervisor, police, and fire department. Next, they should help evacuate the library in accordance with established procedures and assist patrons in moving at least 100 yards from the facility. Finally, a floor plan of the library should be made available to officials who are required to search the premises.[7]

QUESTION 98
How Can Librarians Respond to Homeless Patrons Who Seem Potentially Volatile?

One group that has received increasing attention in the library literature is the homeless who use the library as their place of residence during the day.[8] Reactions to the presence of this population have ranged from dictatorial to supportive. Some librarians are fearful of this population and see the homeless as negatively influencing the library environment. They point out that many of the homeless have a history of mental illness. While most are not prone to violence, the possibility always exists for those with psychiatric impairments to become aggressive.

To deal with this problem, some libraries have attempted to use authoritarian and restrictive controls. Although a legal case can be made that homeless people have the right to use public facilities, it is incumbent upon management to establish policies and procedures to protect library employees and patrons from potentially violent individuals.[9] Library administrators also need to deal with this problem through establishing relationships with community agencies.[10] The responsibilities of community mental health centers, state psychiatric facilities, social-service agencies, shelters, and law enforcement agencies in resolving this larger social problem should not be overlooked.

An example of establishing linkages with community service organizations occurred in San Francisco when an attorney, Lisa Parsons, advocated library cards for the homeless. In 1989, the homeless could not check out library materials because they could not provide an address to verify residency. Although administrators were sympathetic to the plight of the homeless, they also pointed out that they had a responsibility to manage library resources in a prudent manner.

Essentially, library administrators viewed the library card as a credit voucher entitling the holder to borrow up to $400 of library materials at any one time. To assure appropriate handling of overdue materials, they needed prompt and effective notification procedures. Library managers and homeless service providers worked together to solve the dilemma between responsible risk management and nondiscriminatory practices toward all patrons. A library card was issued to a homeless patron if a service provider issued a statement on agency letterhead stating that the library could use the agency address for mail services.[11]

QUESTION 99
What Causes Staff Members to Engage in Violent Acts?

Patron violence is more likely than staff member violence, but employee killings of supervisors and peers have risen at an astonishing rate. In 1980, acts of employee violence were virtually nonexistent; lately coworker slayings have averaged eighteen per year. However, it is impossible to tell if any individual employee is likely to commit an atrocity in the library.

Mental health experts say they cannot predict this type of violent behavior because of its relative infrequency, but the profile of the typical perpetrator is a middle-aged man who is a loner with a history of violence. Other possible characteristics include low self-esteem, paranoid ideation, fascination with guns and combat, an unstable family life, and chronic disputes with people at work. Finally, there is often a history of alcohol or drug abuse.

Those employed in service professions such as librarianship seem particularly susceptible to alcohol and drug abuse for a couple of reasons. First, idealistic expectations that professionals develop about their ability to help others can cause great emotional stress, leading to burnout. *Burnout* is a state of physical, emotional, and mental exhaustion that occurs as a result of intense involvement with staff and patrons over long periods of time in emotionally demanding situations. It is characterized by chronic fatigue, feelings of helplessness and hopelessness, low self-esteem, and depersonalization of others. Many attempt to escape feelings of burnout by using drugs and alcohol.

Another factor that indirectly facilitates chemical abuse in the library setting is the hesitancy to report impaired colleagues. "Helping" people don't want to be responsible for others losing their jobs. This results in a conspiracy of silence where the abuse is recognized but never reported. Some librarians may excuse or rationalize a coworker's dependency problem. Others may actually protect or rescue the impaired worker—covering up the impairment. In the collegial library setting, employees often grow as close as family members. To report a peer's problem may be interpreted as betrayal. Thus, library workers are susceptible to becoming enablers—individuals whose actions allow substance abuse and dependency to continue in others.

Among U.S. workers, the drug most frequently abused is alcohol. There are many possible symptoms of alcohol abuse, including changes in life style to accommodate alcohol use, changes in activity level, inconsistency between statements and actions, a compulsion to justify one's actions, feeble attempts to project an aura of self-control, irritability, pessimism, isolation, depression, deterioration in appearance, vaguely described illness or injuries, and increased tardiness or absenteeism.

Impairment among library administrators and professionals is more difficult to detect than impairment in workers at lower hierarchal levels. Librarians typically do not punch time cards, so tardiness and absenteeism are difficult to monitor. Productivity is also difficult to measure in the professional and administrative ranks. And even if performance deficits are detected, nonprofessional staff members can usually be blamed for the problems. The primary symptom of chemical abuse among librarians is *job shrinkage,* which occurs when individuals continue to perform adequately but accomplish fewer and fewer tasks. They apply familiar solutions to new problems, make acceptable rather than optimal decisions, and fail to seek new challenges.

To identify cases of chemical dependency among applicants and employees, some libraries provide screening through urine or blood tests. Drug testing can be done on a preemployment basis, on a random basis, or on a just-cause basis after accidents. While preemployment and just-cause testing are generally acceptable to constituents of the library, random testing is often interpreted as an unnecessary invasion of privacy.

Once substance abuse has been confirmed, libraries face the choice of terminating the offending employee or placing him or her in an employee assistance program (EAP). The main purpose of an EAP is to improve the job performance of employees who are suffering from a broad spectrum of problems, including alcohol and drug abuse. The library manager has primary responsibility for identifying performance problems and referring staff members to an EAP. Rather than diagnosing drug or alcohol abuse, the supervisor is advised to act only as a referral source. Drinking and drug abuse should be discussed only if the employee appears to be under the influence of a substance, is taking chemicals during work hours, or has failed a screening test.

Library Management Tip

The recommended intervention style for dealing with drug or alcohol abuse is *constructive confrontation.* The supervisor confronts the employee about the documented deteriorating work performance. The employee is told that continued poor performance could lead to disciplinary action. Underlying this confrontation is the ultimate threat of job loss if the poor performance continues. In the second part of the intervention strategy, the supervisor offers the constructive message that help is available through an EAP. Thus the supervisor communicates support and concern to the employee by suggesting that she or he see the EAP counselor so that a satisfactory level of performance can be regained.[12]

Research shows that 85 percent of impaired workers who seek treatment can return to the work force as productive employees. But even after successfully completing rehabilitation programs, many recovering substance abusers fear reemployment. They avoid returning to work as they must resume interactions with colleagues who are aware of their past problems. In many cases such fears are realistic. Coworkers avoid relying upon previously impaired peers. And managers may resent impaired librarians for disrupting order and degrading the profession. One tool to help employees reenter the library is the return-to-work contract. Signing the contract publicly commits the impaired employee to abstain from abusing alcohol or drugs, continue with regular mental health appointments and support group meetings, establish performance objectives, and submit to drug or alcohol testing. This detailed contract minimizes the ambiguity faced by the impaired employee returning to the library.

QUESTION 100
What Steps Can Managers Take to Minimize Workplace Violence?

There are several emotional workplace situations which seem to provoke employee violence. These include traumatic events such as grievance handling, discipline, layoffs, and firings. For example, in January 1993, a former employee went into the Tampa, Florida, workplace where he had previously been employed. He yelled, "this is what you all get for firing me." He then shot and killed three former supervisors and colleagues, and subsequently shot himself.

To decrease the risk of violence, exit interviews can be conducted to assess the emotional trauma experienced by the displaced employee. Outplacement services can also be provided to assist employees who have been laid off. Further, supervisors should receive sensitivity training in handling emotionally charged situations. The staff similarly needs training in patron relations to help prevent explosive behavior.

In some cases, the physical characteristics of libraries can be altered to minimize damage resulting from violent outbursts. Precautions include the installation of "panic buttons" for public service desks, scream alarms for restrooms, and portable alarms for workers in isolated areas.[13] Other considerations include metal detectors, surveillance cameras, and even bulletproof glass. Also, security guards can be hired to protect staff members and modify the inappropriate behavior of some patrons.

To protect employees from patron violence, management should develop a culture where staff members are encouraged to verbalize their concerns about safety issues. Also, the library should be designed so that someone can't easily walk off the street and confront the librarian at the circulation desk. The library can use state laws prohibiting threats to press charges against offenders. In library branches where staff members work alone, service hours can be shifted so that low-use hours are minimized. And volunteers can be scheduled to work with librarians during quiet times.

To control employee violence, administrators should develop policies that deal with employee intimidation and take quick disciplinary measures when these policies are violated. Training should be provided to supervisors so that they recognize important signs that may signal future violence—in 70 percent to 80 percent of the cases, there are early warning signs.[14] For example, supervisors should be trained not to discount employees' complaints about job-related stress. They should be advised to be alert to changes in employee behavior such as increased verbal aggression or agitation. Further, supervisors should take all veiled and overt threats seriously. Finally, to prevent potential domestic violence from spilling over into the library, administrators should not allow workers' family members to have free access to back work areas.

Library Management Tip ——————————————————————————

If violence does occur in the library, counseling should be provided to victims for as long as necessary. Some workers may need time off. Others may have a need to blame management for the incident—even if management is clearly blameless. Library administrators should handle victims' anger and grief by meeting with employees. A debriefing should be held as soon after the crisis as possible, and staff members should be told exactly how the incident unfolded. Managers should listen carefully, openly, and sympathetically to victims' reactions. If such incidents are not handled sensitively, library managers can expect to see declines in morale and productivity as well as increases in turnover.

QUESTION 101

Is There a Chance That Concerns about Personal Safety May Induce Dysfunctional Responses among Library Staff?

Whenever individuals fear for their personal safety or health, protectionary reactions, such as the "fight-or-flight" response, may be evoked. When staff members operate in threatening situations, the library manager must be aware that frazzled nerves and fatigue may actually ignite negative interactions where none might have normally existed.

In extreme cases, staff members may actually become "paranoid" in the library. Workplace paranoia is usually transitory or situational rather than persistent—spurred by events such as exposure to a frightening occurrence or even overly intense scrutiny by managers. Some psychotherapists suggest that paranoid people are projecting their hostile feelings onto others. Other experts attribute it to a need for excessive love to neutralize hate, while some blame childhood parental rejection.

But whatever the underlying dynamics, paranoia causes individuals to believe that others think of them as inferior—leading to feelings of isolation, alienation, and defensiveness. Common workplace symptoms include oversensitivity to being left out of decisions, fear of being taken advantage of, feelings of being "set up" by coworkers, inability to acknowledge deficiencies, holding grudges long after workplace conflicts, questioning the commitment and trustworthiness of peers, and communicating in an argumentative fashion.

Workplace paranoia can be effectively addressed through several managerial interventions. First, library managers can engage in efforts to raise the self-esteem of staff members. This can be accomplished through praising specific workplace behaviors. Notably, value judgments or general commendations should be carefully worded, since they may be mistrusted by the paranoid worker. Second, the library manager may encourage staff members to talk over their fears or concerns with peers or supervisors. And finally, any behavior that may increase paranoia should be avoided.

REFERENCES

1. Miller, W. (April 26, 1993). How to reduce potential for workplace violence. *National Underwriters,* 14, 30.

2. 1993, the final look back (January 24, 1994). *Library Hotline,* 4.

3. St. Lifer, E. (August 1, 1994). How safe are our libraries? *Library Journal,* 35–6.

4. Cool heads prevent injuries in Salt Lake hostage ordeal (March 14, 1994). *Library Hotline*, 1.

5. Librarian honored for bravery during Salt Lake library siege (March 21, 1994). *Library Hotline*, 1.

6. McLaughlin, C. (August 1, 1994). Salt Lake City: A model. *Library Journal*, 37.

7. Mantell, M., and S. Albrecht (1994). *Ticking bombs: Defusing violence in the workplace*. Burr Ridge, Ill.: Irwin.

8. Anderson, A. J. (April 15, 1990). What would Mother Theresa do? *Library Journal*, 63–4.

9. Maminski, D. (April 15, 1990). Not philosophy, but action. *Library Journal*, 64–5.

10. McDonald, P. (April 15, 1990). A challenge to the community. *Library Journal*, 65.

11. Landraf, M. N. (November 1991). Library cards for the homeless. *American Libraries*, 946–9.

12. Carson, K. D., and D. B. Balkin (December 1992). An employee assistance model of health care management for employees with alcohol-related problems. *Journal of Employment Counseling*, 29, 146–56.

13. Baron, S. Anthony (1993). *Violence in the workplace: A prevention and management guide for business*. Ventura, Calif.: Pathfinder.

14. Barcilea, S. (May 8, 1994). Most companies are not prepared for increase in workplace violence. *The Clarion-Ledger* (Jackson, Miss.), 5C.

PART II
The 102nd Solution

CHAPTER 19
Total Quality Management

Up to this point in the *Deskbook*, many of the solutions offered have been "prescriptive"; that is, they were offered with the intent of fixing a problem that had already occurred. But significant resources in time, money, and emotional energy might be saved if problems could be averted before managerial intervention was required. Thus, what may be more valuable than a "prescription" is a "vaccination"—a vaccination designed to inoculate the library against incidents and problems before, rather than after, they surface; a vaccination that can be administered even before dysfunctional symptoms appear. Such a vaccine—"Total Quality Management"—is offered by the 102nd solution. Total Quality Management (TQM) is an emerging managerial philosophy that encourages continuous improvement of all systems and processes in the library. If TQM is implemented, less effort may be directed toward retrospectively treating problems and more toward prospectively strengthening the library.

One librarian had the following to say about management theory:

> The development of new management theories sometimes reminds me of seeing the wave performed in a large football stadium. Begun by a few committed individuals, the process rapidly gains support and soon sweeps its way around the arena. Since there is no logical stopping point in the circular stadium, the wave eventually dies out from sheer boredom.
>
> After a while, and particularly if the game is one-sided, someone will start a new wave. During all of this, librarians may be sitting in the upper end zone seats. The first few passes of the wave go by before they even notice, but eventually they try to participate because it is important to belong to the group.[1]

So it goes with Total Quality Management. The library science field is witnessing the publication of numerous articles on this "new" management philosophy.[2] Monographs, such as *Integrating Total Quality Management in a Library Setting,* are also being written to offer guidance on TQM implementation. Getting in on the TQM act are professional associations, supporting the movement by providing education to their respective memberships. For example, the Special Libraries Association offers a six-hour course entitled "The Quality Imperative: An Introduction to TQM for Information Professionals."

History of the Quality Management Movement

The term "quality" initially entered into management's vocabulary with the 1911 publication of Frederick Taylor's *The Principles of Scientific Management.* In this historical treatise, Taylor suggested that managers should not only plan and direct workers' activities but also inspect the quality of their output. Because of the confusion that existed in productive organizations during the Industrial Revolution, managers embraced his ideas of mass production and quality inspections. Today, some management practitioners and academicians take Taylor out of his historical context and blame him for the quality problems that have plagued American industry in the past few decades. They suggest that scientific management not only alienated the worker from management, but also failed to integrate quality into the production process.

A 1931 book by Walter A. Shewhart, entitled *Economic Control of Quality of a Manufactured Product,* marked the second stage of the quality management movement. Shewhart was a member of a group investigating quality problems at Bell Telephone Laboratories. It was during this work that he recognized the incidence of quality variations could be predicted using probability and statistics. Further, he felt that post-production inspection of all output was inefficient. Thus, he helped develop sampling formulas so that only a certain proportion of items needed to be inspected, and the quality of those random items could then be generalized to the entire production lot. His sampling procedures were further refined in World War II when the U.S. Army was attempting to obtain a large number of quality firearms and ammunition from multiple suppliers.

The third historical stage of the quality management movement entailed a paradigm shift from postproduction inspection of product samples to companywide preproduction processes that would ensure quality output. No longer was quality seen as a function of the quality assurance department—it was viewed as a companywide coordination responsibility of top administration. Armand Feigenbaum, while a doctoral student at Massachusetts Institute of Technology in 1951, developed the concept of "total quality control" emphasizing the interdependence of quality activities throughout the organization. Feigenbaum advocated the use of quality engineers to ensure that products were planned, developed, and produced with quality standards in mind. In that same year, Joseph Juran wrote the first edition of his *Quality Control Handbook*. Like Feigenbaum, he challenged organizations to approach quality from a companywide perspective. Unfortunately, these experts were generally ignored in the United States. Instead, it was the Japanese who pursued quality in the years after World War II.

In 1950, the Union of Japanese Scientists and Engineers asked W. Edwards Deming—another U.S.-born quality expert—to deliver a series of lectures on quality control. Four years after Deming's invitation, Joseph Juran was also asked to help teach Japanese executives about quality management. But it was Deming who gained international prominence through his consultative work with Japanese manufacturing firms. He was so successful in his pursuits that the Japanese people attributed their industrial prosperity to his philosophy. While Japan was busy focusing on improving quality, the United States concentrated on increasing efficiency. This pursuit of production "quantity" rather than quality appears to have contributed to the United States's eventual competitive decline.

The United States did not wake up to the notion of quality until three decades after Japanese enterprises had implemented their initiatives. Finally, the fourth stage of the quality movement occurred following the 1980 NBC documentary *If Japan Can Do It, Why Can't We?*, which brought Deming celebrity status in America. At this same time, major U.S. corporations began using Juran as a consultant. Adding to this interest was Philip Crosby's best-selling 1979 book, *Quality Is Free*. Major corporations finally began implementing Deming's, Juran's, and Crosby's approaches to quality during the 1980s. Today, many libraries are also pursuing continuous quality improvement.

HOW CAN QUALITY LIBRARY SERVICE BE DEFINED?

[Q]uality has much in common with sex. Everyone is for it. (Under certain conditions, of course.) Everyone feels they understand it. (Even though they would not want to explain it.) Everyone thinks execution is only a matter of following natural inclinations. (After all, we do get along somehow.) And, of course, most people feel that all problems in these areas are caused by other people. (If they would only take time to do things right.)[3]

Although most library managers talk about quality, the term is often misunderstood. It is difficult to have a meaningful dialogue about quality because there is no agreement about the definition of the concept. This ambiguity is perpetuated by those who perceive quality in the way the late Supreme Court Justice Potter Stewart perceived pornography. He stated, "I can't define [it], but I know it when I see it."

In attempting to clarify the definition of quality, David Garvin, a management researcher from Harvard, identified five common conceptualizations. The *transcendent* perspective is synonymous with "innate excellence." Here, quality is a viewed as a property that can't be analyzed, but can be universally recognized through experience. Given its elusiveness, the transcendent approach offers no guidelines for libraries in pursuit of quality. However, Garvin's other definitions explain quality in more concrete terms.

His *product-based* perspective identifies quality as a precise and measurable factor—variations in quality are the result of product or service differences in the quantity of desired attributes. The *user-based* perspective focuses on satisfaction of patron preferences. Since library users have different wants and needs, each has an individualistic and personal view of what constitutes quality. According to Genichi Taguchi, a Japanese statistician, the *manufacturing-based* definition of quality is determined by the degree to which product characteristics meet established standards. The final approach, *value-based*, defines a quality product or service as one that performs as expected based on the price. Since people want to get what they pay for, the value-based approach is the one adopted by many consumers when evaluating quality.

While patrons perceive quality from a personal standpoint—based on the individual attention and treatments they receive—other library stakeholders view quality service delivery from different perspectives. Staff members are concerned with the quality of their work lives, for example. And society defines library quality from an aggregate perspective, asking what is the net utility/benefit for the community and citizenry as a whole.

Some professionals contend that the library consumer's perception of quality service is distorted. These professionals point out that the patron's view is often inaccurate because he or she doesn't have the requisite knowledge for judging technical competence in the library. Because the technical aspects of librarianship can be difficult for patrons to evaluate, they assess the quality of library services by their impressions of the level of competence and professionalism displayed by staff members. Perceptions of competence are formed when librarians appear to be skilled, capable, and proficient. Here, patrons rely on cues such as whether the library services were provided in an organized fashion, with sufficient attention to detail. Impressions of professionalism are formed when the patron perceives the librarian as exhibiting integrity, warmth, and consideration in the interaction. With the TQM approach, quality is determined not by conformance to professional library standards but by compliance with the expectations of patrons.

Marketing researchers offer ten dimensions that influence customers' evaluations of service delivery.[4] These are: (1) tangibles, such as attractiveness of the library facility, appearance of staff members, and the characteristics of other patrons; (2) reliability, the dependability of library service; (3) responsiveness, the willingness and promptness of staff members in delivering service; (4) competence, the knowledge of the librarian; (5) understanding the patron, efforts to learn the library users' needs and provide individualized attention; (6) access, including location, parking availability, and hours of operation; (7) courtesy, politeness of staff members; (8) communication, the ability of employees to explain the services available in understandable terms; (9) credibility, the trustworthiness of the staff; and (10) security, including physical safety and the confidentiality of materials checked out.

Of these ten service dimensions, the most important one is reliability—the staff's ability to perform the service dependably, consistently, and accurately.[5] The patron wants the library to deliver on the promised services. If it doesn't, apologies, excuses, and friendliness are not going to serve as substitutes for unreliable services. Not making mistakes in the first place will do more to improve relationships with library users than any other act. TQM is the one modern management approach that, at its core, focuses on building quality into processes so that the patron will not have to suffer from service mistakes.

WHAT DO THE QUALITY GURUS HAVE TO SAY TO LIBRARIANS

W. Edwards Deming

W. Edwards Deming was born in 1900. As a young adult, he studied at the University of Wyoming. Following this, he pursued a Ph.D. in mathematical physics at Yale University. During his graduate education, he worked summer months at the Hawthorne Plant of Western Electric in Chicago, developing his expertise in statistical quality control. Though Deming was not aware of the classical Hawthorne experiments being conducted by researchers from Harvard University, like those who were conducting the famous studies, he began to develop ideas about human motivation. There, he learned workers hated the quota system in which they were told to accomplish a specified amount of work in a particular time period. In addition to being unpopular, Deming observed, production quotas resulted in poor quality of work and lost productivity.

Deming graduated from Yale in 1928 and began his lifelong work of denouncing quota systems and focusing on quality outcomes. He attempted to institute his ideas in U.S. organizations, but received little attention. Finally, after receiving accolades for his work in Japan, he began preaching his broad management philosophy at home— an impassioned philosophy referred to as "Demingism" by some and "revolutionary evangelism" by others.

Many came to hear his caustic words about management and his exalting words about quality. Until the time of his death in December 1993, the aging Deming conducted twenty seminars per year throughout the United States, lecturing to an estimated audience of ten thousand who paid more than one thousand dollars each to hear him. In his speeches, Deming relentlessly blamed management, not staff members, for low quality. He continually stated that 94 percent of all errors are due to system problems over which management has control. Only 6 percent of errors are the fault of staff members.

Deming's rather loosely knit management philosophy consists of fourteen points, which may be applied to libraries as follows:

1. Establish constancy of purpose for service improvement. Libraries should avoid short-term "band-aid" solutions to quality problems. Instead, long-term planning at the board and administrative levels must consider how quality service delivery can best be achieved.

2. Adopt the new quality philosophy. Those who work in libraries must adopt a philosophy in which negativism and poor service are unacceptable. Unhappy patrons not only cease visiting libraries (which reduces the need for staff), but also resist tax hikes and avoid making financial contributions to support the library.

3. Cease dependence upon mass inspection. Continuous improvement—not quality assurance—is the key to excellent service. With a quality assurance approach, staff members will assume their errors will be detected by others, and thus may underemphasize the importance of doing things right the first time. Quality breakdowns are more difficult to fix after than before the fact.

4. End the practice of awarding vendor business based on price alone. Rather than constantly searching for cheaper suppliers, long-term relationships should be established with vendors. For example, when choosing a CD-ROM service, more than price should be considered. The capabilities of the system and service support will be important to the librarian.

Vendors have also used TQM as a way to improve and promote their services. For example, the National Technical Information Service (NTIS) instituted a quality program in 1992. Today, they advertise that—because of their TQM initiative—they can fill millions of orders for reports, data files, and software programs with 99.9 percent accuracy at a 50 percent faster processing time.

5. Improve constantly and forever every system of service. TQM is not a one-time effort, nor even something that is ever accomplished. Instead, it is a journey. Once this journey is embarked upon, management is obligated to continually improve the library. Because of the high level of interdependency among organizational members in a library, a team approach is required for making decisions about quality improvements.

6. Institute training procedures. Staff members often learn their jobs from colleagues who were improperly trained themselves. When this occurs, new members cannot adequately perform. Instead, organization members should receive proper training through activities such as in-services, professional conferences, and continuing education.

7. Adopt and institute leadership. Managers should go beyond telling employees what to do and actually lead by example. Leadership means discovering and removing barriers that prevent individuals from taking pride in their work.

8. Drive out fear so that everyone can work effectively. Library staff members must feel secure if quality is to improve. They must be able to ask questions, report quality problems, and take a firm position on necessary improvements without fear of reprisal.

9. Break down barriers between departments. One department's goals can interfere with another's. Therefore, departments must be able to communicate with each other. Departmentalism must be replaced by an identification with the mission of the entire library.

10. Eliminate slogans, exhortations, and targets for the workplace. Management slogans (such as "if it's worth doing, it's worth doing right") can breed resentment among staff members as these messages (erroneously) imply that improvement will follow increased effort on their part.

11. Eliminate numerical quotas, including management-by-objectives. Work standards place a cap on productivity, since very few will be motivated to produce beyond the expected level. Moreover, numerical quotas do not focus on quality issues. In fact, Deming feels that the emphasis on numbers by American management impedes quality improvement more than any other single factor.

12. Remove barriers that rob people of pride in workmanship. Barriers such as outdated equipment, substandard materials, and authoritarian managers stand in the way of quality improvement. Annual ratings and merit pay heighten conflict and competition. The humanity of the workforce must be fostered through true delegation and autonomy—not through pseudo-participation.

13. Institute a vigorous program of education and self-improvement for everyone. Management, professionals, and nonprofessional staff members should be continually educated. People are important assets, and they must acquire new knowledge and skills to keep up with changing technology and advances in the field of librarianship.

14. Create a structure that puts everybody in the organization to work accomplishing the transformation. Administrators must communicate a new vision for the library. They should be accessible to organization members and provide a structure in which people can contribute to the quality mission.

Joseph M. Juran

A second quality guru, Joseph M. Juran, was born in 1900 in Eastern Europe. When he was twelve years old, his family emigrated to the United States. After graduating from the University of Minnesota in 1924, Juran accepted a job at the Western Electric's Hawthorne Plant in Chicago; he continued to work for the Bell Telephone System until World War II. In 1954, Juran went to Japan, having developed a more coherent, integrated, and structured approach to quality management than that of Deming.

Juran suggests that quality improvement be an integral part of an organization's strategic plan. He rejects the notion of postproduction inspections by quality control departments, insisting instead that quality issues be the domain of top management. Juran advocates a "quality trilogy" approach which includes quality planning, quality control, and quality improvement. "Quality planning" includes four steps: identifying customers, determining their needs, designing services that meet those needs, and delivering the desired services. "Quality control" involves evaluating actual services, comparing actual services with planned services, and taking corrective action if there are discrepancies. Finally, quality improvement compels the organization to deliver increasingly higher levels of quality service.

The concept of *benchmarking*—another important quality management activity—is encouraged by Juran. Benchmarking is the continual process of identifying, monitoring, and evaluating innovative service delivery techniques and adapting superior techniques so that they may be implemented in a particular environment—in this case, the library. One important consideration is the selection of processes and outcomes to be benchmarked. In the library, there are several areas which should be tracked. For example, data can be collected for benchmark comparisons on turnaround time, usability of forms, overall organizational performance, utilization statistics, and patron satisfaction.

Three types of benchmarking have been identified.[6] The first type—and probably the easiest to institute in large library organizations—is *internal* benchmarking. Internal operations are examined, and superior techniques duplicated in departments that use less effective procedures. *Competitive* benchmarking against other library providers is often complicated by a lack of access to data. Competitive benchmarking does, however, force managers to look externally for superior industry practices. A third type of benchmarking, *functional,* involves examining organizational leaders in other industries. For example, a bookstore might be used as a benchmark to improve access to collections.

Philip B. Crosby

Philip B. Crosby, author of best-sellers such as *Quality without Tears: The Art of Hassle-Free Management* and *The Eternally Successful Organization: The Art of Corporate Wellness,* is recognized as a third leader in the American quality movement. In the 1960s, Crosby became the director of quality at the Martin Company which assembled Pershing missiles for the U.S. Army. In building the missiles, the Martin Company understandably strove for zero defects—a concept that Crosby took with him to ITT, where he became corporate vice-president for worldwide quality. In 1979, he retired from ITT and established a quality consultation firm, Philip Crosby Associates.

There are four major principles associated with Crosby's philosophy: (1) the only acceptable standard is zero defects; (2) quality is defined as conformance to service requirements; (3) prevention—or "do it right the first time" (DIRT-FooT)—is the true avenue to quality; and (4) poor quality costs organizations money. Crosby believes management must be responsible for "injecting" their organizations with a "vaccination serum" that contains five ingredients. These include (1) policies that clearly outline quality standards and expectations; (2) positive reinforcement from management to encourage and recognize employees; (3) adequate training and proper tools for staff members to meet the established standards; (4) a systems approach to the organizationwide prevention of defects, and (5) integrity in providing promised services to the customer.

The Major Principles of TQM for Libraries

TQM programs in library organizations are based on three major principles: patron focus, process improvement, and employee empowerment.[7] Patron focus specifies that library organizations must be responsive to the user. Process improvement is built on the notion that consumers of a library organization can best be served by reducing system deficiencies through a structured procedure using project teams. Finally, employee empowerment involves efforts to utilize the talents of all staff members in the library.

PATRON FOCUS

Librarianship literature reports that over 50 percent of the questions presented to reference librarians are answered incorrectly or insufficiently. Because of quality problems such as these, there has been an increased emphasis on evaluating patrons' satisfaction with services. Factors affecting patron satisfaction include such issues as the competency of the staff, the size of collections, suitability of study space, quality of photocopy machines, relevancy of library programs, convenience of library hours, attractiveness of the facility, safety of the location, fairness of library policies, sophistication of searches, and capability of computers.[8]

To fully engage the library patron, marketing researchers suggest that library users actually be encouraged to criticize the services, because there are many who do not complain to staff but go away dissatisfied. Therefore, it must be easy for library users to give feedback on the services they receive. The use of comment cards is one avenue for learning of patrons' perceptions of the service, but this may not be enough. Since patrons are unlikely to initiate the feedback process, more proactive strategies may be necessary. For example, a manager can ask patrons who are leaving the library how services might have been better rendered.

To successfully manage quality, it may be necessary to go beyond assessing satisfaction to determining patrons' needs and expectations. Simply asking patrons to complete satisfaction questionnaires often does not provide the baseline information needed for intervention and quality improvement. Rather than questions about satisfaction, the questions asked should facilitate the development of improvement plans and actively engage the patron in the quality process. An example of such a question is, "How well did the librarian train you in using the CD-ROM?"

A focus on the needs of the ultimate customer—the library patron—seems particularly important in these days of changing technology.[9] But there are some professionals who wonder if the patron should be viewed as a customer at all. When this businesslike orientation occurs, the value systems of the librarian and the customer can be in conflict. For example, some librarians worry that consumer satisfaction will result in "good" books being replaced by "popular" books. This trend toward customerization and commercialization has been labeled the "Big Mac approach" to librarianship.[10]

However, there are some cases in which libraries have had to become more business oriented to survive. For example, the Phillips Laboratory Research Library at Hanscom Air Force Base had to change its way of thinking about its customers.[11] Staff members were accustomed to receiving a yearly budget for purchasing journals and performing online searches to serve the scientific divisions. However, executives shifted the funding policy so that support functions—such as the research library—had to charge back the cost of the services requested by scientists. At the same time, funds for the library's operating budget were substantially decreased. Thus, to make up for the shortfall, the library had to identify billable customers. This new orientation meant that the library staff had to market their services to the patrons, hold down the cost of online searching, and survey their customers to determine current and future needs.

In order to survive and thrive, academic libraries are also engaging in a fundamental switch in how they think about their services. Librarians can no longer view themselves as working in the great warehouses of knowledge—rather, librarians must be active agents of information transfer.[12] With changing technology, most academic customers prefer not to visit the library to find needed information. Instead, many access materials through online information systems from their offices, laboratories, and homes.

While patron involvement is valuable for assessing and improving service systems, there are numerous other "customers" that also require consideration. The late Kaoru Ishikawa, former president of Musahi Institute of Technology near Tokyo, developed the concept of the "internal customers"—colleagues in the next department or down the hall—who depend upon services provided by others in the same library. Every staff member has both an internal supplier and an internal customer who depends upon receiving quality output in order to perform his or her job. For example, reference staff effectiveness is dependent upon the holdings purchased by the collection development staff and also upon the materials processed by the technical service staff.

PROCESS IMPROVEMENT

The second major principle of TQM is process improvement. To eliminate useless steps in the process and improve the quality of outcomes, a team approach to quality is recommended. At the upper levels of management, the top administrators typically form a quality council. These top-level council meetings are used to prioritize quality issues that are to be handled by lower-level project teams. Membership on a project team includes representatives from different departments and different levels of the organizational hierarchy who temporarily join together to solve a quality problem.

In some cases, even top administrators serve on project teams—for as John Dewey once noted, the search for truth is a cooperative activity.[13] However, these cooperative searches for truth and quality are more difficult in large organizations such as universities. In such settings, the library often participates in the institution-wide improvement effort by appointing a coordinator to the quality council. For example, at Pennsylvania State University, an associate dean of libraries serves as the liaison to the university-wide Continuous Quality Improvement Center.[14] This council decides on the major quality objectives to be tackled by the project teams on a university-wide basis.

Project teams require the joint efforts and expertise of a number of different staff members—each with her or his divergent perceptions of goals, time frames, and values. Given the need for cooperation within and among these eclectic groups, one researcher has suggested six practical tips to project team coordination: (1) don't focus exclusively on the task and ignore the psychosocial needs of members, (2) remember that cooperation is vital as diverse inputs can result in high levels of project team performance, (3) focus on the superordinate goal as this helps facilitate cooperation, (4) ensure that members have access to each other during meetings, (5) facilitate interactions between meetings by paying attention to the physical proximity of group members, and (6) establish common ground rules to regulate and facilitate cross-functional cooperation.[15]

Quality management requires a structured process in which a project team tackles a particular quality problem. In attempting to eliminate quality breakdowns, the project team systematically performs five activities: problem definition, problem documentation, measurement, analysis, and solution implementation.

Documentation and Control Tools

Since the project team represents a cross-section of organizational members, its members need to have a clear understanding of exactly what symptom(s) the quality council wants them to address. Therefore, the team first carefully defines the problem. Rather than taking quick action, project teams must develop a clear understanding of the quality problem (or opportunity for improvement) so that an appropriate intervention can be established. A service map, or flow diagram of sequential steps of the examined process, is the most common tool used to document the problem. The diagraming of service maps often highlights discrepancies between visions of what the process should be and what it is in reality. This flow chart helps team members visualize how work processes actually take place through and across departments.

The service map provides four functions: (1) it allows the team to identify the current internal and external customers in the process; (2) it provides the team with a clear understanding of the steps in the process; (3) it is useful in identifying inefficient and redundant steps; and (4) it provides a framework for determining how to improve the process. The symbols used in a simple service map are illustrated in figure 9.[16]

Figure 9. The Reference Process

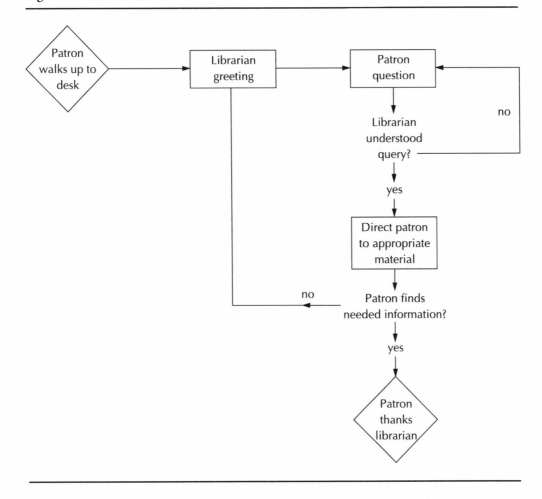

The TQM process utilizes data and measurement to assess the discrepancy between customers' expectations and actual service delivery. Therefore, the project team is interested in collecting data on inputs and outcomes such as books added, number of journal subscriptions, size of staff, amount of budget dollars, quantity of circulation items, responses to reference questions, attendance at programs, waiting times for check-out, queuing time for xeroxing, billing errors, address errors, and unfilled requests for materials.

Project groups also use certain control tools to accomplish their tasks. Two of these tools are the Gantt chart and the PERT network. The Gantt chart is simply a bar chart graphically illustrating the amount of time to be spent on each activity in the accomplishment of a major project (*see* figure 10). This chart is named for its founder, Henry L. Gantt.

Figure 10. Gantt Chart for Starting a New Branch Library

	Week 1	Week 2	Week 3	Week 4	Week 5
1. Renovate building	********************				
2. Order equipment		*****************			
3. Recruit staff			******************		
4. Orientation				*******	
5. Train technicians					****************
6. Liaison with community leaders			************************************		

The second control tool used by project teams is the PERT network (Program Evaluation and Review Technique network) originally developed for the U.S. Navy Special Projects Office in 1958. The PERT network allows library managers to visualize a project in its entirety. Here, the events required to complete a project are shown in network form with the time required for each activity (*see* figure 11). In addition to the overall display, the one path containing the most time-consuming activities is identified. This longest sequence, or critical path, helps identify the earliest possible project completion date. The library manager should pay particular attention to the critical path so that delays are minimized.

Figure 11. Incorporating TQM into the Library Using PERT

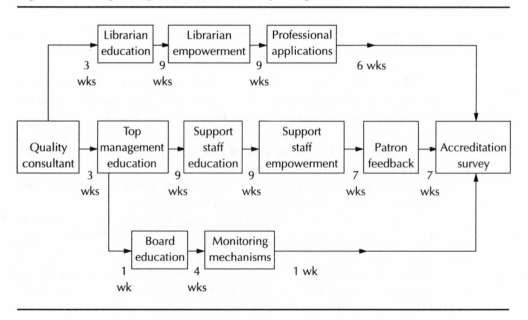

Quality Tools

In addition to the traditional production-oriented techniques discussed previously, the quality management literature offers several additional control analysis tools. These include the fishbone diagram, Pareto chart, histogram, scattergram, run chart, control chart, and the plan-do-study-act cycle.

The fishbone diagram, or cause-and-effect diagram, was developed by a Japanese executive, Kaoru Ishikawa. It is a diagram that aids project teams in differentiating among symptoms, secondary causes, and root causes of quality breakdowns. The fishbone gets its name from its shape (*see* figure 12). The quality problem the team wants to address is placed at the far right (at the fish's head). On the larger lines (large bones of the fish) of the diagram are the major factors contributing to the problem—such as policies, procedures, staff, and equipment. On the smaller lines (little bones of the fish) are issues that might possibly enhance or moderate the major factors contributing to the problem. The team examines these factors and circles the ones they believe have the most significant impact on the problem.

Joseph Juran developed a second analytical tool, the Pareto chart, which was named after a nineteenth-century Italian economist who suggested that 80 percent of the wealth was owned by 20 percent of the people. Reapplying this concept, Juran observed that 80 percent of the quality problems in organizations were the result of only 20 percent of all possible sources (thus, the "eighty-twenty" rule was born). To depict the major sources of the problem, a bar chart is used. Different causes are listed on the horizontal axis and percentages of occurrences are listed on the vertical axis, as in figure 13.

Figure 12. Fishbone Diagram on Literature Support for Faculty

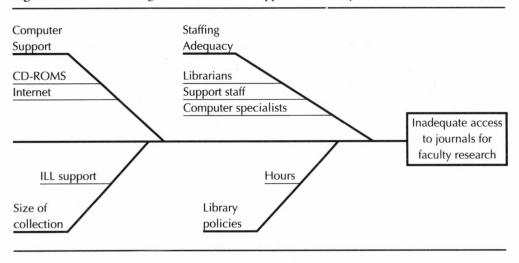

Figure 13. Pareto Chart on Phone Service Complaints

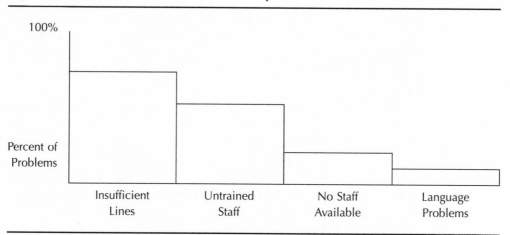

100%

Percent of
Problems

| Insufficient Lines | Untrained Staff | No Staff Available | Language Problems |

The histogram is simply a frequency distribution bar chart that shows the dispersion of selected variables (*see* figure 14A). The scattergram, sometimes called the scatter diagram, is also a visual mechanism for analyzing data. But rather than examining only one factor, it compares the relationship between two variables (*see* figure 14B).

Figure 14A. Histogram Showing Age Distribution

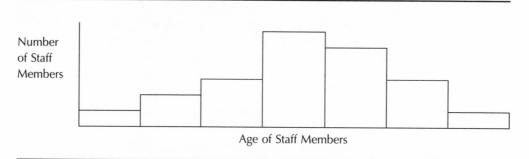

Number
of Staff
Members

Age of Staff Members

Figure 14B. Scattergram on Age vs. Commitment to the Librarianship Profession

Age

Organizational Commitment to the Librarianship Profession (as measured by a survey)

One is shown on the horizontal axis, and the second is shown on the vertical axis. If there is a positive correlation between the two variables, there will be a clustering of points from the lower left corner to the upper right corner. A lack of correlation between the variables is shown by the random dispersion of the points.

A run chart is a trend chart or time series chart in which baseline data are plotted over time (*see* figure 15A). These data are needed to establish a statistical process control chart like the one shown in figure 15B, which indicates whether service provision is within tolerable limits. The upper control limit (UCL) and the lower control limit (LCL) indicate the maximum allowable variation in any given process. Fluctuations within the limits are called common variance and are caused by the system. Fluctuations outside the limits are called special variance. Once special negative variance is removed, library management must change the system to minimize common variance.

The Plan-Do-Check-Act (PDCA) cycle was developed by Walter Shewhart (*see* figure 16). The first step in this cycle is to develop hypotheses about the possible causes of the problem. This diagnosis step is translated into a "plan" to correct the causes. Next, the project team is expected to "do" pilot studies or experiments based on their plan. Using this experimental approach, the team "checks" the hypotheses to see which correctly describes the root cause. The team

Figure 15A. Run Chart on Interlibrary Loan Transactions Handled

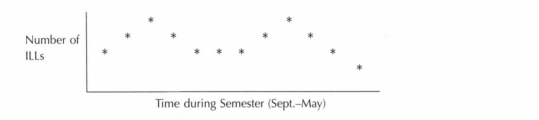

Figure 15B. Control Chart on Turnaround for Interlibrary Loans

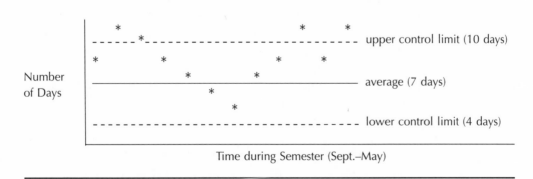

Figure 16. The Plan-Do-Check-Act Cycle

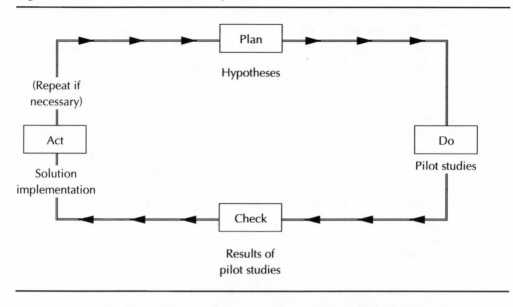

then implements or "acts" on the most desirable solution, taking into account both the technical aspects and the human aspects of change. Finally, progress made with this remedy is tracked so that potential gains can be maintained.

EMPLOYEE EMPOWERMENT

The TQM approach provides libraries with the appropriate culture necessary for improving quality services. Its customer-centered philosophy allows staff members more responsibility in anticipating, preventing, and handling day-to-day problems. The traditional authoritarian style of management, with its rigidity and control, is not workable in a TQM environment. Instead, there is an emphasis on decentralization of decision making. That is, authority is being pushed down the organizational hierarchy instead of concentrated only in top administration.

Decentralization and TQM initiatives do not threaten the existing authority hierarchy in the library, however.[17] Administrators continue to engage in regular management behavior such as monitoring performance, improving procedures, and implementing changes. But, those in power positions are expected to change the ways they relate to staff members. They are to become more accessible in receiving information and processing suggestions, to engage all members of the staff in transformation to a quality culture, and to empower the staff.

An important aspect of the empowerment process is delegation. Delegation involves allowing employees to exercise independent judgment. However, the library manager retains responsibility for over-seeing the completion of tasks, establishing quality standards, and ensuring staff members have the necessary knowledge to perform. In addition, staff members must have access to appropriate resources for the empowerment process to work. If a staff member is having trouble carrying out a task, the manager should assist, rather than reprimand, the worker. Rescinding authority when staff members encounter problems is not beneficial to the worker or to the library. In fact, the withdrawal of power can lower self-esteem and create feelings of estrangement.

Empowerment represents more than just sharing with the staff. Even when employees have access to the resources needed to overcome quality problems, they must feel capable and confident in applying those resources to problems in the library. Thus, empowerment must also take into account the internal state of the employee—staff members only feel personal empowerment when they have confidence in their capability to get the job done.

Personal empowerment requires employee confidence and self-efficacy—the belief that one can accomplish a specific job. In libraries, a variety of factors can serve to lower a staff member's self-efficacy. Fortunately, these can be overcome through proper management. When the organization is bureaucratic with formal communication channels, employees experience feelings of powerlessness. They experience similar problems when library managers are anarchistic or unduly negative. Finally, staff members do not feel empowered when roles are ambiguous, autonomy is not allowed, or the goals seem insignificant.

The library manager can institute certain practices to reduce impediments to self-efficacy. Training can be provided to enhance skills, policies can be adapted to encourage self-direction, open communication channels can be instituted, and jobs can be redesigned to foster skill variety and relevance. Library managers can also strengthen interpersonal relations with employees by being considerate, showing trust, and displaying respect.

Self-efficacy messages can be reinforced through realistic goals, role modeling, words of praise, and a positive, understanding atmosphere. Staff members should come to believe that goals are actually attainable. They should also trust that they will be appropriately rewarded for achieving objectives. When they believe they can, empowered staff members will overcome many obstacles in pursuit of quality goals.

When confidence is shown in a staff member's ability to handle crises, organization-based self-esteem (OBSE) heightens. OBSE develops when staff members regard themselves as important and effective members of the library. These empowered employees feel trusted, valuable, and able to make a difference. Employees with a high degree of OBSE are likely to display better job performance, helpful citizenship behavior toward others, and commitment to the library's goals, values, and culture.

A properly implemented TQM program should enhance staff members' OBSE as well as their ability to respond effectively to patron needs and expectations. However, when responding to the library user, staff members must feel assured that no management retaliation will occur if they happen to overstep their traditional limits of authority. To establish this trust, management must give up traditional policing activities. This is not to imply that the interaction between management and employees should be totally conflict-free. Rather, understanding between the two parties is the objective. Under a TQM approach, both management and staff members strive consistently to do things right, but they may have honest disagreements about how this is best accomplished. This is the nature of participation.

Participative management consists of more than merely asking staff members their opinions about work issues. Broadly speaking, it means involving employees directly in setting goals, making decisions, and solving problems. Some theorists suggest that participative management is the only ethical way to manage. They point out that employees are adults who should have a say in their workplace. Their basic needs should not be frustrated, and no harm should come to them from unilateral mandates issued by management. Indeed, research suggests that participation has positive effects for both the library and the individual: it increases job satisfaction, decreases confusion about expectations, and promotes creativity.

One formal mechanism used to increase employee participation is the use of quality circles. Quality circles are typically comprised of eight to twelve staff member volunteers, who meet once a week to focus on solving workplace problems. Their recommendations are then made directly to top management for possible implementation.

Quality circles were most prominent in libraries during the 1980s. During this period, they were eagerly introduced by some top administrators and often met with enthusiasm by staff members. Gains were typically seen in the first couple of years following formation. Staff members eagerly made suggestions, such as the need for glare-free screens for computer monitors, the feasibility of placing terminals closer to the reference desk, and the improvement of service through better signage in the library. But as months passed, recommendations typically decreased and enthusiasm waned. With passing time, quality outcomes went back to their pre-quality-circle levels. Rather than remaining as adaptable problem-solving groups, quality circles became a part of the old bureaucracy. Today, most library administrators have given up on quality circles and are focusing on more widespread involvement.

Real involvement of staff members seems to result in improved attitudes, but current research indicates that it has little long-term impact on increased productivity. Also problematic is that some library supervisors resent participative techniques, as they equate staff involvement with a reduction in their power and authority. These supervisors argue that participation is not an inherent right of staff members. They appropriately point to instances in which management is forced to exercise power unilaterally, as when an employee must be fired for unethical conduct.

Though management power must be used on occasion, it seems that today's staff members thrive best in a considerate and participative environment. But even when there is reasonable harmony in the library, mistakes will inevitably occur. When a patron is unhappy with the quality of services rendered, action must be taken immediately to ensure that a temporarily dissatisfied library user becomes a satisfied one. Action taken to alter the negative feelings of a patron is called "service recovery." The empowered employees in a TQM environment should have the authority and power to take immediate action to solve a problem or compensate the patron for an inconvenience. This strategy can prevent the loss of a patron and minimize criticism of the library in the community.

Rather than writing their complaints, many patrons will let their concerns be known verbally. When this happens, they want a quick and personal response. If no action is taken when they complain, dissatisfaction increases. They are doubly dissatisfied because of poor service in the first place and failure to take corrective action in the second place. Patrons want performance, not just polite sympathy. Therefore, staff members must be empowered to take service recovery action. For service recovery to be effective, library staffers must be able to "right a wrong" as soon after it occurs as possible. If a paraprofessional can take immediately action to correct a minor billing error, for example, a patron can be quickly appeased.

TQM or Not TQM?

Since management theories pass in and out of favor, some library administrators contend that TQM is just another fad. Skeptics have used the acronym "TQM" to refer to the "Total Quality Mistake." Still others refer to TQM as the management equivalent of the leisure suit. Therefore, the question for many is whether TQM is "just another gust of wind"? The probable answer to this query is not a simple "yes" or "no."

It is certainly possible that TQM will be relabeled in the next decade. But the focus on quality service is here to stay. Of course, many would argue that the focus has always been around—that the library profession has consistently pursued excellence as its first priority.[18] This is a reasonable argument—but as Donald Riggs, Dean of Libraries at the University of Michigan, notes, "who can argue with the improvement of quality in libraries?"[19] Few would debate that nearly every process in the library can be improved. In fact, the processes most easily tackled by TQM techniques are those bordering on drudgery, such as processing books and checking in periodicals. Elimination of useless steps in these processes can result in cost savings while reducing error rates.

However, knowing about TQM techniques and implementing them are two different beasts. There are some situations where the TQM approach is particularly difficult to institute. For example, if a library faces downsizing due to economic constraints, the layoff of colleagues will undermine the trust needed between management and staff members for successful implementation. Also, some library managers get tired of being blamed for all of the system's failures. Because quality experts often attribute organizational problems to the administration rather than to the staff, managers often feel like they have signs on their backs reading "CALL 1-800-BLAMEUS." Other library managers object to the heavy emphasis on team projects. Some sarcastically refer to TQM teams as "posses"—when things go wrong, a few managers, librarians, support staff members and even patrons are brought together to ritualistically "ride off, find the problem, and literally analyze it to death."

Another difficulty with TQM is the lengthy time it requires to be fully implemented on a systemwide basis. It is not a quick-fix approach—a library must actively follow its tenets for years to realize major benefits. Of course, it can be difficult to maintain enthusiasm for TQM programs over this extended period. To ease the burden for overworked professional librarians, it is recommended that they not be required to attend unproductive mandatory meetings. Efforts to involve librarians should be directed toward issues that are salient, important, and conducive to TQM analysis. For example, a TQM focus on interlibrary loan transactions can result in the reduction of average turnaround time from fourteen days to six days. This kind of result is reinforcing, thus maintaining the interest of librarians.

In addition to a focus on clear-cut goals, managers can sustain the involvement of professional librarians in a number of other ways. These include training a few interested librarians and having these "champions of TQM" sell the program to colleagues and integrating TQM agenda items in staff meetings. Finally, librarians can be shown ways TQM can be applied to remove barriers to work enjoyment—such as the elimination of burdensome paperwork.

REFERENCES

1. White, H. S. (June 15, 1993). The library implications of individual and team empowerment. *Library Journal,* 47.

2. O'Neil, R. M., R. L. Harwood, and B. A. Osif (Winter 1994). A TQM perspective: The busy manager's bookshelf. *Library Administration & Management,* 49–52.

3. Crosby, P. B. (1979). *Quality Is Free.* New York: McGraw Hill, pp. 13–14.

4. Zeithaml, V. A., L. L. Berry, and P. Parasuraman (1990). *Delivering quality service: Balancing customer perceptions and expectations.* New York: Free Press.

5. Berry, L. L., A. Parasuraman, and V. A. Zeithaml (1994). Improving service quality in America: Lessons learned. *Academy of Management Executive,* 8(2), 32–6.

6. Camp, R. C. (1989). *Benchmarking.* Milwaukee: Quality Press.

7. Tenner, A. R., and I. J. DeToro (1992). *Total quality management: Three steps to continuous improvement.* Reading, Mass.: Addison-Wesley.

8. Shaughnessy, T. W. (Winter 1993). Benchmarking, total quality management and libraries. *Library Administration & Management,* 7–12.

9. Riggs, D. E. (1992). Strategic quality management in libraries. *Advances in Librarianship,* 16, 93–105.

10. Brewer, R. (November 1, 1990). Analysis 1: Respond—but take charge! *Library Journal,* 65–6.

11. Duffek, E., and W. Harding (1993). Quality management in the military: An overview and a case study. *Special Libraries,* 84(3), 137–40.

12. Stuart, C., and M. A. Drake (1993). TQM in research libraries. *Special Libraries,* 84(3), 131–6.

13. Bechtel, J. M. (1993). Leadership lessons learned from managing and being managed. *Journal of Academic Librarianship,* 18(6), 352–7.

14. O'Neil, R. M., R. L. Harwood, and B. A. Osif (Fall 1993). A total look at total quality management: A TQM perspective from the literature of business, industry, higher education, and librarianship. *Library Administration & Management,* 244–54.

15. Pinto, M. B. (Winter 1990). Gaining cooperation among members of hospital project teams. *Hospital Topics,* 15–21.

16. For a more detailed service map see Mackey, T., and K. Mackey (May 15, 1992). Think quality! The Deming approach does work in libraries. *Library Journal,* 57–61.

17. Lawler, E. E. (1994). Total quality management and employee involvement: Are they compatible? *Academy of Management Executive,* 8(1), 68–76.

18. Lawes, A. (1993). The benefits of quality management to the library and information services profession. *Special Libraries,* 84(3), 142–6.

19. Riggs, D. E. (November 1992). TQM: Quality improvement in new clothes. *College & Research Libraries,* 481–3.

Management Maxims: Guidelines for Browsers

References are to page numbers.

Communication Issues

1	Library managers spend about 80 percent of their working time communicating with others.
2	The use of jargon is both pervasive and problematic in the library and information science profession.
2–5	Active listeners are empathetic and try to determine what the speaker is saying from the speaker's point of view.
3	Like overload, information underload creates stress and role ambiguity.
3	Distortion is particularly likely when the message will make staff members look bad or when an employee is afraid the supervisor will "shoot the messenger" bearing bad news.
4	As messages travel downward, they typically expand and become more negative.
4	Newcomers entering a library setting are particularly in need of information—for even though they may have had occupational training or experience, they will lack specific knowledge about organizational culture and protocols.
5	In situations involving personal interaction, there is immediate feedback, and many cues such as body language and facial expressions are exchanged—cues that may be more revealing than words themselves.
6	Information is disseminated by the grapevine quickly and accurately. In fact, up to 90 percent of informal communications are reliable, and errors are mostly due to omission rather than commission.
6	Unfortunately, nearly two-thirds of workers claim they receive more information about their workplace from the grapevine than from any other source.

7	Research indicates that as much as 90 percent of a message is communicated through body language and other nonverbal signals.
7	The emotions of fear, excitement, frustration, confidence, and anger are easily interpreted by individuals in most societies through facial configurations.
10	Library managers are no longer trying to provide service to the "melting pot" of the American culture. Rather, most view the communities they serve as representing a "salad bowl."
10	To respond to diversity issues, the library needs to provide collections that reflect its patrons' needs.
11–2	By the turn of the century, the majority of U.S. citizens in 95 percent of all urban areas will be from four "minority" groups: African-Americans, Asian-Americans, Hispanics, and Native Americans.
12	Marketing techniques will vary depending upon the background and acculturation of the patrons as differences among people arise, in part, from their cultural heritage.
13	Serving patrons in their preferred language can often lead to better utilization of the library.
13	When multilingual staff are not available, the library may want to have a series of brochures to provide answers to the most commonly asked questions.
14	To provide better service, library administrators in culturally diverse areas are trying to increase the number of bilingual and bicultural staff members to better serve their diverse populations.
15	Though affirmative action programs are designed to make up for past discrimination, current enrollment in library schools suggests that recruitment of minorities will continue to be a problem.
16	Managing diversity includes recognizing new types of staff members, learning to understand the needs and desires of nontraditional workers, and creating an environment in which minorities can succeed.
16	Because of the complexities of managing cultural diversity in the library setting, a three-pronged approach may be necessary: awareness building, discrimination control, and prejudice reduction.
19	Only when individuals feel they are being tremendously overcompensated compared to others do they tend to feel guilty.
20	When there is a perception of distributive justice and procedural justice, staff members are likely to be both satisfied and committed to the library.

20   Dissimilarities in learning styles can cause friction between staff members, as they will have disparate perceptions of their world.

21   Of the 267 professional librarians listed in one large research database, the four-letter diagnostic code revealed that a majority scored as ISFJ: Introverted (61%), Sensing (54%), Feeling (67%), Judging (64%).

21   Although library administrators only reluctantly admit to reliance upon intuition, evidence suggests many good decisions are made based on managers' "gut feelings."

22   Despite long-held skepticism, intuition is finding its way out of the closet and into library management circles.

22   Today, management theorists recognize that some conflict is helpful in the library environment.

22   When conflict exceeds appropriate limits, it usually means that staff members' disagreements no longer focus on library issues but rather on personal agendas.

23   Recognizing that some constructive conflict is desirable, the library manager can use groups for creative decision making when complex problems require a variety of opinions.

23   High quality group decision making is typically accompanied by free expression of ideas, diversity, and flexibility.

24   Groupthink occurs in overly cohesive groups where there is so much pressure for consensus that individual members lose their capacity to evaluate alternatives realistically.

24–5   Instead of striving for the agreement and consensus associated with groupthink and polarization, groups should attempt to achieve harmonies of difference, in which the diverse opinions of members are reconciled and integrated into a common solution.

27   Legitimate, reward, and coercive powers are collectively known as "positional" bases for they emanate from the job held by the manager rather than from any individual characteristics or attributes of the manager.

27   Alternatively, referent and expert powers are "personal" bases, as they are earned by the manager rather than bestowed with a promotion or appointment to the management team.

27   The mirror effect results when staff members' treatment of patrons mirrors management's treatment of staff members.

28   While reward power only influences performance, coercive power surprisingly has no effect on performance.

28	Power is often perceived differently by managers and staff members.
28	While a library manager may believe that subordinates are executing requests because of expert power, they may really be doing so to avoid coercion.
30	Additionally, when employees begin focusing on earning extrinsic rewards, the joy of performing their work may be diminished.
30	A reward may be perceived as a bribe, leading to perceptions that the library manager is manipulative.
31	Expert power results from being consistently approachable by staff members with questions, a willingness to share information, and a desire to help staff members solve work-related problems.
31	When relationships are based on referent power, staff members tend to imitate the supervisor's behaviors and adopt the supervisor's attitudes—which can eliminate workplace conflicts and facilitate efficient services.

Professional Issues

34	To many patrons, everyone who works in a library—from those staffing the reference desk, to those shelving books, to those behind the circulation counter—is a "librarian."
35	Another suggestion is to include position titles on name tags clearly identifying professional staff members.
36	The cosmopolitans will bring to the library innovative and creative ideas implemented by other institutions, preventing organizational stagnation.
36	But once professionals are employed, managers should avoid placing them in situations where they must choose between the values of the profession of librarianship and those of the employing organization.
37	The field of librarianship seems to attract people who are willing to sacrifice themselves for the greater good.
37	Library education is designed not only to teach practical skills, but also to socialize students to the values and theories of the profession.
38–9	Under a matrix structure, staff members "specialize" in both a functional and in a "product-line" department.
40	When employees have two supervisors, stress is often created by conflicting expectations, role overload, and ambiguity.

40   In organizations that employ highly trained and qualified profession-als, decisions made jointly will generally be more acceptable than those made unilaterally by administrators.

41   If the wrong alternative is chosen, the challenge facing library man-agers is to prevent the professional staff from engaging in "escalation of commitment"—becoming overcommitted to a losing course of action.

42   Managers of geographically separate library branches are most effec-tive when they are both autonomous, able to exercise independent discretion and make decisions on their own, and committed, identi-fying with the goals and values of the whole library organization.

42   To transform these managers into effective professional supervisors, the director can control the type and amount of information passed to these managers through vertical communication linkages (up and down the hierarchy) and/or horizontal communication linkages (be-tween peers).

45   Many libraries are expanding their hiring of paraprofessionals while simultaneously decreasing the hiring of professional librarians.

46   Illustrative of their elevated status in the field, paraprofessionals are becoming increasingly involved in library association activities.

46   One way in which employees can be recognized is through the "be-stowing" of a position title that commands respect.

46   No matter what term is chosen, library managers should realize that carefully considered titles can enhance the self-esteem and ultimately the productivity of the support staff.

47   There is much consensus among those involved in the profession that not everyone who works in a library is a "librarian."

47   While very few libraries today require their paraprofessionals to have earned a graduate degree (interestingly, nearly one-quarter of aca-demic and research libraries do), many libraries do require support staff members to have a college degree.

50   So the challenge facing library managers is how to keep the parapro-fessional staff motivated to perform in an environment where they may feel they are treated as second-class citizens.

50   Thus, when the library manager feels that both quantity and quality performance are important, goals should be established with the paraprofessional for *both* dimensions.

53   Extrinsic feedback can serve as a significant source of reinforcement; this may explain why reference department employees are often the most satisfied in the library.

53	Paraprofessionals who are too closely supervised may lack a perception of autonomy.
53	Although they are not on the payroll, volunteers should not be thought of as just a free source of labor.
54	Volunteers should be nurtured with support and recognition.
56	Research has shown that a mentor can expedite advancement for some librarians.
57	While women librarians most often recognize their mentors for teaching them "tricks of the trade" and serving as competent role models, men librarians tend to acknowledge those who encouraged them to enter the field of librarianship.
57	"In-groupers" are often expected to help the supervisor run the library department.
57	Out-group members are often assigned unchallenging work, because the supervisor lacks confidence in their ability to accomplish difficult tasks.
58	When the occupational choice results in a good fit with one's personality, individuals are more satisfied, make fewer job changes, and achieve greater professional success than those who choose a vocation dissimilar from their interests.
59	By the "late-career stage," many library administrators are eager to retire.
60	With a dual career ladder, the specialist has the potential to earn more money and prestige without being forced into becoming a manager.
60	With a spiral career path, individuals make occupational moves every five or ten years in pursuit of stimulation and personal growth.
61	In the absence of constructive ways to deal with the isolation accompanying plateauing, entrapped employees may feel depressed.
62	Neglect is a coping mechanism where the worker retires on the job.
63	In a survey of public librarians, it was reported that over half are experiencing medium to high levels of burnout.
63	The manager needs to be clear that while upward advancement is unlikely, the employee can still contribute to and be valued by the library.

Employment Issues

65	Job descriptions contain information about the duties and responsibilities of a job as well as the context in which a job is performed.

66 In the library environment, rapid technological advances and personnel cutbacks brought about by budgetary constraints serve to make job descriptions rapidly obsolete.

69 Job descriptions can be used for several purposes, including offering information about what aspects of performance should be evaluated during employee appraisals.

69 Job descriptions aid in the recruitment and selection process by outlining the skills, knowledge, and abilities an incumbent needs to successfully perform a job.

69 Some supervisors perceive that a job description serves as a rigid and inflexible barrier undermining their ability to delegate, make decisions, and exercise authority.

69 Some staff members fear that if they reveal too much detail about their jobs, others will be able to perform them and the incumbent will become dispensable.

71 To facilitate the hiring of those disabled, employers are required to make "reasonable accommodations" (which might include altering the work schedule or modifying equipment and facilities) unless doing so would cause "undue hardship."

71 Currently, employers can ask candidates to take physical exams only after employment has been offered, when there is necessary reason, if the organization pays for the exam, and when all employees are subject to being examined.

72 The minimum wage and overtime provisions protect only those who are "nonexempt" from the law—that is, those who are not managerial, supervisory, technical, or professional staff members.

72 If the library is charged with pay discrimination, job descriptions can demonstrate that the work involved in different positions is substantially unequal and thus should be compensated at different rates.

74 The effect of technology on staffing patterns is that it changes the type rather than the number of workers needed.

75 In order to minimize disappointment, all nonhired applicants should be rejected with tact.

76 Given legal and ethical mandates to avoid discrimination, certain questions commonly asked by application forms and interviewers should either be avoided, modified, or justified to applicants.

76 Candidates often fabricate or distort information to enhance their probability of being hired.

79   While the court upheld the director's right to require the degree, it was necessary to demonstrate that this educational criterion was relevant and necessary to successful performance on the job.

79   Personality tests (or any other devices, such as graphology, that attempt to assess personality) should *not* be included in selection batteries.

80   The library manager who receives a reference call must be cautious when answering queries about the personal character of past employees.

80   A manager should answer questions only about work-related behaviors—not about personality or attitude.

82   The second form of discrimination, adverse impact, can be established by applying the Rule of Four-Fifths (or the 80 Percent Rule).

83   The best defense to a discrimination charge is to establish "job relatedness" by statistically demonstrating that a selection criterion (e.g., 5 years previous experience) is valid or related to high performance on the job.

86   Since employee handbooks may be legally binding, they must be carefully worded, frequently updated, and inclusive in terms of content.

86   Manuals should not contain any rules that are not consistently enforced.

86   Newcomers with disabilities may need the handbook available on audio or closed-captioned video cassette.

87   Throughout the manual, beware of any wording which may imply continued employment—such as "permanent staff," "job security," "career path," or "just cause."

88   Once clear, reasonable rules are developed and communicated, they must be enforced consistently, fairly, and without discriminatory intent.

89   When mitigating circumstances surround a rule infraction, disciplinary action may not be warranted.

89   The first step in progressive discipline is normally an oral warning, which should be recorded in the employee's personnel file immediately following its administration.

89   The final stage is termination or discharge.

90   Staff members who believe they have been inappropriately discharged from a library have the right to file a "wrongful termination" suit.

90   In wrongful termination cases heard by a jury, the defendant (the library being sued) faces a 70 percent chance of losing.

90   While keeping such close tabs on workers may be perceived as an invasion of privacy, this is not likely the legal case.

92   Currently, only two in five employee thieves are prosecuted.

93   Examples of atypical scheduling include "compressed work weeks," "flextime," "telecommuting," and "permanent part-time" employment.

95   From an organizational perspective, part-timers can be a source of stable, dedicated, and relatively inexpensive labor, as most part-timers do not receive benefits.

95   The progression of withdrawal behaviors typically begins with tardiness, intensifies to absenteeism, and culminates in voluntary turnover.

96   The technique found to be most effective at controlling absenteeism is the "paid-leave bank."

96   Dysfunctional turnover results when good performers leave the job.

97   Functional turnover results when poor performers leave the job.

98   Moonlighters tend to have a strong work ethic as well as a zest for life and are willing to bear discomforts associated with holding multiple jobs.

98   To raise awareness about potential conflicts of interest associated with moonlighting, the employing library may annually ask staff members to complete a form listing "Outside Professional Activities."

99   Child care is the fastest growing employee benefit.

99   Since 12 percent of individuals who take care of elderly relatives are forced to quit their jobs to do so, some libraries are beginning to offer geriatric day-care benefits in addition to child care.

Personnel Issues

101   Given the natural tendency to overestimate individual performance, employees who receive negative appraisals are likely to grow defensive and resentful.

101   Nearly three-quarters of all supervisors question the usefulness of evaluating subordinate performance.

102   How can a staff member admit to needing training when that admission may lead to disciplinary action?

102   How can appraisers give accurate ratings if they will diminish trust between the supervisor and the worker?

102   In over 75 percent of all libraries, a staff member's direct supervisor will be the one and only evaluator.

103   While supervisory and self-ratings are most often used to evaluate the performance of nonmanagerial staff, subordinate evaluations are increasingly being used to assess the performance of library managers.

104   The appraisal instrument should provide guidance and direction for performance improvement.

104   Given the deficiencies surrounding the graphic rating scale, behaviorally based performance appraisal systems are recommended by personnel experts in the librarianship field.

107   Employees hope to capitalize on their appraiser's recency error when productivity improves, tardiness ceases, and coffee breaks shorten just prior to their evaluation.

107–8   Another perceptual bias is the "halo effect," which occurs when exceptional performance on one dimension positively influences performance ratings on all other dimensions.

109   Pay-for-performance is an appealing concept to both employers (who believe that employees will work harder if they expect the increased effort will result in higher pay) and employees (who believe that doing a job well will be recognized and rewarded).

110   Merit pay differentials between superior and average performers must be sizeable enough to motivate excellence.

110   In general, female librarians are paid 12 percent less than their male counterparts with similar education and experience.

110–1   Comparable worth is based on the notion that while the true value of jobs may be similar, some jobs (typically held by women) are often paid at lower rates than other jobs (typically held by men).

111   For employee evaluations to effectively inform training initiatives, developmental performance appraisals must accurately diagnose areas of deficiency.

112   Although supervisors should be familiar with jobs performed by subordinates, they may not possess enough specific, detailed knowledge to instruct them.

112   The most common form of on-site/off-job training in the librarianship field is the formal lecture.

112   Library managers who value continuing education will typically reimburse professionals for conference attendance.

114   Training tends to be more successful when trainees actively participate in instructional programming—as opposed to being passive recipients of information.

115   During times of fiscal crises or budgetary constraints, the training budget is often the first line item to be slashed. Such a response is, however, short-sighted.

115   By the mid-1990s, the number of library school closings has reached well into the double digits.

116   There is little debate as to the fact that librarians are currently undervalued—even in the university setting where they would appear to be critical to the success of the entire academic community.

118   The first library union was formed in 1914.

118   Like other workers, library employees join unions when they are dissatisfied with compensation and supervision, object to workplace conditions, perceive "safety in numbers," and believe the union can achieve more than they can individually.

120   It is conceivable that union and professional organization membership may be compatible and even complementary.

120   Many librarians perceive that they receive greater direct economic benefits from the union than from professional organizations.

120   Hoping that labor would be the impetus for pulling the United States out of the Great Depression, the first piece of legislation aimed at protecting workers' rights to unionize in private organizations was passed in 1935.

121   The Labor-Management Relations Act (LMRA; also known as the Taft-Hartley Act) was designed to rebalance the scales of power that had been tipped in the favor of unions by the Wagner Act.

122   Support for a union is demonstrated when employees sign authorization cards, which are nonbinding, noncontractual statements certifying that the worker wishes to be represented by a named union.

122   While the union is collecting authorization card signatures, library managers typically engage in a campaign of their own.

123   Notably, bargaining in good faith does not mean one party must agree to another's offer or proposal, nor does it require making concessions.

123   "Mandatory" bargaining issues are those relating to wages, hours, and other critical terms and conditions of employment. These issues must be discussed and settled before a contract can become effective.

124   Mediation involves inviting a third party into the dispute to make nonbinding recommendations about settlement.

124   Arbitrators are neutral third parties who make legally binding recommendations to resolve a dispute.

126 Each and every grievance filed by a bargaining unit member must be processed by management, regardless of its merit.

126 Grievance proceedings are conducted during working hours, and participants are paid regular wages during their involvement in the process.

Liability Issues

127 Sexual harassment is legally defined as unwelcome sexual advances, requests for sexual favors, and other verbal or physical conduct that constitutes a hostile environment.

127 Nearly 80 percent of librarians report they have been harassed on the job—and 70 percent report they are victimized at least monthly.

128–9 Males are afforded the same legal rights to a hostility-free workplace as are female victims.

129 It has been soundly established in the legal arena that employers can be held personally (and financially) responsible if employees are being harassed—whether or not the employers acknowledge they were aware of such harassment.

131 No matter what moral philosophy is adopted to define an ethical dilemma, outcomes are dependent, in part, upon the decision makers' personal development.

131 Those low in moral development are self-centered and seem to lack understanding about justice and personal rights.

132 Intentionally amoral managers think that different rules apply to their decisions at work than to other parts of their life.

132 Because whistle-blowing puts both the employee and the library administrator in precarious positions, a better course is for libraries to set up formal communication channels for reporting unethical practices.

133 The library administrator would be well advised to formulate written policies for conflicts of interest.

134 As a rule of thumb, the librarian should avoid even the suspicion that a conflict exists.

137 Only about 19 percent of libraries have a systematic, clear-cut catastrophe reaction plan, and only an additional 17 percent are working on one.

137 It is important that these plans be revised annually and not be allowed to gather dust on the shelf.

137	In cases of large-scale regional disasters (e.g., earthquakes, hurricanes, or floods), management must also determine the effect the disaster has had on the personal lives of the employees.
138	Profound losses, such as those often associated with disasters, can elicit common grief reactions.
138	Besides natural catastrophic events, risk management also focuses on such problems as preventing patron injuries, limiting exposure to hazardous materials, controlling liability for transportation accidents, eliminating embezzlement, protecting against lawsuits claiming breach of contract, and defending against defamation charges.
139	Prelitigation activities occur immediately after an incident and are designed to avoid claims or lawsuits. Postlitigation activities involve attempts to lessen financial and reputational losses.
141–2	An organization may be financially responsible for problems that arise because of staff member negligence.
142	To apply tort law, the complainant must establish that there was a breach of duty resulting in harm—inflicted either intentionally or unintentionally.
142	Change is inevitable and occurs even when staff members prefer stability.
144	Participation and involvement are considered to be the most effective mechanisms for overcoming resistance, as they can build commitment to the program of change.
146	Librarians typically spend more than 90 percent of their workday indoors—a matter of some concern, since the Environmental Protection Agency estimates that exposure to dangerous pollutants is two to five times greater indoors than it is outdoors.
147	Large volumes of paper housed in the library introduce much airborne dust, aggravating many human allergies.
147	Library administration has a threefold mandate to protect staff members, patrons, and the collection from dangerous indoor pollutants.
147	While 55 degrees Fahrenheit is optimal for the collection, such a low temperature would prove to be uncomfortable for human occupants of the library.
149	Ergonomic furnishings are biologically designed to minimize physical strain and exertion in the work environment.
149	While ergonomic furnishings may avert many muscular-skeletal injuries, supervisors should be trained in detecting potential situations that may induce carpal tunnel syndrome.

149   Although over 90 percent of all libraries utilize computers in their operations, over 30 percent of all workers fear them.

150   Library managers must find friendly ways to communicate with apprehensive users, particularly since manuals and instruction guides are often dense, cold, and incomprehensible.

150   Worker's Compensation is a state-regulated insurance program designed to protect workers from loss of income due to injuries and illnesses contracted due to employment.

151   To avoid legitimate claims, the library manager should regularly inspect the facility to identify known and potential hazards.

152   In 1970, Congress passed the Occupational Safety and Health Act—a law designed to protect workers in their places of employment.

152   OSHA deals with two distinct types of threats: (1) safety risks (such as cuts, burns, and broken limbs), which impair an employee's physical well-being and lead to occupational injuries; and (2) health hazards (such as exposure to chemicals, dust, and fumes, loud noises, and inappropriate lighting), which impair not only physical well-being, but also mental and emotional well-being.

154   Violence is the leading cause of death in the workplace among U.S. women: an average of fifteen people are killed on the job each week.

154   Librarians are increasingly the targets of random acts of violence.

155   Although it is difficult to prepare for all contingencies, staff training can help prepare employees for general responses needed to manage violent incidents.

155   It is important to have a positive working relationship with the police so that there is an early response mechanism established with local authorities.

156   Although a legal case can be made that homeless people have the right to use public facilities, it is incumbent upon management to establish policies and procedures to protect library employees from potentially violent individuals.

156   The responsibilities of community mental health centers, state psychiatric facilities, social service agencies, shelters, and law enforcement agencies in resolving this larger social problem should not be overlooked.

157   Patron violence is more likely than staff member violence, but employee killings of supervisors and peers have risen at an astonishing rate.

158	The primary symptom of chemical abuse among librarians is job shrinkage, which occurs when individuals continue to perform adequately but accomplish fewer and fewer tasks.
160	Precautions include the installation of "panic buttons" for public service desks, scream alarms for restrooms, and portable alarms for workers in isolated areas.
160	To protect employees from patron violence, management should develop a culture where staff members are encouraged to verbalize their concerns about safety issues.
161	Workplace paranoia is usually transitory or situational rather than persistent—spurred by events such as exposure to a frightening occurrence or even overly intense scrutiny by managers.
161	Common workplace symptoms include oversensitivity to being left out of decisions, fear of being taken advantage of, feelings of being "set up" by coworkers, inability to acknowledge deficiencies, holding grudges long after workplace conflicts, questioning the commitment and trustworthiness of peers, and communicating in an argumentative fashion.

Total Quality Management

167	TQM is the one modern management approach that, at its core, focuses on building quality into the processes so that the patron will not have to suffer from service mistakes.
172	To fully engage the library patron, marketing researchers suggest that library users actually be encouraged to criticize the services, because there are many who do not complain to staff but go away dissatisfied.
173	Every staff member has an internal supplier and an internal customer who depend upon receiving quality output in order to perform his or her job.
174	Quality management requires a structured process in which a project team tackles a particular quality problem.
174	The diagraming of service maps often highlights discrepancies between visions of what the process should be and what it is in reality.
180	The traditional authoritarian style of management, with its rigidity and control, is not workable in a TQM environment.
183	For service recovery to be effective, library staffers must be able to "right a wrong" as soon after it occurs as possible.

183   It is certainly possible that TQM will be relabeled in the next decade. But the focus on quality service is here to stay.

184   It is not a quick-fix approach—a library must actively follow its tenets for years to realize major benefits.

INDEX

Absenteeism, 93, 95, 96
Academic librarians
    attitudes toward union membership, 120
    gender-based pay differentials, 110
    value to academic community, 116
Acceptance, as natural disaster response, 139
Accommodation, as conflict resolution style, 22
Acquired immune deficiency syndrome (AIDS),
    10–1
Adverse impact, as workplace discrimination,
    81, 82
Advocacy, of librarians, 37–8
Affirmative action, 14–5
African-Americans, 11–2, 14
Age Discrimination in Employment Act of
    1967, 81
Agency law, 141–2
Age-related discrimination, 61, 81
AIDS *see* Acquired immune deficiency
    syndrome
Air pollution, indoor, 146–8
Albany, New York, public librarians'
    unionization in, 119
Alcohol abuse, by librarians, 157–9
American Indian Library Association, 15
American Library Association
    Black Caucus, 15
    code of ethics, 133–5
    Gay and Lesbian Task Force, 10
    Independent Librarians' Exchange Round
        Table, 97
    policy toward homophobic discrimination,
        15
Americans with Disabilities Act of 1990, 67–8,
    70–1, 72, 81
Appointments, to consult with professional
    librarians, 35

Arbitrators, of labor disputes, 124, 126
Asian-Americans, 11–2, 13, 14, 16
Assessment centers, 112–3
Association of College and Research Libraries,
    48
Association of Independent Information
    Professionals, 97
AT&T, 112
Attrition rates, 75
Autonomy, of staff members, 20
    of paraprofessionals, 53
Avoidance, as conflict resolution style, 22–3
Awareness building, with multicultural staff
    members, 16

Baby-boom generation, 11, 61
Back injuries, prevention, 151
Bargaining, as natural disaster response, 138
BARS (behaviorally anchored rating scale), 105
Benchmarking, 170–1
Benefits, employee manual coverage of, 85
Bias, in performance evaluations, 105–8
"Big Mac" approach, to librarianship, 172
Bjoring, Robyn, 136
Body language, 5, 7–8
Bomb threats, 156
Bookmobiles, electronic monitoring of, 90
Borrowing privileges, of minors, 140
Boyd, Alex, 15
Brainstorming, 23
Branch managers, autonomy and commitment
    of, 42–3
Breach of contract, 142
Bribery, 133
    rewards as, 30
Buckeye Public Library, 154–5
Bureaucracy, professional, 48–9

Burnout, 62–4, 157
Bush, George, 70

Caldwell-Wood, Naomi, 15
Career anchors, 60
Career citizenship behaviors, 64
Career commitment, 58–9
Career management issues, 56–64
    alternative career paths, 59–60
    burnout, 62–4, 157
    career stages, 58–9
    mentoring, 56–7, 64
    plateauing, 60–4
    preferential treatment, 57–8
Career paths, 59–60
Carpal tunnel syndrome, 148–9
Carter County Library, 136
Case analyses, 113
Caterpillar, Inc., 142
Cause-and-effect diagrams, 177
Change, organizational
    crisis-related, 138
    planned, 142–4
Charts
    Gantt, 175, 176
    Pareto, 177–8
    run, 179
Child-care needs, of staff members, 99
Chinese Civil Service, 101
Cincinnati, Ohio, anti-gay discriminatory policy
    of, 15
Circulation records, confidentiality, 134
Civil Rights Act of 1964, 71, 72–3, 81
Closed-shop provisions, 121
Code of ethics, 133–5
Coercion, as power base, 26, 27, 28, 32
Collaboration, as conflict resolution style, 23
Collection policies, 10
Collective bargaining, 123–4
Comment cards, 172
Commitment
    of branch managers, 42–3
    career, 58–9
    dual professional/organizational, 35–6
    escalation of, 41–2
    organizational, 38
    power bases and, 27
    professional, 47, 48
    social, 37–8
Common law, 141–2
Communication
    breakdowns in, 1–2
    departmentalization as obstacle to, 169

    privileged, 134
    as quality service delivery component, 167
Communication issues, 1–9
    active listening, 2–3
    body language, 6, 7–8
    conflict resolution, 22–3
    creativity, 20, 23–4
    grapevine, 6–7
    information acquisition by new staff
        members, 4–6
    information overload, 3
    information underload, 3
    intuition, 21–2
    multilingual services, 13–4
    noise distortion, 1–2
    overconformity, 24–5
    patron and staff diversity, 10–8
    personality differences, 19–21
    power bases, 26–33
    selective perception, 2
    serial transmission effect, 3–4
    unethical behavior reporting, 132
Community of interest doctrine, 121
Comparable worth doctrine, 110–1
Compensation
    employee manual coverage of, 85
    equity of, 19–20
    gender-based differentials, 110–1
    legislation regarding, 110–1
    merit pay, 109–10, 169
    for overtime work, 50, 72, 93–4
    for volunteers, 53–4
Competence
    managerial, 75
    professional, 166, 167
Competition, merit pay-related, 110, 169
Compliance, 27, 32
Compressed workweek, 93
Compromise, as conflict resolution style, 23
Compustress, 149
Computer anxiety, 149–50
Computer crime, 91
Computers
    health hazards caused by, 147, 148–50
    usage monitoring of, 90
Conferences
    as continuing education, 112
    paraprofessionals' attendance at, 48
Confidentiality, librarian-patron, 134
Conflict
    constructive, 22
    insufficient, 24–5
    merit pay-related, 169

Conflict resolution, 22–3
Conflicts of interest
    moonlighting-related, 98
    vendor-related, 133–4
Continuing education, 112–3, 114, 169
Contract law, 141, 142
Contracts
    breach of, 142
    implied, compliance with, 84–92
    return-to-work, 159
    union-negotiated, 123–4, 125, 126
Coping strategies, of plateaued librarians, 61–2
Court system, 141–2
Creativity, 20, 23–4
Crises, staff members' responses to, 137–8
Crosby, Philip, 165, 171
Cues, in information transmission, 5, 7
Cultural brokers, 13–4
Cultures, differentiating characteristics, 12
Cyberphobia, 149

Day-care, 99
Decentralization, 180
Decision making
    ethical, 130–2
    group, 23–4
    problem diagnosis and, 40–2
Delegation, in empowerment, 180–1
Delphi technique, for group decision making,
    23–4
Deming, W. Edwards, 165, 167–70
Denial, as natural disaster response, 138
Denver, Colorado, anti-gay discriminatory
    policy of, 15
Denver Public Library, 53
Deontology, 131
Departmentalization
    as communication obstacle, 169
    functional, 38–9
    matrix, 39–40
    product line, 39
Depression, as natural disaster response, 138
Dewey, John, 173
Dewey, Melvil, 31, 47
Directors, nonlibrarians as, 37
Disabled persons, 70–1
    discrimination toward, 71
    as patrons, 71
    as staff members, 67–8, 71, 86
    see also Americans with Disabilities Act of 1990
Discharge, of staff members
    "at-will," 89–90
    as disciplinary penalty, 88, 89

as employee violence cause, 159
as implied contract issue, 85, 88, 89–90
Discipline, 85, 88–9
    progressive, 32, 88, 89
Discrimination
    age-related, 61, 81
    toward disabled persons, 71
    in hiring practices, 72–3, 76, 79, 81–3
    homophobic, 15
    legislative protection against, 72–3, 81
    reverse, 15
Discrimination control, 16–7
Disparate treatment, as workplace
    discrimination, 81–2
"Do it right the first time" (DIRT-FooT), 171
Document retention policies, 142
Domestic violence, 160
Dominance, as conflict resolution style, 22
Drug abuse, by librarians, 156–7
Drug testing, 158
Due process, 32
Dwyer, Mary Jo, 140

Economic Control of Quality of a Manufactured
    Product (Walter Shewhart), 164
Ego strength, 20
80 Percent Rule, 82
80–20 Rule, 151, 177
El Nuevo Herald, 12
Elder-care responsibilities, of staff members, 99
Elderly persons
    as patrons, 11
    see also Older workers
Electronic communication
    effect on work scheduling, 94
    information transmission via, 5
Electronic monitoring and surveillance, 90–2
Embezzlement, 91
Emergencies
    natural disasters, 136–8
    workplace violence, 154–62
Emotions, communication of, 7
Employee assistance programs (EAP), 158 159
Employee manuals, as implied contracts, 84–92
    communication of contents to employees,
        86–8
    contents, 84–6
    rule-breaking responses and, 88–9
Employment issues
    hiring practices, 74–83
    implied contract compliance, 84–92
    job descriptions, 65–73
    work scheduling, 93–100

Employment testing, 79
Employment-at-will, 89–90
Empowerment, of staff members, 28
    delegation in, 180–1
    in Total Quality Management, 171, 180–3
English language
    sexist nature of, 2
    word definitions in, 1
Enlightened egoism, 131
Environmental Protection Agency (EPA), 146
Equal Employment Opportunity Act, 141
Equal Pay Act of 1963, 72, 110
*The Eternally Successful Organization: The Act
    of Corporate Wellness* (Philip Crosby), 171
Executive Order 11246 of 1965, 81
Executive orders, 141
Exit, as coping strategy, 61–2
Exit interviews, 96, 159
Expertise, as power base, 27, 29, 30–1, 32
Eye contact, 8

Facial expressions, as nonverbal
    communication, 7
Fair Labor Standards Act of 1938, 49–50, 72,
    93–4
Federal Emergency Management Assistance
    (FEMA), 136
Federal government, branches, 141
Federal Mediation and Conciliation Service
    (FMCS), 121
Feedback
    from patrons, 103, 172
    performance, 50, 52–3
    for volunteers, 54
Feigenbaum, Armand, 164–5
Field-dependency, 20
Final Exit (Derek Humphrey), 140
Firing, of staff members *see* Discharge, of staff
    members
First Amendment rights, of patrons, 140
First impressions, of staff members, 107
Fishbone diagrams, 177
Flextime, 93, 94
Fraud, 91
Furnishings
    arrangement, 8
    ergonomic, 149

Gambling, legalized, 116
Gantt, Henry L., 175
Gantt charts, 175, 176
Garvin, David, 166
Gender roles, in Mexico, 12

Gestures, as nonverbal communication, 7
Goal setting, 50–1
Grand Canyon Community College Library, 136
Grapevine, in organizational communication,
    6–7
Grief, as natural disaster response, 138
Grievances, filing of, 89, 126
Griggs v. *Duke Power Company*, 103
Groupthink, 24–5

Halo effect, 107–8
Health hazardous exposure *see* Safety and
    health issues
Hiring practices, 74–83
    discrimination in, 76, 79, 81–3
    interviewing of job applicants, 76–8
    reference inquiries, 79–80
    rejection of job applicants, 75–6
    screening of job applicants, 74–6
Hispanics, 11–2, 14
Histograms, 178
Hofstede, Geert, 12
Holland, J. L., 58
Homeless patrons, 156–7
Homosexuals
    as disabled persons, 70–1
    discrimination toward, 15
    as patrons, 10–1
    as staff members, 16
"Hot-stove" rule, of discipline, 88–9
Human resource planning, 74

If Japan Can Do It, Why Can't We? (television
    documentary), 165
Illnesses, work-related, 72, 147–9, 152–3
In Search of Excellence (Tom Peters), 114–5
In-basket simulations, 112–3
Information overload, 3
Information transmission
    distortion of information during, 3–4
    methods, 5–6
    to new staff members, 4–6
Information under-/overload, 3
Information-seeking techniques, of new staff
    members, 4–5
In-group members, 57–8, 61
Injuries, work-related, 148–9, 150–2
*Integrating Total Quality Management in a
    Library Setting*, 164
Interviews
    exit, 96, 159
    preemployment, 76–8, 80
    by search committees, 80

Intuition, 21–2
Ishikawa, Kaoru, 173, 177
ITT, 171

Japan, quality management in, 165, 168, 170
Jargon, 1–2
Jewett, Charles Coffin, 31
Job applicants
  educational requirements, 77, 78–9
  interviewing, 76–8
  literacy, 76
  rejection, 75–6
  screening, 74–6
Job characteristics model, 52
Job descriptions, 65–73
  benefits of, 68–9
  employment legislation compliance and,
    70–2
  information contained in, 65–8
  for newly hired personnel, 86
  "person specifications" documents and, 68
  provision to injured employees' physician,
    152
  resistance to, 69–70
Job enlargement, 51
Job enrichment, 51–2
Job loading, horizontal and vertical, 51–2
Job performance evaluations *see* Performance
  evaluations
Job shrinkage, 158
Jung, Carl, 20
Juran, Joseph, 165, 170–1, 177

Labor disputes, arbitrators, 124, 126
Labor force
  demographic changes, 93
  female, 99
  minority-group, 14, 16
  union membership, 118
Labor relations laws, 120–1
Labor relations process, 118
Labor-Management Relations Act of 1947, 121
Labor-Management Reporting Disclosure Act
  of 1959, 121
Larceny, 91
Law librarians, professional liability, 140
Law libraries, paper recycling, 87
Law of agency, 141–2
Laws
  types, 141
  see also specific laws
Lawsuits
  health hazards exposure-related, 72

wrongful termination-related, 90
Leaderless group discussions, 113
Leadership, 169
Lectures, as training method, 112
Lesbians
  discrimination toward, 15
  as patrons, 10–1
  as staff members, 16
Letters, of reference, 79–80
Liability and legal issues
  affirmative action, 14–5
  fundamental issues, 141–2
  professional liability, 139–40
  risk and change management, 136–40
  unethical behavior, 127–35
  workplace crime and violence, 154–62
  workplace safety and health, 146–53
Librarians
  as agents of information transfer, 173
  distinguished from paraprofessionals, 34–5,
    47–8
  married, 96
  professional liability, 139–40
  professionalism, 34–44
  violence toward, 154–5
  see also Academic librarians; Medical
    librarians; Public librarians
Librarianship
  "Big Mac" approach, 172
  as knowledge-based profession, 37
Library Administration and Management
  Association, Library Safety/Security
  Discussion Group, 154
Library associations
  conferences, 48, 112
  paraprofessionals' participation in, 48
  union membership and, 119–20
Library buildings, sick-building syndrome,
  146–8
Library cards
  for the homeless, 156–7
  for minors, 140
Library design, 38–40
Library education
  librarians' attitudes toward, 37
  see also Library schools; Master of Library
    and Information Science (MLIS) degree
Library Mosaic, 46
Library of Congress, lack of affirmative action
  by, 14
Library schools
  closings, 115–6
  minority-group students, 15

Library science professors, average age, 116
Linguistic noise, 1
Listening, active, 2–3
Literacy, of job applicants, 76
Literature searches, biomedical, 139–40
Lockouts, 124–5
Locus of control, 20
Loyalty, 31, 62

Management, participative, 49, 182–3
Management-by-objective, 169
Management-by-walking around (MBWA), 4
Managerial activity, effect of professionalism on, 36–8
Managers, number of employers supervised by, 40
Marginalization, of librarianship, 36–8
"Master and Servant" (Horace Wood), 89
Master of Library and Information Science (MLIS) degree
librarians' attitudes toward, 37
as professional librarianship job requirement, 78–9
Matrix departmentalization, 39–40
McCune, Bonnie, 53
Media, information transmission via, 5–6
Medical librarians
gender-based pay differentials, 111
professional liability, 139–40
Medicare regulations, 11
MEDLINE, 139
Mentoring, 56–7, 64
Merit pay, 109–10, 169
Merrivine v. *Mississippi State University,* 79
Mexicans, cultural values, 12–3
Miami-Dade County Public Library system, 12, 137
Minimum wage, 50, 72
Minority-group members
employment-related discrimination towards, 82
as library school students, 15
as patrons, 10–4
recruitment, 14–5
as staff members, 14–7
Minors, restricted borrowing privileges, 140
Mirror effect, 27
Monitoring, electronic, 90–2
Moonlighting, by staff members, 97–8
Moral development, 131
Multiculturalism, 10, 13–4
of library staff, 14–7, 31
Multilingual library services, 13–4

Musahi Institute of Technology, 173
Myers-Briggs Type Indicator, 20–1

Name tags, position titles on, 35
National Labor Relations Act (NLRA) of 1935, 120–1, 123, 141
National Labor Relations Board (NLRB), 121, 122, 123
National Technical Information Service (NTIS), 168
Native Americans, 11–2
American Indian Library Association, 15
Natural disasters, 136–8
Neglect, as coping strategy, 62
Negligence, 141–2
Newspapers
gay and lesbian, 11
Spanish-language, 12
Noise, as communication obstacle, 1–2
Nominal group technique, 23
Nuevo Herald, El see El Nuevo Herald

Occupational choice, 58
Occupational Safety and Health Act of 1970, 72, 152–3
Occupational Safety and Health Administration, 152
Older workers, job discrimination toward, 61, 81
Open-door policy, 5
Oral communication, 5
Ordinances, 141
Organizational design, 38–40
Orientation programs, 86–8
Ormsby, Rita, 60
Outcome/input ratios, 19
Out-group members, 57–8
Overconformity, in group decision making, 24–5
Overjustification effect, 30
Overtime, compensation for, 50, 72, 93–4
Owens, Robert, 101
Oxford University Libraries, performance evaluations, 101

Page, Gwen, 155
Paid-leave bank, 96
Panizzi, Anthony, 31
Paper recycling programs, 87–8
Paranoia, workplace, 161
Paraprofessionals, 45–55
distinguished from professional librarians, 34–5, 47–8
importance, 45–6
job enrichment, 51–3

motivation, 48–51
position titles, 46
promotion, 49
volunteers as, 53–4
Pareto chart, 177–8
Pareto rule, 151
Parsons, Lisa, 156
Part-time employment, 94–5
Patron focus, in Total Quality Management, 171, 172–3
Patrons
  as customers, 172–3
  disabled, 71
  diversity, 10–1
  feedback from, 103
  homeless, 156–7
  homosexual, 10–1
  minority-group, 10–4
  perception of librarians' professionalism, 34–5
  perception of library service quality, 166–7, 172–3, 183
  privacy rights, 133, 134
  service recovery for, 183
  sexual harassment by, 130
  violent, 154–7
Pay-for-performance system *see* Merit pay
Peer evaluations, 102–3
Peer modeling, 112
Pennsylvania State University, Continuous Quality Improvement Center, 174
Performance, effect of power usage on, 28
Performance evaluations, 101–7
  behaviorally based format, 104–5
  bias in, 105–8
  central tendency error in, 105–6
  contrast error in, 106–7
  criteria, 103–5
  employee compensation and, 109–11
  employee training and, 111–5
  evaluators for, 102–3
  graphic rating scale format, 104
  halo effect in, 107–8
  history, 101
  "horns effect" in, 108
  leniency error in, 106
  negative, 101
  potential problems with, 101–8
  primacy error in, 107
  purposes, 102
  recency error in, 107
  severity error in, 106
Performance feedback, 50, 52–3

Periodicals, gay and lesbian, 10, 11
Person specifications documents, 68
Personality differences, 19–21
Personality tests, 79
Personnel issues
  performance evaluations, 101–17
  unionization, 118–26
PERT (Program Evaluation and Review Technique) network, 175, 176
Peters, Tom, 114–5
Phillips Laboratory Research Library, Hanscom Air Force Base, 172–3
Photocopiers, health effects, 147
Physical examinations, preemployment, 71
Plan-Do-Check-Act (PDCA) cycle, 179–80
Plateauing, 60–2
Polarization, 24–5
Pornography, 166
Position titles, 65
  on name tags, 35
  of paraprofessionals, 46, 65
Posture, 7
Power bases, 26–33
  choice of, 27–8
  coercive, 26, 27, 28, 29, 32
  expert, 27, 29, 30–1, 32
  legitimate, 26, 27, 28, 29, 31, 32
  Library Manager Power Profile for, 28, 29
  personal, 27, 30–2
  positional, 27
  referent, 26, 27, 28, 29, 31, 32
  reward, 26, 27, 28, 29–30, 32
Precedents, legal, 141
Preferential treatment, of staff members, 57–8
Pregnancy Discrimination Act of 1978, 81
Prejudice reduction, 16, 17
The Principles of Scientific Management (Frederick Taylor), 164
Privacy rights
  of patrons, 133, 134
  of staff members, 90–1
Problem diagnosis, 40–2
Process improvement, in Total Quality Management, 171, 173–80
Productivity, work standards and, 169
Product-line departmentalization, 39
Professional associations *see* Library associations
Professional issues, 34–44
  career management, 56–64
  paraprofessionals, 45–55
Professionalism, 34–44
  criteria, 47–8
  effect on managerial activity, 36–8

Project team approach, to Total Quality
Management, 169, 173–80, 184
documentation and control tools in, 174–6
quality tools in, 177–80
Promotion
internal, 75
of paraprofessionals, 49
relationship to mentoring, 57
Proxemics, 8
Public librarians, burnout, 63

Quality
conceptualizations of, 166
in library service, 165–7
see also Total Quality Management
Quality circles, 182
Quality control, 170
Quality Control Handbook (Joseph Juran), 165
Quality improvement, 170
Quality Is Free (Philip Crosby), 165
Quality management movement, 164–5
Quality planning, 170
*Quality without Tears: The Act of Hassle-Free
Management* (Philip Crosby), 171
Quotas, numerical, 169

Recruitment
internal, 75
of minority-group applicants, 14–5
Recycling programs, 87–8
Reference librarians
appointments to consult with, 35
staffing requirements, 75
Reference questions, incorrect and inadequate
answers, 172
References, employment, 79–80
Reinforcement theory, 29
Relativism, 131
Reliability, as quality service delivery
component, 167
Resistance
to coercive power, 27
to organizational change, 142–4
Retention, of multicultural staff members, 16–7
Return-to-work contracts, 159
Reverse discrimination, 15
Reward, as power base, 26, 27, 28, 31, 32
Riggs, Donald, 184
Right-to-know rules, 72
Right-to-work legislation, 121
Risk and change management, 136–40
Risk avoidance, 138
Risk prevention, 138, 139, 140

Risk shifting, 138–9
Rogers, Will, 115
Role ambiguity, 3
social, 38
Role play, 113
Rule of Four-Fifths, 82
Rule-breaking, disciplinary response to, 85,
88–9
Run charts, 179

Sabbaticals, 63
Safety and health issues, 146–53
computer-related health hazards, 147,
148–50
employee manual coverage of, 85
sick-building syndrome, 146–8
workers' compensation claims, 150–2
St. Louis Public Library, 140
Salaries
of paraprofessionals, 49, 50
see also Compensation
Salt Lake City Public Library, 155
Scattergrams, 178–9
Search committees, 80
Security
as quality service delivery component, 167
staff's sense of, 169
Security devices, 160
Security guards, 160
Security methods, for sexual harassment
prevention, 130
Selective perception, 2
Self-efficacy, of staff members, 181–2
Self-ratings, by staff members, 103
Serial transmission effect, 3–4
Service delivery, patrons' evaluation of, 167
Service maps, 174–5
Service recovery, 183
Sexism, of English language, 2
Sheldon, Brooke, 30
Shewhart, Walter A., 164, 179
Sick time, 96
Sick-building syndrome, 146–8
Skinner, B. F., 29
Slogans, 169
Social advocacy, of librarians, 37–8
Socialization, 87
Spanish-speaking library staff, 13–4
Spanish-speaking population, 11–3
Span-of-control, 40
Spatial distance, in nonverbal communication,
8
Special Libraries Association, 164

Specialists, dual career ladder, 59–60
Staff members
    attrition rates, 75
    as "cultural brokers," 13–4
    disabled, 81
    empowerment, 28, 171, 180–3
    first impressions of, 107
    hierarchical positions, 35
    homosexual, 16
    interdependency, 173
    as "internal customers," 173
    job performance evaluations *see* Performance
        evaluations
    multicultural, 14–7, 31
    natural disaster responses, 137–8
    negligence of, 141–2
    new, information acquisition by, 4–6
    organizational change responses, 142–4
    preferential treatment of, 57–8
    Spanish-speaking, 13–4
    views of fairness and justice, 19–20
    violence by, 154, 159, 160
    violence responses, 155–6
        see also Librarians; Paraprofessionals
Staffing requirements, 74–5
Statutes, 141
Stewart, Potter, 166
Stress, natural disaster-related, 138
Strikes, 124–5
Structure, organizational, 170
Substance abuse, by librarians, 156–7
Supervisors, subordinates' evaluations of, 103
Surveillance, electronic, 90–2
Suspension, 89

Taft-Hartley Act, 121
Taguchi, Genichi, 166
Tardiness, 94, 95–6
Taylor, Frederich, 164
Technology
    impact on librarianship, 37
    impact on library use, 172–3
    impact on staffing requirements, 74
Telecommuting, 93
Teleology, 131
Telephone references, 79, 80
Tenure, for paraprofessionals, 49
Termination, wrongful, 89–90
    see also Discharge, of staff members
Testing, preemployment, 79
Theft, organizational, 91–2
Thinking styles, 20–1
Time theft, 91

Tort law, 141, 142
Total Quality Control, 164–5
Total Quality Management, 163–85
    barriers to, 169
    disadvantages, 183, 184
    employee empowerment in, 171, 180–3
    history, 164–5
    implementation, 183–4
    patron focus in, 171, 172–3
    patrons' expectations and, 166–7
    principles, 167–83
    process improvement in, 171, 173–80
    as "Total Quality Mistake," 183
Touching, as nonverbal communication, 7–8
Training
    entry-level, 111–2, 114
    evaluation criteria, 113–5
    for job performance improvement, 111–5
    off-site, 112–3
    on-the-job, 63, 111–2, 114–5, 116
    of paraprofessionals, 47
    for violent incident response and prevention,
        155, 156, 159, 160
Training procedures, 169
Turnover, 96–7
    of paraprofessionals, 49
    of search committee hires, 80

Unethical behavior, 127–35
    American Library Association's code of
        ethics for, 133–5
    ethical decision making and, 131–2
    sexual harassment as, 127–30
Unfair labor practices, 120–1
Union of Japanese Scientific Engineers, 165
Unionization, 118–26
    collective bargaining and, 123–4
    grievance filing and, 126
    labor relations laws and, 120–1
    motivations for, 118–9
    opposition to, 119, 122
    organizing campaigns for, 121–3
    professionalism and, 119–20
    strike prevention techniques and, 124–5
Unions
    definition, 118
    legislative regulation, 121
Unity of command concept, 40
University of Guam Library, 136
University of Oregon, Graduate School of
    Librarianship, 115

Vacation time, 96

Vendors
    conflicts of interest with, 133–4
    Total Quality Management and, 168
Victims, of violent incidents, 160
Violence, 154–62
    domestic, 160
    as paranoia cause, 161
    by patrons, 154–7
    prevention, 159–60
    sexual, 127
    by staff members, 154, 159, 160
Voice, as coping strategy, 62
Volunteers, management of, 53–4

Wagner Act *see* National Labor Relations Act
    (NLRA) of 1935
Weber, Max, 48

Whistle blowing, 132
Williamson, Charles C., 47
Withdrawal behaviors, 95–7
Women, in labor force, 99
Words, differing definitions, 1
Work scheduling, 93–100
    flextime, 93, 94
    impact on staffing requirements, 74
    ineffective, 95–6
    part-time employment, 94–5
    telecommuting, 93, 94
    temporary employment, 95
Work stoppages, 124–5
Worker's compensation claims, 150–2
Written communication, 5–6

Zero defects, 171